Hurdle: The Book on Business Planning

How to develop *and implement* a
successful business plan.

By: **Tim Berry**

Palo Alto Software Second Edition, December1998

Publisher:

Palo Alto Software, Inc.
144 E. 14th Ave.
Eugene, OR 97401
USA
Fax: 1 (541) 683-6250
Email: info@palo-alto.com
Website: www.palo-alto.com

Library of Congress Catalog Number: 98-86285

ISBN 0-9664891-0-1

Cover design by Paul Berry. Book layout by Teri Epperly

About the Author

Tim Berry's latest book is *CPA's Guide to Business Planning*, published in 1998 by Harcourt Brace Professional Publishing. His other books on business planning with spreadsheets were published in the 1980s by Dow-Jones-Irwin, Microtext/McGraw-Hill, and Hayden Books. His business software has been published by Palo Alto Software and M & T Publishing. He has been a professional business planner since 1974, as an employee of Business International and vice president of Creative Strategies, as a consultant to Apple Computer, as a member of the board of directors of Borland International, and as president and founder of Palo Alto Software. He has given seminars on business planning in 10 countries on three continents.

Berry holds a Stanford MBA degree, an MA with honors from the University of Oregon, and a BA *magna cum laude* from the University of Notre Dame.

Acknowledgements

I want to thank Paul Berry for not just cover design, but for inspiration as well. I was recently introduced to the phrase "Entrepreneur in Heat." If you have to ask what that means, then you've never been involved with somebody starting a business. The shortcut is simply "EIH." Paul has been EIH a lot lately.

Teri Epperly has done a wonderful job with this book, designing the layout, editing, managing the graphics and patiently waiting me through the ups and downs of my developing software, writing this and one other book, and managing a company at the same time.

For Kristi Wharfield, Vie Radek, Doug Wilson, Cristin, Megan, and most of all Vange, thanks for putting up with me while this was coming together.

Sample Business Plans

This book includes two complete sample business plans, printed after the main text. One sample is a computer store that is actually a composite of several computer reseller businesses the author consulted with during the early 1990s. The other was a consulting company that was accepted for financing by a major venture capital firm, although it was never actually formed. Both were originally published as part of Business Plan Pro™ and Business Plan Toolkit™, published by Palo Alto Software, Inc.

"A practical business plan includes 10 parts implementation for every one part strategy."

"A business plan is worth the results it creates."

"Good plans are full of specifics--dates, deadlines, budgets, and specific people responsible--that can be measured and tracked."

"Specifics and tracking create the results."

"If this book can save you from starting a bad business, it has done you a great favor."

Table of Contents

Chapter 1: It's About Results 1

From the start, remember that business plans aren't about ideas, analysis, or presentation; they are about results. The plan is ultimately worth the decisions that you make because of it. A good plan is full of specifics that can be measured and tracked because tracking produces results.

Chapter 2: Initial Assessment 7

Start your business plan with a quick assessment. Even for an ongoing business, take the time to step away from the business and look at the basics. Do your business numbers make sense? One of my business school professors used to refer to this process as finding out "is there a there there?"

Chapter 3: Pick Your Plan 13

As we noted in Chapter 1, business planning is about results. Make the contents of your plan match your purpose. Don't accept a standard outline just because it's there.

Chapter 4: Know Your Market 19

What's the first thing, the most essential element, you need in business? No, not a plan: you need customers. In Chapter 2, Initial Assessment, you took a good first look at whether or not your business has (or will have) enough customers to keep it healthy. For the next step, you need to go further into a market analysis. It doesn't have to be academic, necessarily, and it doesn't have to be a huge project that stalls your planning process. What you want, ultimately, is to know your customers.

Chapter 5: The Business You're In 31

With your initial market analysis done, you're still not through a standard business plans's market analysis chapter. In addition to the information you've already developed, you also need to explain the type of business you're in.

Chapter 6: What You Sell 45

This step in the process is much more important for a plan going to external readers, the banks or investors, than for internal plans. A complete business plan describes what you sell: either products, services, or both. This part of the plan is mainly description. Sometimes it will include tables that provide more details, such as a bill of materials or detailed price lists. More frequently, however, this section is mainly text. It normally comes as Chapter 3.0 in the plan, after the company description, but before the market analysis.

Chapter 7: Forecast Your Sales 51

The next step is developing your sales forecast. Don't fear--it isn't as hard as most people think. Think of your sales forecast as an educated guess. Forecasting takes good working knowledge of your business, which is much more important than advanced degrees or complex mathematics. It is much more art than science. Whether you have business training or not, don't think you aren't qualified to forecast. If you can run a business, then you can forecast its sales. Most people can guess their own business' sales better than any expert device, statistical analysis, or mathematical routine. Experience counts more than any other factor.

Chapter 12: Cash is King 89

So, as we looked at business numbers in the previous chapter, we focused on the critical difference between cash and profits. This chapter looks at how to plan for cash in a business plan, understanding the critical elements that affect cash flow. You don't want to be one of those businesses that goes broke even while producing profits.

Chapter 13: Finish the Financials 99

If you've really followed through with the cash plan, your financials are almost done. The balance sheet should be completed by the time you have a cash flow working. Business ratios should be almost automatic too, because they draw all of their information from tables you've already finished.

Chapter 14: Strategy and Tactics 107

With most of the financials now done, it's time to turn to strategy and tactics. You've been developing strategy throughout, I know, because you can't do the numbers without thinking about the strategy. However, now you want to explain your strategy and develop the implementation. If you refer back to the text outline we discussed in Chapter 3, you probably have several topics still blank in your plan document. But not in your mind. Its time to write your thoughts on strategy and tactics into your text outline.

Chapter 15: Print and Publish 115

So you're about ready to print your plan. Please make sure to run it through a final critical edit. Then make sure to publish it so that commitments made by managers are clearly known and acknowleged. Also make it clear that you will be tracking results, and comparing your actual results to the planned results, and discussing the difference.

Chapter 16: Planning for Implementation 117

Some plans are more likely to be implemented than others. Successful implementation starts with a good plan, one that is full of specific information on milestones, managers, responsibilities, dates and budgets. Beyond the plan itself, however, there are other factors also critical to implementation. Are you going to track results, comparing the planned results to the actual results? Are you going to follow up with your management team, making revisions and checking on performance?

Chapter 17: Starting a Business 131

I'll always remember a talk I had with a man who had spent 15 years trying to make his sailboat manufacturing business work, achieving not much more than aging and more debt. "If I can tell you only one thing," he said, "it is that you should never take money from friends and family. If you do, then you can never get out. Businesses sometimes fail, and you need to be able to close it down and walk away. I wasn't able to do that." If I could make only one point with budding entrepreneurs, it would be that you should know what money you need and understand that it is at risk. Don't bet money you can't afford to lose. Know how much you are betting.

Chapter 18: Getting Financed 137

Contrary to popular belief, business plans do not generate business financing. True, there are many kinds of financing options that require a business plan, but nobody invests in a business plan. Investors need a business plan as a document that communicates ideas and information, but they invest in a company, in a product, and in people.

Sample Plan: Acme Consulting 145

Sample Plan: AMT, Inc. 173

Appendix A: Glossary 213

Appendix B: Index 221

Workbook 225

CHAPTER 1:

It's About Results

From the start, remember that business plans aren't about ideas, analysis, or presentation; they are about results. The plan is ultimately worth the decisions that you make because of it. A good plan is full of specifics that can be measured and tracked because tracking produces results.

About 10 years ago, I was having lunch with Professor James March, a business school professor whose class I'd enjoyed a few years earlier, as a grad student. I was then in my late 30s, making my living mostly through business plan consulting. I'd had some successes. One of my plans was for a company that went from zero to more than $100 million of sales in four years. Apple Computer's Latin American group increased sales from $2 million to $27 million during the four years I'd done its annual plan. I'd

had some failures too, but we don't mention those.

"So what is the value of a business plan?" Professor March asked at one point.

"Thousands of dollars," I answered. "Tens of thousands, in some cases."

"Wrong," he answered, to my shock. "Very wrong."

The value of a plan is the decisions it influences, he explained, and ultimately, how much money is in the bank as a result.

He was very right, although I was fairly smug about my successes, and didn't like his response. And the underlying lesson is vital to this book.

A business plan is worth the results it creates:
Good plans are full of specifics – dates, deadlines, budgets, and specific people responsible – that can be measured and tracked. Specifics and tracking create the results.

Illustration 1-1: Planning is a Process, Not Just a Plan

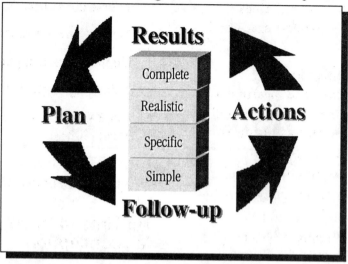

A business plan will be hard to implement unless it is simple, specific, realistic and complete. Even if it is all these things, a good plan will need someone to follow up and check on it.

I've absorbed the idea into my work on business planning. Plans should be measured by results. No matter how well researched, beautifully written, or excellently presented, what really makes a difference is how it impacts the results of the business.

What Makes A Good Plan?

Illustration 1-1 shows the a business plan as part of a process. You can think about the good or bad of a plan as the plan itself, measuring its value by its contents. There are some qualities in a plan that make it more likely to create results, and these are important. However, it is even better to see the plan as part of the whole process of results, because even a great plan is wasted if nobody follows it. The plan depends on the human elements around it, particularly the process of commitment and involvement, and the tracking and follow-up that comes afterward. I'm going to deal with those elements in coming chapters of this book. They are vital. But for now, let's look at the qualities that make the plan itself better or worse.

Successful implementation starts with a good plan. There are elements that will make a plan more likely to be successfully implemented. Some of the clues to implementation include:

1. Is the plan simple? Is it easy to understand and to act on? Does it communicate its contents easily and practically?

2. Is the plan specific? Are its objectives concrete and measurable? Does it include specific actions and activities, each with specific dates of completion, specific persons responsible and specific budgets?

3. Is the plan realistic? Are the sales goals, expense budgets and milestone dates realistic? Nothing stifles implementation like unrealistic goals.

4. Is the plan complete? Does it include all the necessary elements? Requirements of a business plan vary, depending on the context. There is no guarantee, however, that the plan will work if it doesn't cover the main bases.

Use of Business Plans

Preparing a business plan is an organized, logical way to look at all of the important aspects of a business. First, decide what you will use the plan for, such as to:

- Define and fix objectives, and programs to achieve those objectives.

- Create regular business review and course correction.

- Define a new business.

- Support a loan application.

- Define agreements between partners.

- Set a value on a business for sale or legal purposes.

- Evaluate a new product line, promotion, or expansion.

No Time to Plan? A Common Misconception

"Not enough time for a plan," business people say. "I can't plan. I'm too busy getting things done."

Too many businesses make business plans only when they have to. Unless a bank or investors want to look at a business plan, there isn't likely to be a plan written. The busier you are, the more you need to plan. If you are always putting out fires, you should build fire breaks or a sprinkler system. You can lose the whole forest for too much attention to the individual trees.

Keys to Better Business Plans

- Use a business plan to set concrete goals, responsibilities, and deadlines to guide your business.

- A good business plan assigns tasks to people or departments and sets milestones and deadlines for tracking implementation.

- A practical business plan includes10 parts implementation for every one part strategy.

- As part of the implementation of a business plan, it should provide a forum for regular review and course corrections.

- Good business plans are practical.

Business Plan "Don'ts"

- Don't use a business plan to show how much you know about your business.

- Nobody reads a long-winded business plan: not bankers, bosses, nor venture capitalists. Years ago, people were favorably impressed by long plans. Today, nobody is interested in a business plan more than 50 pages long.

A Business Plan Fable

Once upon a time there were three entrepreneurs who set out to seek their fortunes. Each of them developed a business plan.

The first business plan was built of straw. It was easy to complete, but it was mostly just puffery. For example, it had objectives like "being the best" and "excellence in customer satisfaction" without any way to measure results. It had a lot of talk, but few specifics. I'd almost say it was written like a sales or public relations piece, except that not even those can really afford to skip the hard facts.

The second business plan was built of sticks. It was built on what a venture capitalist I know calls "hockey stick" forecasts. You can probably guess what that means. I've seen a lot of them. Sales grow slowly in the past but the forecast shoots up boldly with huge growth rates, just as soon as something happens. Usually the something that is supposed to happen is investment, usually with other people's money, and as soon as this plan gets the money wonderful things will happen. As one of my favorite teenagers would say, rolling her eyes with eloquent sarcasm, "yeah, right," and "oh, brother."

The third business plan was built of bricks. You can see them in Illustration 1-1. Bricks are specifics, especially "ownership," as in specific job responsibilities, specific people in charge of well-defined activities. Bricks are

---

Business plans don't sell new business ideas to venture capitalists. Venture capitalists invest in people and ideas, not plans. A business plan, though necessary, is only a way to present information.

milestone dates, deadlines, budgets, and concrete, measurable objectives.

Then came the real world, as awesome as the big bad wolf in a similar fable. The real world was phone calls and daily routine. It was business problems and changes in economic environment, customers paying slower than expected, costs going up on one product, down on another. In business school they called it the RW, prounounced "are-dub." I won't say anything about huffing and puffing.

The real world blew the plan of straw apart in an instant. It was worthless, forgotten, lost somewhere in a drawer, never to be referred to again. Nobody remembered what it said. It was useless.

The real world blew the plan of sticks apart too, in just a few instances. Nobody had paid much attention anyhow, because the forecasts were so wildly optimistic. Nobody had been given responsibility, and nobody would have taken it. The plan was simply ignored. It was useless.

The plan of bricks, however, stood up to the real world. As each month closed, the plan of bricks absorbed plan-vs.-actual results. Managers looked at the variance. They made adjustments. Each manager kept track of milestones and budgets, and at the end of each month the actual results were compared to the plan. Managers saw the performance of their peers. Changes were made in the plan--organized, rational changes--to accommodate changes in actual conditions. Managers were proud of their performance, and good performances were shared with all. And the company lived happily ever after.

Summary

Beyond specifics in the menus, please remember that your plan is yours. It doesn't belong to your software or your software publisher. You can easily omit the company chapter, for example, in an internal plan, or the marketing or personnel chapters, for that matter. The plan is yours, and the choices are yours.

This page intentionally blank.

CHAPTER 2:
Initial Assessment

*Start your business plan with a quick assessment. Even for an ongoing business, take the time to step away from the business and look at the basics. Do your business numbers make sense? One of my business school professors used to refer to this process as finding out "is there a **there** there?"*

For a first look, consider your objectives, mission statement and keys to success.

Objectives

Objectives are business goals. Set your market share objectives, sales objectives, and profit objectives. Companies need to set objectives and plan to achieve them.

Make sure your objectives are concrete and measurable. Be specific, such as achieving a given level of sales or profits, a percentage of gross margin, a growth rate, or a market share. Don't use generalities like "being the best" or "growing rapidly."

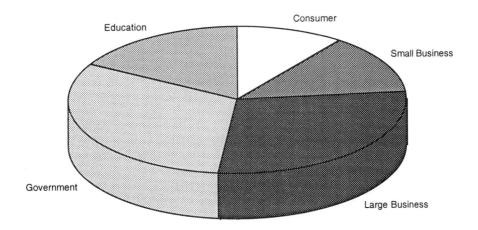

For example, "being the best" or "maximize customer satisfaction" are not serious business plan objectives, because they cannot really be measured. Much better objectives would set measurable goals such as holding gross margin to 25 percent as a minimum, or selling more than $3 million, or achieving six percent profit on sales and 10 percent return on equity.

If less tangible goals are critical to a plan, find a way to measure them. For example, if image and awareness are vital, then plan for statistically valid surveys to measure the improvements in image and awareness. You can also set goals for market share, and purchase research to measure the actual share. Or if you want to focus on customer satisfaction, plan for a survey to quantify satisfaction, or specify numerical objectives regarding returns or complaints.

The Mission Statement

Use the mission statement to define your business concept. A company mission statement should define underlying goals (such as making a profit) and objectives in broad strategic terms, including what market is served, and what benefits are offered.

What Business Are You In

Ask yourself what business you are in, and don't narrow yourself down. One of the classic business examples is the railroads, which lost a chance to expand in the twentieth century because they misdefined themselves. They thought they were in the business of running trains on tracks. They didn't understand they were in the business of transporting goods and people. When trucks and buses and highways grew, the railroads were left behind.

My company, Palo Alto Software, is not in the business of software development. It is in the business of helping people do business plans by themselves, providing business know-how through software and documentation. The broader definition helps us understand what we're up to.

Include Customer Satisfaction

Leading experts in developing customer satisfaction look to a mission statement to define customer satisfaction goals. Developing customer care programs depends on spreading the idea and importance within a company. That should normally start with a statement included in your mission statement.

Include Workplace Philosophy

Some mission statements also define internal goals such as maintaining a creative work environment and building respect for diversity. Experts in employee relations look immediately to a mission statement for a definition of a company's stand on some of these fundamental issues.

Value Propositions and Value-Based Marketing

Experts developed the value-based marketing framework to help companies understand their business better. This framework starts with a business value proposition, which states what benefits a business offers to whom, and at what relative price level. For example:

- This automobile manufacturer offers reliable, safe automobiles for familes at a relative price premium.

- This fast food restaurant offers quick and consistent lunches at a low price.

Keys to Success

Focusing on what I call "keys to success" is a good idea for getting a better view of the priorities in your business. Just about any business imaginable is going to depend a lot on three or four most important factors. In a retail business, for example, the classic joke is that the keys to success are "location, location, and location." In truth, that might be, for example, location, convenient parking, and low prices. A computer store's keys to success might be knowledgeable salespeople, major brands, and newspaper advertising.

Focus is very important, and the key to success framework helps you develop focus. There is what I call a law of inverse focus. I can't prove it with detailed research, but I've seen many times that beyond three or four key items, the more items on a priority list, the less chance of implementation. Thinking about keys to success is a great way to focus on the main elements that make your business work.

Stick to three or four items on a list of priorities, no more. The more items on the list, the less chance of implementating any of them.

Break-even Analysis

Next comes a simple Break-even Analysis table as shown in Illustration 2-1. Make the following three simple assumptions:

- Average per-unit sales price (per-unit revenue):

  The price that you charge per unit. Take into account sales discounts and special offers. For non-unit based businesses, make the per-unit revenue $1 and enter your costs as a percent of a dollar.

- Average per-unit cost:

  The incremental cost of each unit of sale. If you are using a Units Based Sales Forecast table (for manufacturing and mixed business types), you can project unit costs from the Sales Forecast table. If you

are using the basic Sales Forecast table for retail, service and distribution businesses, use a percentage estimate. For example, a retail store running a 50% margin would have a per-unit cost of .5, and a per-unit revenue of 1.

- Monthly Fixed costs:

  Technically, a break-even analysis defines fixed costs as costs that would continue even if you went broke. Instead, you may want to use your regular running fixed costs, including payroll and normal expenses. This will give you a better insight on financial realities.

Illustration 2-2 shows a Break-even chart. As sales increase, the profit line passes through the zero or break-even line at the break-even point.

Illustration 2-1: Break-even Analysis

Break Even Analysis:	
Monthly Units Break-even	1,030
Monthly Sales Break-even	$353,480
Assumptions:	
Average Unit Sale	$343.04
Average Per-Unit Cost	$248.15
Fixed Cost	$97,778

The break-even analysis calculates a break-even point based on fixed costs, variable costs per unit of sales, and revenue per unit of sales.

Illustration 2-2: Break-even Chart

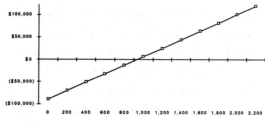

The Break-even chart shows that the company needs to sell almost 1,000 units per month to break even.

Illustration 2-2 shows that the company needs to sell approximately 1,000 units in order to cross the break-even line. This is a classic business chart that helps you consider your bottom-line financial realities. Can you sell enough to make your break-even volume?

Of course the break-even analysis depends on assumptions made for average per-unit revenue, average per-unit cost and fixed costs. These are rarely exact assumptions.

Market Analysis

You don't need to do major market research for this initial market analysis. You may want to, and even need to, do real research later on, and we talk about this in detail in Chapter 4 (nowadays that is almost all Internet research). For now, however, you want to get a good educated guess about how many potential customers you might have.

What you want at this point is a reality check. You've already developed a quick break-even analysis that ties your initial business numbers to your required sales. So now you're going to look at how many customers you might have, so you can think about the importance of breaking even.

Develop a basic Market Analysis table. This table gives you a simple list of market segments. Each segment is a group of customers. Define the groups according to what needs you supply, demographic characteristics, buying habits, preferences, or whatever other classification system works for your plan. Fill in the total potential customers estimate for each segment, and the annual growth rate expected for each segment.

Illustration 2-3 shows a Market Analysis table, and its corresponding chart is displayed on the first page of this chapter. You can use a Market Analysis chart as a visual guide to your market segments

Illustration 2-3: Market Analysis Table

Potential Customers	Total Cust's	Growth rate
Consumer	12,000	2%
Small Business	15,000	5%
Large Business	33,000	8%
Government	36,000	-2%
Education	19,000	0%
Total	115,000	n.a.

This analysis table lets you show the estimated total customer base and your projected growth rate for each group.

Pause for Reflection

At this point you've defined your business, your financial break-even point, and your total potential market. How does your business look from this viewpoint? Does it make sense? Can you make the sales you need to break even? Is the market big enough? Are your projections realistic? Can you bring together the keys to success?

At this point, especially for potential start-up companies, a moment of reflection is critical. Many people dream of starting a business, but that dream turns into a nightmare if the new business isn't successful.

Summary

If you think you can make your break-even numbers work, and you believe you have enough customers to make it, then go on to develop the plan. If not, either do more research and revise the idea, or give up and try something else.

CHAPTER 3:
Pick Your Plan

As we noted in Chapter 1, business planning is about results. Make the contents of your plan match your purpose. Don't accept a standard outline just because it's there.

In the United States business market, at least, there is a certain standardization about business plans. You can find dozens of books on the subject, about as many Web sites, two or three serious software products, and courses in hundreds of business schools, night schools, and community colleges. Although there are many variations on the theme, a lot of it is standard.

The Standard Business Plan Outline

So there are predictable contents of a standard business plan. For example, a business plan normally starts with an Executive Summary, which should be short and interesting. People almost always expect to see sections covering the company, the market, the product, the management team, strategy, and financial projections. The order of the sections might change from one plan to another, but those basic contents will almost always be there.

The table on the following two pages includes a complete standard business plan outline. You'll notice that I don't recommend developing the plan in the same order you present it as a finished document. For example, although the Executive Summary obviously comes as the first section of a business plan, I recommend writing it after everything else is done. It will appear first, but you write it last.

This book, therefore, discusses the business plan in the order you develop a plan, not in the same order as the document outline. The table on the next two pages explains, in detail, where the different tables and topics fall in a standard outline, and where you can find the related discussions in this book.

Outline order and sequence in a standard business plan.	Where the process is covered in this book.
1.0 Executive Summary 1.1 Objectives 1.2 Mission 1.3 Keys to Success	Chapter 14, *Strategy & Tactics,* helps you write the main summary. Chapter 2, *Initial Assessment*, talks about Objectives, Mission, and Keys to Success.
2.0 Company Summary 2.1 Company Ownership 2.2 Company History (for ongoing companies) or Start-up Plan (for new companies. 2.3 Company Locations and Facilities	Chapter 10, *Describe Your Company*, covers the company text section in your business plan as well as the related tables, either the Start-up or the Past Performance table.
3.0 Products (or services, or both) 3.1 Product (or service, or both) Description 3.2 Competitive Comparison 3.3 Sales Literature 3.4 Sourcing 3.5 Technology 3.6 Future Products	This is in Chapter 6, *What are You Selling*.

4.0 Market Analysis Summary
4.1 Market Segmentation
4.2 Target Market Segment Strategy
   4.2.1 *Market Needs*
   4.2.2 *Market Trends*
   4.2.3 *Market Growth*
4.3 Industry Analysis
   4.3.1 *Industry Participants*
   4.3.2 *Distribution Patterns*
   4.3.3 *Factors of Competition*
   4.3.4 *Main Competitors*
	We cover this in Chapter 4, *Know your Market*. Also included is the market analysis table and chart.
	
	This is all in Chapter 5, *The Business You're In.*

Outline order and sequence in a standard business plan. (cont.)	Where the process is covered in this book. (cont.)

5.0 Strategy and Implementation Summary

5.1 Strategy Pyramids

5.2 Value Proposition

5.3 Competitive Edge

5.4 Marketing Strategy

   5.4.1 Positioning Statement

   5.4.2 Pricing Strategy

   5.4.3 Promotion Strategy

   5.4.4 Marketing Programs

5.5 Sales Strategy

   5.5.1 Sales Forecast

   5.5.2 Sales Programs

5.6 Milestones

6.0 Management Summary

6.1 Organizational Structure

6.2 Management Team

6.3 Management Team Gaps

6.4 Personnel Plan

7.0 Financial Plan

7.1 Important Assumptions

7.2 Key Financial Indicators

7.3 Break-even Analysis

7.4 Projected Profit and Loss

7.5 Projected Cash Flow

7.6 Projected Balance Sheet

7.7 Business Ratios

7.8 Long-term Plan

Much of this is covered in Chapter 14, *Strategy & Tactics,* which also covers the recommended Milestones table. Implementation and plan-vs.-actual analysis comes up again in Chapter 16, *Planning for Implementation.*

The sales forecast discussions and the forecast itself are all the subject of this book's Chapter 7, *Forecast Your Sales.*

Chapter 8, *Your Management Team,* covers this text and the Personnel Plan table.

Chapter 9, *The Bottom Line,* covers the Profit and Loss and General Assumptions tables. Chapter 2, *Initial Assessment,* includes the Break-even table as part of the Initial Assessment. You deal with Cash Flow and the Cash Flow table in Chapter 10, *Describe Your Company,* the Balance Sheet table in Chapter 11, *About Business Numbers,* the Business Ratios table in Chapter 13, *Finish the Financials,* and the Long-term table in Chapter 14, *Strategy & Tactics.*

Standard Tables and Charts

There are also some business tables and charts that are normally expected in a standard business plan.

Cash flow is the single most important numerical analysis in a plan, and should never be missing. Most plans will also have sales forecast, and profit and loss statements. I believe they should also have separate personnel listings, projected balance sheet, projected business ratios, and market analysis.

 I also believe that every plan should include business charts that use bar charts and pie charts to illustrate the numbers.

Form Follows Function

However, as we noted in Chapter 1, business planning is about results. Make the contents of your plan match your purpose. Don't accept a standard outline just because it's there.

For example, if you are developing an internal plan for corporate use, you don't need to include a section about the company. If your plan focuses on well-known existing products or services and is intended for internal use only, you may not even need to include the details about the products.

Another example that comes up frequently is the level of detail required in your market analysis. Business plans looking for investors need to have some convincing market data, but a plan for a small local business, to be used mainly by a small group of people close to the company, may not need as much research. Is there an opportunity to improve the company and the plan by learning more about the market? Then do it. If not, it may be overkill.

Investor Summaries and Loan Applications

When a plan is used to back up a loan application or to explain a business to potential investors, it may require a special summary document as well as a complete plan. Many investors like to see a brief summary, and a loan application doesn't always require a complete plan. If you develop your plan in the right way, you can use the summary paragraphs of the main sections--company, market, product, etc.--to create these summary documents.

Timeframes: Is Three Years Enough?

Regarding the span or length of focus of a business plan--its timeframe--opinions vary. I believe a business plan should normally project sales by month for the next 12 months, and annual sales for the following two years. This doesn't mean businesses shouldn't plan for a longer term than just three years, not by any means. It does mean, however, that the detail of monthly forecasts doesn't pay off beyond a year, except in special cases. It also means that the detail in the three-year forecasts probably doesn't make sense beyond three years. Plan your business for five, 10, and even 15-year timeframes; just don't do it within the detailed context of business plan financials.

Summary

Beyond specifics in the menus, please remember that your plan outline is yours. It doesn't belong to your software or your software publisher. You can easily omit the company section, for example, in an internal plan, or the marketing or personnel sections, for that matter. You make the choices that best suit your needs.

This page intentionally blank.

CHAPTER 4:
Know Your Market

What's the first thing, the most essential element, you need in business? No, not a plan: **you need customers**.

In Chapter 2, Initial Assessment, you took a good first look at whether or not your business has (or will have) enough customers to keep it healthy. For the next step, you need to go further into a market analysis. It doesn't have to be academic, necessarily, and it doesn't have to be a huge project that stalls your planning process. What you want, ultimately, is to know your customers.

Simple and Practical Market Research

Some of the best market research is simple, practical, and even obvious. You don't get it from reference sections in libraries, or even from the Internet. Get it from real people, particularly customers or potential customers. Here are some practical examples.

Study Similar Businesses

Always take a good look at other businesses similar to your own, as a very good first step. If you're looking at starting a new business, you may well be starting one similar to one you already know. If you're doing a plan for an existing business, you are even more likely to know the business well. Even so, you can still learn a lot by looking at other similar businesses.

• **Look at existing, similar businesses.**

   If you are planning a retail shoe store, for example, spend some time looking at existing retail shoe store businesses. Park across the street and count the customers that go into the store. Note how long they stay inside, and how many come out with boxes that look like purchased shoes. You can probably even count how many pairs of shoes each customer buys. Browse the store and look at prices. Look at several stores, including the discount shoe stores and department store shoe departments.

- **Find a similar business in another place.**

  If you are planning a local business, find a similar business in another place, far enough away that you won't compete. For the shoe store example, you would identify some shoe stores in similar towns in other states. Call the owner, explain your purpose truthfully, and ask about the business.

- **Scan the local newspapers for people selling similar businesses.**

  Contact the broker and ask for as much information as possible. If you are thinking of creating a shoe store and you find one for sale, you should consider yourself a prospective buyer. Maybe buying the existing store is the best thing. Even if you don't buy, the information you gain will be very valuable. Why is the owner selling? Is there something wrong with the business? You can probably get detailed financial information.

- **Always shop the competition.**

  If you're a restaurant business, patronize the competition once a month, rotating through different

restaurants. If you're a shoe store, shop the competition once a month, at different stores.

Talk to Customers

If you're considering starting a new business, talk to potential customers. In the shoe store example, talk to people coming out of the stores. Talk to your neighbors, talk to your friends, talk to your relatives. Ask them how often they buy shoes, what sizes, where, at what price, and whatever else you can think of. If you're starting a restaurant, landscape architecture business, butcher shop, bakery, or whatever, talk to customers.

At most business schools, when they teach business planning, students have to do a market survey as part of the plan. The plan isn't complete unless they go out and ask a credible number of people what they want, why, where they get it, how much they pay, and so forth. Although you may not go through the formality of a customer survey for your business, this information is vital.

At Palo Alto Software, we put a customer survey on two of our three Web sites on the Internet. People browsing the Internet looking for material and information on business plans find our sites including **www.palo-alto.com**, **www.bizplans.com**, and

www.bplans.com. Two of those sites do no selling, but provide free information including free downloadable sample plans, outlines, and discussions (none of them nearly as complete as this manual, by the way, so don't be tempted to drop this book and turn to the Web instead; there is more information here on the printed page.) We asked people stopping by our business plan Web sites to answer a few quick questions that concerned us. The invitation promises just a few questions, and promises also that we won't ask their names or e-mail addresses, and we won't follow up with sales information. As of this writing, we get about 300 responses a month, which provides us with valuable information about the concerns people have as they consider writing a business plan.

If you have an ongoing business, the process of developing a plan should include talking to customers. Take a step away from the routine, dial up some of your customers, and ask them about your business. How are you doing? Why do they buy? How do they feel about your competitors? It is a good idea to take a customer to lunch once a month, just to keep yourself in touch.

Count Potential Customers

Most business plans contain an analysis of potential customers. We saw that in Chapter 2, as part of the initial assessment. As an essential first step, you should have a good idea of how many potential customers there are. The way you find that out depends on your type of business. For example, a retail shoe store needs to know about individuals living in a local area, a graphic design firm needs to know about local businesses, and a national catalog needs to know about households and companies in an entire nation.

Good sources depend on what you need. Government and commercial statistics are usually more than enough, but for some plans you may end up purchasing information from professional publishers or contract researchers.

For general demographic data about a local area, if you have no easier source, ask the reference desk at a local library. A local university library is even better, particularly a business library. Chambers of Commerce usually have general information about a local market. In the United States, there is the federal government's U.S. Census Bureau. Nowadays the quickest route to the census bureau is the Internet Web site at **www.census.gov**.

The official statistics are good for business information as well. You should be able to find a count of local businesses, with some measure of size such as sales or employees. The U.S. Census Bureau has a lot of information on businesses, and you can find free information at the Chamber of Commerce and probably at a local library.

Before the Internet became so prevalent, I frequently turned to vendors of mailing lists for general information about people and types of business. The mailing list vendors often have catalogs listing total numbers of types of people and types of business. For example, to find out how many attorneys or CPA offices there are in the United States, I might look at the lists for sale at a list broker.

Magazines provide another good source of demographics. If you're selling to computer stores, for example, call *Computer Retail Week* and *Computer Reseller News* and ask both publications for a media kit. The media kit is intended to sell pages of advertising to potential advertisers. They are frequently full of demographics on the readers. For information on any specific type of business, get the media kits for the magazines that cater to those types of businesses as readers.

Just browsing the census bureau Web site while preparing this draft, it took me about 10 minutes to discover that my home county has 378 general contractors, of which 360 have fewer

than 20 employees and the remaining 18 have between 20 and 100. There are 238 legal businesses in my county, of which only 12 have more than 20 employees. Also, following the shoe store example, there are 32 shoe stores in Lane County, OR, none of them having more than 20 employees. And there are 111,000 households in the county, 61 percent of them owner occupied, and an average of 2.49 people per household. Some 22 percent of adults in the county are college graduates, and the median household income is $26,000. All of this information was available for free at the U.S. Census Bureau Web site at **www.census.gov**.

Know the Customers

Aside from just counting the customers, you also want to know what they need, what they want, and what makes them buy. The more you know about them, the better. For individuals as customers, you probably want to know their average age, income levels, family size, media preferences, buying patterns, and as much else as you can find out that relates to your business. If you can, you want to divide them into groups according to useful classifications such as income, age, buying habits, social behavior, values, or whatever other factors are important. For the shoe store, for example, shoe size is good, but you might also want activity preferences and even--if you can find it--psychographics.

Psychographics divides customers into cultural groups, value groups, social sets, motivator sets, or other interesting categories that might be useful for classifying customers. For example, in literature intended for potential retailers, First Colony Mall of Sugarland, Texas, describes its local area psychographics as including "25% Kid & Cul-de-Sacs (upscale suburban families, affluent), 5.4% winner's circle (suburban executives, wealthy), 19.2% boomers and babies (young white-collar suburban, upper middle income), and 7% country squires (elite exurban, wealthy)." Going into more detail, it calls the Kids & Cul-de-Sacs group "a noisy medley of bikes, dogs, carpools, rock music and sports." The winners circle customers are "well-educated, mobile, executives and professionals with teen-aged families. Big producers, prolific spenders, and global travelers." The country squires are "where the wealthy have escaped urban stress to live in rustic luxury. No. 4 in affluence, big bucks in the boondocks."

Stanford Research Institute (SRI) provides another example. Its VALS service offers information on U.S. customers classified according to the value sets shown in Illustration 4-1. Customers and potential customers are divided into groups including fulfilleds,

Illustration 4-1: SRI's Psychographics

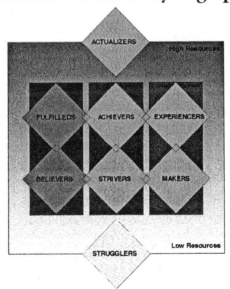

The diagram illustrates SRI's VALS values and lifestyles psychographics research that divides the U.S. market into various types of potential customers.

achievers, experiencers, and others. More information about that is available from SRI at the Web site **http://future.sri.com/VALS/valsindex.html**. The e-mail is vals@sri.com, and the main telephone number is (650) 326-6200.

The Internet Revolutionizes Business Plan Research

I'm old enough to remember when gathering information was a problem. Business consultants could make money just collecting the kind of information you need for a good business plan market analysis. These days, however, the problem is much more sorting through all the information than it is gathering information. The World Wide Web on the Internet has completely changed research, especially practical business research.

This is far too much a topic to cover in this book, but it is also vital to modern business. By the time you're looking at developing a business plan, I think you should know how to use the World Wide Web on the Internet. At the very least, know how to find Yahoo at **www.yahoo.com** and sort through its catalog of business information. You should also go to Excite at **www.excite.com**, and know how to search for business information on that search engine. New search engines and new searching techniques appear all the time, so please try to stay current.

Illustration 4-2: The Yahoo Internet Catalog

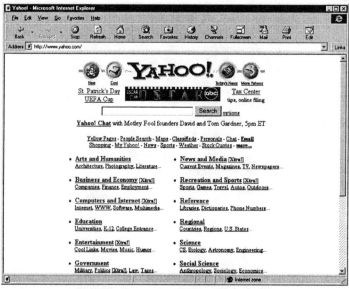

The Yahoo site (www.yahoo.com), probably the best-known Internet navigational aid, sorts and catalogs the World Wide Web according to logical categories. It is a frequent first stop for information gathering.

Just as an example, Illustration 4-2 shows Yahoo's main page.

As you click on any of the underlined words, the view opens up to more information and more specifics. Illustration 4-3 shows the main search page at Excite.

Your Market Segmentation Scheme is Critical

The market segmentation concept is crucial to market assessment and market strategy. Divide the market into workable market segments — age, income, product type, geography, buying patterns, customer needs, or other classifications. Define your terms, and define your market.

Segmentation can make a huge difference in understanding your market. For example, when a local computer store business defines its customer segments as "high-end home office" and "high-technology small business," its segmentation says a lot about its customers. The segmentation helps the company plan focus on the different types of potential customers. When I was consulting for Apple Computer in the middle 1980s, we divided the markets into workable categories including home, education, small business, large business, and all others. Some other groups in Apple also focused

Illustration 4-3: Searching the Net with Excite

The Excite Internet search engine at www.excite.com is another leading Internet search site that you can use to help you locate market and business information.

on government as a specific market segment. As you define the segment you point toward an understanding of the market. In the 1970s, I knew a company that was selling candy bars through retail channels. They segmented the market in a way that defined a range of products as "oral satisfacters" (their term, not mine). That included candy, cookies, soft drinks, and bagged chips. The segmentation helped the marketers understand their real competition, which wasn't just other candy bars, but also other products targetting the same customer money. That understanding of competition improved the marketing and sales programs.

In today's business it's easy to see segmentation in action. Consider the different tone, content, and media for ads that sell kids products to kids, compared to those that sell the same product to parents. Car companies change their advertising substantially from one type of program to another. Stand-up comedian Richard Klein used to joke about the beer company ads that changed the style of the music to match the audience. He complained that he kept getting the country music version, but he liked the blues version better. The company that did those ads used the styles of music to address different target customer groups.

In developing segmentation, consider what factors make a difference in the purchasing, media, and value patterns of your target groups. Does age matter in choice of restaurants, or is style and food preference more important? Is income level a key factor? Education? I suspect some restaurants will sell more meals to college graduates than others. Is this because of education, age, or income levels? That depends on your business.

In your initial assessment you may have already developed your first basic Market Analysis worksheet for analyzing potential customers. It will help you define your market and understand your key market segments. As you complete your market analysis, look at your segmentation critically, and strategically. Is this the best segmentation? Be sure to revise and polish your numbers.

The Market Analysis Table and Chart

As part of the business plan, you should generate enough information to develop a basic Market Analysis table. Illustration 4-4 gives you a simple example implemented as a spreadsheet table.

This sample table gives you a simple list of market segments. Each segment is a group of customers, classified according to the market segments you define. You can create a simple market analysis by estimating the number of potential customers for each segment, and the growth rate, as shown in the example. Once you have those numbers it should be a simple step to develop the corresponding chart in Illustration 4-5.

Filling Out the Text

After you find out about your market for a business plan, you also want to communicate that knowledge to the readers of your plan. Keep your explanations clear and concise. The depth of detail in market analysis will

Illustration 4-4: Market Analysis Table

Potential Customers	Total Cust's	Growth rate
Consumer	12,000	2%
Small Business	15,000	5%
Large Business	33,000	8%
Government	36,000	-2%
Education	19,000	0%
Total	115,000	n.a.

This table shows a simple classification of market segments, each segment defined by its total potential customer count and its estimated growth rate.

Illustration 4-5: Market Analysis Chart

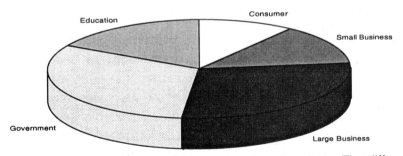

This simple pie chart shows the potential market as the plan starts. The different segments of the pie show the relative sizes of different target market groups.

depend a lot on the type of plan. You may not need to provide a complete market study in a plan developed for internal use, when all of your team knows the market well. Maybe you'll just cite the type of customers you attract, and the part of town you serve. The market analysis section in a business plan is the section that is most likely to require research for information from outside your business, while most others require thinking and analysis of factors within your business.

This is a good point to add a word of caution about the level of detail required. Please remember that planning is about making good decisions, applying focus and enforcing priorities. A good useful business plan doesn't necessarily include a market analysis suitable for a Ph.D. candidate in market research. Planning is not about testing your knowledge. If you are looking for investment, then you may have to use this section to display your wisdom and understanding of your industry, but don't overdo it. If you are planning an internal plan and have no audience other than your own team, we recommend enough market research to make sure you're not missing key points.

The value of information is limited by its impact on decisions. If more market information is not going to help you do something better, then don't bother.

Begin With a Summary

Your market section should begin with a simple summary. You should generally describe the different groups of target customers included in your market analysis, and refer briefly to why you are selecting these as targets. You may also want to summarize market growth, citing highlights of some growth projections, if you have this information available.

Assume that this paragraph might be included in a loan application or investment summary, so you need it to summarize the rest of the section. What information would be most important, if you had only one brief topic to include about your market? One good technique is to skip this topic until you have finished the rest of the section. Then go back to the summary to write the highlights.

Explain your Segmentation

Make sure to explain and define the different segments in your table, particularly since you refer to them and they are the basis of your strategy. What distinguishes small business from large business, if this is part of your segmentation? Do you classify them by sales, number of employees, or some other factor? I've seen segmentations that define customers by the channels they buy in, as in the retail customer compared to the wholesale or direct customer, also compared to the Internet download customer. Have you defined which segment is which, and why?

As you deal with segmentation, you should also introduce the strategy behind it and your choice of target markets. Explain why your business is focusing on these specific target market groups. What makes these groups more interesting than the other groups that you've ruled out? Why are the characteristics you specify important. This is more important for some businesses than others. A clothing boutique, for example, might focus on one set of upper-income customers instead of another, for strategic reasons. An office equipment store might focus on certain business types whose needs match the firm's expertise. Some fast food restaurants focus on families with children under driving age. Strategy is focus, it is creative, and it doesn't follow pre-written formulas.

Explain Market Needs, Growth, and Trends

All marketing should be based on underlying needs. For each market segment included in your strategy, explain the market needs that lead to this group's wanting to buy your service. Did the need exist before the business was there? Are there other products or services or stores that offer different ways to satisfy this same need? Do you have market research related to this market need? It is always a good idea to try to define your retail offering in terms of target market needs, so you focus not on what you have to sell, but rather on the buyer needs you satisfy. As a shoe store, for example, are you selling shoes or are you satisfying the customer needs for covered feet? Are there really underlying needs, such as style and prestige for fashion footware, or padding for runners, or jumping for basketball players, that relate to selling shoes? Are kids buying status with their basketball shoes?

Understand and explain market trends. What factors seem to be changing the market, or changing the business? What developing trends can make a difference? Market trends could be changes in demographics, changes in customer needs, new sense of style or fashion, or something else. It depends on what business you are in.

For example, a building supply store might note the trend toward remodeling older homes instead of buying new homes, or a trend toward more rooms in larger houses, despite smaller families, because of home offices, dens, and exercise rooms.

A grocery store might note a trend toward Asian foods or spicier foods, or toward fresher, healthier foods, or development of a new shopping area in a different part of town.

A medical supplies store might note demographic trends, as baby boomers age, leading toward more need for estate planning and retirement planning. Look to market trends as a way to get ahead of the market, to know where it is going before it gets there.

You should also understand and explain market growth in each segment. Ideally you cite experts, a market expert, market research firm, trade association, or credible journalist.

Summary

Projecting market growth is particularly important when your plan is related to finding investors, or supporting a loan application, because market growth enhances the implied value of your business.

Cite growth rates in terms that fit the available information, whether growth in the number of potential customers, projected dollar sales, meals served, Web site projects, tax reporting hours, yards to landscape, or whatever you have.

Whenever you can, relate the growth rates cited in expert forecasts to the growth in potential customers that you included in the market analysis table.

CHAPTER 5:
The Business You're In

With your initial market analysis done, you're still not through a standard business plans's market analysis chapter. In addition to the information you've already developed, you also need to explain the type of business you're in.

You'll be expected to explain the general state of your industry and the nature of the business, especially if your plan is going outside your company to banks or investors.

Whether you're a service business, manufacturer, retailer, or some other type of business, you should do an Industry Analysis, describing:

- Industry Participants
- Distribution Patterns
- Competition and Buying Patterns

The following section describes these topics in more detail.

Industry Analysis

A complete business plan discusses general industry economics, industry participants, distribution patterns, factors in the competition, and whatever else describes the nature of this business to outsiders.

The previous chapter brought up the enormous impact of the Internet on the state of business information. Finding information isn't really the problem any more, after the information explosion and the huge growth in the Internet during the 1990s. Even 10 or 15 years ago, dealing with information was more a problem of sorting through it all than of finding raw data. That generality is more true every day.

There are Web sites for business analysis, financial statistics, demographics, trade associations, and just about everything you'll need for a complete business plan. We'll look at that in this chapter after going through some of the topics to cover. I'll also include some of the old-fashioned reference works too, just in case you really need them.

Industry Participants

You can't easily describe a type of business without describing the nature of the participants. There is a huge difference, for example, between an industry like long-distance telephone trunk services, in which there are only a few huge companies in any one country, and one like dry cleaning, in which there are tens of thousands of smaller participants.

This can make a big difference to a business and a business plan. The restaurant industry, for example, is what we call "pulverized," which, like the dry cleaning industry, is made up of many small participants. The fast food business, on the other hand, is composed of a few national brands participating in thousands of branded outlets, many of them franchised.

Economists talk of consolidation in an industry as a time when many small participants tend to disappear and a few large players emerge. In accounting, for example, there are a few large international firms whose names are well known, and tens of thousands of smaller firms. The automobile business is composed of a few national brands participating in thousands of branded dealerships. In computer manufacturing, for example, there are a few large international firms whose names are well known, and thousands of smaller firms.

Distribution Patterns

Explain how distribution works in this industry. Is this an industry in which retailers are supported by regional distributors, as is the case for computer products, magazines, or auto parts? Does this industry depend on direct sales to large industrial customers? Do manufacturers support their own direct sales forces, or do they work with product representatives?

Some products are almost always sold through retail stores to consumers, and sometimes these are distributed by distribution companies that buy from manufacturers. In other cases, the products are sold directly from manufacturers to stores. Some products are sold directly from manufacturer to the final consumer, through mail campaigns, national advertising, or other promotional means.

In many product categories there are several alternatives, and distribution choices are strategic. Encyclopedias and vacuum cleaners are traditionally sold door-to-door, but are also sold in stores and direct from manufacturer to consumer through radio and television ads.

Many products are distributed through direct business-to-business sales, and in long-term contracts such as the ones between car manufacturers and their suppliers of parts, materials, and components. In some industries companies use representatives, agents, or commissioned salespeople.

Technology can change the patterns of distribution in an industry or product category. The Internet, for example, is changing the options for software distribution, books, music, and other products. Cable communication is changing the options for distributing video products and video games.

The Distribution Patterns topic may not apply to most service companies, because distribution is normally about physical distribution of specific physical products. If you are a restaurant, graphic artist, professional services practice, architect, or some other service that doesn't involve distribution, just delete this topic.

For a few services, distribution may still be relevant. A phone service or cable provider, or an Internet provider, might describe distribution related to physical infrastructure. Some publishers may

prefer to treat their business as a service, rather than a manufacturing company, and in that case distribution may also be relevant.

Competition and Buying Patterns

Explain the nature of competition in this market. This topic is still in the general area of describing the industry, or type of business. Explain the general nature of competition in this business, and how the customers seem to choose one provider over another. What are the keys to success? What buying factors make the most difference--Price? Product features? Service, support, training, software? Delivery dates? Are brand names important?

In the computer business, for example, competition might depend on reputation and trends in one part of the market, and on channels of distribution and advertising in another. In many business-to-business industries, the nature of competition depends on direct selling, because channels are impractical. Price is vital in products competing with each other on retail shelves, but delivery and reliability might be much more important for materials used by manufacturers in volume, for which a shortage can affect an entire production line.

In the restaurant business, for example, competition might depend on reputation and trends in one part of the market, and on location and parking in another.

In many professional service practices the nature of competition depends on word of mouth, because advertising is not completely accepted. Is there price competition between accountants, doctors, and lawyers? How do people choose travel agencies or florists for weddings? Why does someone hire one landscape architect over another? Why choose Starbucks, a national brand, over the local coffee house? All of this is the nature of competition.

Main Competitors

List the main competitors. What are the strengths and weaknesses of each? Consider their products, pricing, reputation, management, financial position, channels of distribution, brand awareness, business development, technology, or other factors that you feel are important. In what segments of the market do they operate? What seems to be their strategy? How much do they impact your products, and what threats and opportunities do they represent?

Finding Business Information

You'll end up getting almost everything you need on the Internet, using the World Wide Web. As it turns out, a great deal of business information and small business or entrepreneurial help is readily available. Always start first on the Internet.

Market research firms and industry experts publish much of their information in Web sites, and in trade and business magazines. Reference sites index these magazines, many offer the texts on line, and if not, then libraries stock them. Trade associations publish many listings and statistics, in their Web sites as well as in hard-copy publications. Public stock laws require detailed reporting of financial results and stock market information sources compile industry statistics from financial reports.

You can probably find everything you need on the Internet, using the local library as an alternative. If not, you can turn to university libraries, professional information brokers, and United States government publications.

Since you already have a personal computer (or you wouldn't be using this software), you have most of what you need to access the information on the Internet. These services offer computerized versions of publication indices, statistical abstracts, and even complete text of published articles that are available online. In some cases, you can load information from a remote database into your computer and dump it in a convenient format directly into your business plan.

If you aren't already online, I urge you to get a modem and communications software. Get your Internet access, and learn how to use it. There is no substitute for the facility to dial up to the Internet through a modem and communicate with other people who have questions, advice, and similar interests. The Internet offers an amazing array of information and services. As you read through the more specific suggestions to follow, you can assume that most all of them have Web sites available.

Business Plan Sites

Palo Alto Software maintains two Internet Web sites that offer free downloadable sample plans, tips, outlines, and discussions of topics related to developing a business plan. Look for them at **www.bplans.com** and **www.bizplans.com**. Both of these sites include suggested links to other sources of small business information, including the Small Business Administration (SBA), Small Business Development Centers (SBDCs), and many other valuable sites.

Illustration 5-1 shows Palo Alto Software's main Web site, as it looked when this book was written. The Web site address is **http://www.palo-alto.com.**

It is stocked with latest available information and references to information that might be available elsewhere. For example, this site includes a complete list of Small Business Development Centers and a list of business plan consultants.

Government Sites

We described the U.S. Census Bureau site, **www.census.gov**, in the previous chapter on market analysis. Be sure to visit the Small Business Administration (SBA) Web site at **www.sba.gov**. Illustration 5-2 shows their home page.

Commercial Web Search Engines

Another excellent lead is Yahoo's small business information listing. From the main page at Yahoo, choose Business and Economy, then click on the link at small business information. The specific page address is:

www.yahoo.com/Business_and_Economy/ Small_Business_Information.

Excite's competition for that is a small

business information page that I found at:

http://quicken.excite.com/small_business/

Each one of these Web sites lead to further links, and more information.

RMA Associates

Robert Morris Associates (also called The RMA Associates) is a membership organization sponsored by banks, which publishes an annual listing of standard financial ratios developed by polling member banks for actual business results of thousands of different companies in small business.

The association's publication called *Annual Statement Studies* is a very valuable source of information. That study tells me, for example, that shoe retailers selling less than $1 million per year make an average of 42 percent gross margins, they spend an average of 40 percent on operating expenses, and they net about one percent of sales as profits. That number comes from the RMA *Annual Statement Studies* from 1997.

Illustration 5-1: Palo Alto Software's Main Web site

The Palo Alto Software Web site is intended to provide valuable information to our customers, including market information, sample plans, and links to other sources of information.

The publication sells for less than $30 in hard copy at this writing, and a disk version is less than $150. You can find out more at **www.rmahq.org**, the Web site, or with the association directly at (215) 446-4000. As this is written, the RMA organization is looking at making its numbers more accessible, possibly allowing a direct search on the Web site. We are also looking at offering those numbers on the Palo Alto Software Web site at **www.palo-alto.com**, if possible.

Trade Associations

Many industries are blessed with an active trade association that serves as a vital source of industry-specific information. Such associations regularly publish member directories and the better ones publish statistical information that track industry sales, profits, economic trends, etc.

If you don't know which trade associations apply to your industry, find out. Search the Internet in Yahoo, Excite, and other search engines. Look for the Web site of the trade association for your industry. Ask at the reference section of

Illustration 5-2: SBA Web site

The Small Business Administration Internet site offers a wealth of free information and links to other sources as well.

your library for listings of industry associations. Ask someone else in the same industry. Consult an industry-specific magazine. Look in the readers guide or business index (later in this chapter) or *Ayer's Directory*, published by Gayle Publishers of Philadelphia, which lists periodicals. You can also look for association listings in *Information U.S.A.*, published by Viking Press.

As a specific example, since we mentioned a hypothetical shoe store, the National Shoe Retailers Association publishes a biennial Business Performance Report, a statistical review of more than 1,700 independent shoe retail companies. They sell it for $25 to members, or $50 to non-members. It covers men's, women's, children's, and family shoe companies, and includes standard financials, statistics, and other information.

Business Publications

Business magazines are an important source of business information. Aside from the major general-interest business publications (*Business Week*, *Wall Street Journal*, etc.) there are many specialty publications that look at specific industries.

Specialization is an important trend in the publishing business. Dingbats and Widgets may be boring to the general public, but they are exciting to Dingbat and Widget manufacturers who read about them regularly in their specialized magazines. The magazines are an important medium for industry-specific advertising, which is important to readers as well as advertisers.

The editorial staffs of these magazines have to fill the space between the ads. They do that by publishing as much industry-specific information as they can find, including statistics, forecasts, and industry profiles. Paging through one of these magazines can sometimes produce a great deal of business forecasting and economic information.

Several good reference sources list magazines, journals, and other publications. They also offer indexes to published articles which you can use to search for the exact references you need. These will be kept in the reference section of most libraries.

- *Readers Guide to Periodical Literature* indexes popular magazines. Published by H.W. Wilson of New York. Available in most library reference sections.

- *Business Periodicals Index*, also published by H.W. Wilson of New York. Indexes business magazines and journals only.

- *The Magazine Index*, published by Information Access Co.

Use the indexes to identify published information that might help your marketing plan. When you find an index listing for an article that forecasts your industry or talks about industry economics or trends, jot down basic information on the publication and ask the library for a copy of the publication.

Reference Libraries

Reference librarians follow reference sources as a profession. They are excellent sources of good advice and tips on reference materials that may help you provide the information your business plan requires.

We have found Predicast *Sourcebooks* particularly useful on several occasions. These summarize forecasts that have appeared in any of several hundred business magazines and journals. The presentation focuses on the most important forecast information, and provides the magazine citation--date of publication, page number, etc.--as background.

The Small Business Administration (SBA)

The U.S. Small Business Administration (SBA) is most known for its small business loans, which were covered in the previous appendix. However, it also provides business training, business information, and business services including workshops, individual counseling, publications, and videotapes. It has program offices in every state, the District of Columbia, the Virgin Islands and Puerto Rico. It has business development specialists stationed in more than 100 field offices nationwide. We noted its Web site in Illustration 5-2. The SBA publishes more than 50 business booklets and information products. These products are free, but the SBA suggests a small donation, under $3.00 for most of them. They answer many frequently asked questions and provide important information for business owners and would-be business owners.

If you don't have Web access, you can find out about SBA business development programs and services by calling the SBA Small Business Answer Desk at 1-800-U-ASK-SBA (827-5722). The answer desk "hotline" provides an information and referral service staffed by the organization's office of business initiatives, education, and training. In Washington D.C. the local number is

(202) 205-7333. It operates during normal office hours five days a week.

Small Business Development Centers

Small business development centers (SBDCs) are funded in part by the Small Business Administration (SBA) and also work with local colleges and some other funding agencies. Every state has at least one SBDC, and most states have several offices in several cities. The Palo Alto Software Web site at **www.palo-alto.com** is one of several that list SBDC addresses for several hundred offices.

We've found the SBDCs to be an excellent resource for businesses, offering high quality professional advice at very low prices. SBDCs also work closely with local colleges to participate in and provide courses in business topics such as business planning, bookkeeping, employee management, sales, marketing, and other vital subjects. SBDCs also publish books, surveys and studies, and in some cases, even audio tapes, videotapes and workshops. Palo Alto Software has worked with SBDCs in the past, to provide software and seminar courses related to business planning.

SCORE

The SBA sponsors the Service Corps of Retired Executives (SCORE), which includes more than 13,000 volunteers who provide training and one-on-one counseling at no charge, in 389 offices all over the country. You can find out about SCORE at **www.score.org** on the World Wide Web.

The United States Census Bureau

The United States Census Bureau, part of the Department of Commerce, has a wealth of information available for business and educational purposes. I referred to it specifically and with examples in the previous chapter.

Most of the Census Bureau's reports cover the entire United States and summarize data for the nation. However, the Bureau also publishes information on states, counties in states, and even cities within counties. Among the more valuable special reports are county and city reports that list the number of business establishments by type of establishment in many county and city areas. These are special reports available directly from the bureau and also from some libraries and electronic database services. Many of these reports are available through online services. The Census has an electronic edition called CENDATA. It also has an Internet Web site at **http://www.census.gov**. The U.S. Department of Commerce has a Web site at **http://www.doc.gov**.

Finding Business Assistance

New businesses, small businesses, and business planning are good for an economy. Governments, higher education institutions, and business organizations know that and try to help businesses as much as possible. For you and your business, there is probably a great deal of help available. But you need to know where to ask.

SBDCs and SCORE

We've listed the SBA, SCORE, and SBDCs in the previous section as sources of information. Both SCORE and the SBDCs are also sources of real business assistance. They both exist to help people in small business and entrepreneurs. Not all services are free, but those that aren't free are priced way below market value. For business assistance, go there first. You can get local addresses for SBDCs on our Web

site at **www.palo-alto.com**, and for SCORE you can find local addresses at **www.score.org**.

In this book, I only describe the United States organizations offering help to small business and start-ups. In other markets, similar organizations exist. Check with your chambers of commerce and industry organizations, government development organizations, and business schools.

Consultants, Accountants, and Attorneys

Consultants, accountants, and attorneys are the first line of business assistance. They aren't really the main focus of this chapter, however, and not because they aren't, in general, excellent sources of information. We have the utmost respect for the value of professional advice. In this discussion, however, we deal with relatively low-cost sources of business assistance, such as development agencies, local night schools, and online information services. We don't have a lot to add to the general doctrine of how to choose a good business professional. Let the buyer beware. A good business professional is always worth the money, if you have the money. Unfortunately, not all professionals are good and it's hard to know who's good until you've committed money.

Always try to get some good references on professionals – other clients, satisfied clients – before you use them, and don't forget to check the references. Furthermore, it is not always true that with business consultants you get what you pay for. In our experience there is not always a direct correlation between the fees charged and the value provided.

The SBA says consultants "can be a great asset to a small business owner. A business consultant's fees typically range between $25 and $250 an hour. If you decide to retain the services of a consultant, make sure he/she is reputable and be certain that you understand the fee schedule up-front."

Local Help

Wherever you are, there are probably several local sources of business assistance and information.

Business Organizations

Explore what's available through local business organizations such as the Chamber of Commerce. Many areas have entrepreneurial interest groups, such as a new enterprise forum, entrepreneur's association, or industry associations. Some also have municipal or county development organizations whose main goal is to help companies get started.

Schools and Colleges

Many local community colleges work directly with the SBA to house the Small Business Development Centers (SBDCs) discussed as part of the government resources, in the following section. The community college/SBDC combination is often an excellent resource for workshops, classes, and even business consulting, all of it with experts whose job involves helping small businesses and start-ups, funded at least in part by the school and the government. Call your local community college and ask about business classes.

Libraries

Local libraries regularly carry business periodicals and business books. Reference sections are frequently staffed by experts who are happy to help you find what you need. Look for magazine indexes, trade association annual publications, and government publications.

Banks

Banks are often involved in local development activities, and even when they don't directly offer business help (some do) they will at least know where else you can go for help in the local area. The SBA says "many bank officers have a broad understanding of finance, business operations, and the local economic climate. Do not be afraid to ask your banker questions."

State Development Agencies

Most states have development agencies of one kind or another. They also offer information related to small business and start-ups, and can be a valuable resource. Check with your other resource providers about state agencies; you can also look in your telephone directory for government agencies under the State category.

Trade Associations

In some industries, trade associations can be an excellent source of good information for start-ups. This varies according to your specific industry. Use your library directory of trade associations – the reference librarian should be able to find it for you – to explore associations related to your industry.

Publications

Many publications specialize in your industry, and others specialize in small businesses and start-ups. Explore libraries and bookstores for general business publications; find magazine directories for specialty publications for your specific industry.

Summary

We are in a brave new world of too much information, not too little. It will be hard for you to sort through all the information you'll find on your business or your industry, hard to summarize, hard to decide what is most important. As you do, keep in mind that the business plan is supposed to guide decisions. It is not a school report or even a graduate thesis. If it doesn't have a business purpose--which might be describing the industry for bank or investor, or for your own team, for example, but certainly not just to prove you can--then you shouldn't include it.

This page intentionally blank.

CHAPTER 6:
What You Sell

This step in the process is much more important for a plan going to external readers, the banks or investors, than for internal plans. A complete business plan describes what you sell: either products, services, or both.

This part of the plan is mainly description. Sometimes it will include tables that provide more details, such as a bill of materials or detailed price lists. More frequently, however, this section is mainly text. It normally comes as Chapter 3.0 in the plan, after the company description, but before the market analysis.

Start with a Summary Paragraph

Every section in a business plan should have an opening paragraph that describes the rest of the section. These summary paragraphs can also be used quite effectively in Summary memos and Loan Application support documents. Readers may frequently skip the details, but only when they have an effective summary. It should be a clear and concise single paragraph that can be merged into the executive summary page. For this section, what do you sell, and to whom?

Detailed Description

The previous topic was the summary, so in this topic, you need to provide more detail. List and describe the products or services you sell. For each business offering, cover the main points, including what the product or service is, how much it costs, what sorts of customers make purchases, and why. What customer need does each product or service line fill? You might not want or need to include every product or service in the list, but at least consider the main sales lines.

It is always a good idea to think in terms of customer needs and customer benefits as you define your product offerings, rather than thinking of your side of the equation--how much the product or service costs, and how you deliver it to the customer.

As you list and describe your sales lines, you may run into one of the serendipitous benefits of good business planning, which is generating new ideas. Describe your product offerings in terms of customer types and customer needs, and you'll often discover new needs and new kinds of customers to cover. This is the way ideas are generated.

Competitive Comparison

Use this topic for a general comparison of your offering as one of several choices a potential buyer can make. There is a separate topic, in the market analysis section, for detailed comparison of strengths and weaknesses of your specific competitors.

In this topic you should discuss how your product lines and retail offering compare in general to the others. For example, your outdoor store might offer better ski equipment than others, or perhaps it is located next to the slopes and caters to rental needs. Your jewelry store might be mid-range in price but well known for proficiency in appraisals, remounts, and renovation. Your hobby shop has by far the largest selection of model trains and airplanes.

In other words, in this topic you want to discuss how you are positioned in the market. Why do people buy from your business instead of from others in the same market? What do you offer, at what price, to whom, and how does your mix compare to others? Think about specific kinds of benefits, features, and market groups, comparing where you think you can show the difference. Describe the important competitive features of your products and/or services. Why do people buy from you instead of others? Do you sell better features, better price, better quality, better service, or some other factor?

Sourcing and Fulfillment

In this section, you want to explain your product sourcing and the cost of fulfilling your service. Manufacturers and assemblers should present spreadsheet output showing standard costs and overhead. Distributors should present discount and margin structures. Service companies should present costs of fulfilling service obligations.

For example, sourcing is extremely important to a manufacturing company. Your vendors determine your standard costs and hold the key to continued operation. Analyze your standard costs and the materials or services you purchase as part of your manufacturing operation. Look for strengths and weaknesses.

Manufacturing companies want to have ample information about resource planning and sourcing of vital materials, especially if you are preparing a plan for outsiders such as bankers or investors, or for business valuation. In this case, you may have additional documentation you can copy and attach as appendices, perhaps even contracts with important suppliers, standard cost breakdowns, bills of materials, and other information.

Where materials are particularly vital to your manufacturing, you might discuss whether second sources or alternative sources are available, and whether or not you use them or maintain relationships with them. This is also a good time to look at your sourcing strategy, and whether or not you can improve your business by improving your product sourcing.

But sourcing is not just for product-based companies. For example, a professional service company, such as an accounting practice, medical practice, law practice, management consulting firm, or graphic design firm, is normally going to provide the service by employing professionals. In this case, the cost is mainly the salaries of those professionals. Other service businesses are quite different. The travel agency provides a service through a combination of knowledge, rights, and infrastructure, including computer systems and databases. The Internet provider or telephone company provides a service by owning and maintaining a network of communications infrastructure. A restaurant is a service business whose costs are a combination of salaries (for kitchen and table waiting) and food costs.

Technology

In this section, explain how technology affects your business, the products you sell, the means you use to sell them, and the needs of the customers you serve.

In some cases this might be a change in scanning technology, retail point-of-sale systems, or even video displays. In others, technology changes the nature of the goods or services you sell, such as the cellphones or high-density videos that didn't even exist a few years ago. Do you want to include the Internet? Will a Web site change the way you do business?

Sometimes, technology can be vital to a service company, such as the case of the Internet provider that uses wireless connections as a competitive edge, or the local company that offers conference rooms for video conferencing. An accounting practice might gain a competitive advantage from proprietary software or wide area network connections to its clients. A medical laboratory might depend completely on certain expensive technologies for medical diagnostics. A travel agency might depend on its connection to an airline reservation system.

Technology can be critical to a manufacturing business in at least two ways: first, the technology involved in assembly or manufacturing, such as in the manufacture of computer chips; and second, the technology incorporated in your product, such as proprietary technology that enhances the value of the product. In either case, technology can be a critical competitive edge. If you are writing a plan for outsiders, then you need to describe the technology and how well or thoroughly you have the technology protected in your business through contracts, patents, and other protection.

Technology might be a negative factor, something to be included in a plan because a threat should be dealt with. For example, that same travel agency that depends on a computerized reservation system might also note growing competition from Internet reservations systems available to consumers who prefer to buy direct.

Not all businesses depend on technology. Technology might also be irrelevant for your business. If so, you can delete this topic if it doesn't seem important.

Future Products

Now you want to present your outlook for future products or services. Do you have a long-term product strategy? How are products developed? Is there a relationship between market segments, market demand, market needs and product development?

Here again, what you include depends on the nature of your plan. In some cases future products are the most important point for investors looking to buy into your company's future. On the other hand, a bank is not going to lend you money for product development or hopes for future products; so in a plan accompanying a Loan Application, there would probably be much less stress on this point.

You may also need to deal with the issue of confidentiality. When a business plan includes sensitive information on future products, then it should be carefully monitored, with good documentation of who receives copies of the plan. Recipients might reasonably be asked to sign non-disclosure statements and those statements should be kept on file.

Include Sales Literature

It is generally a good idea to include specific pieces of sales literature and collateral as attachments or appendices to your plan. Examples would be copies of advertisements, brochures, direct mail pieces, catalogs, and technical specifications. When a plan is presented to someone outside the company, sales literature is a practical way to both explain your services and present the look and feel of the company.

If it is relevant for your business, you should also use this topic to discuss your present situation regarding company literature and your future plans. Is your sales literature a good match to your services and the image your company wants to present? How is it designed and produced? Could you improve it significantly, or cut the cost, or add additional benefits?

Summary

Depending on the purpose of your plan, you should provide good, practical information on the products or services you sell. Give your plan readers what they will need to evaluate the plan. Make sure they understand the need you serve, how well you satisfy that need, and why your customers buy from you instead of somebody else. Ideally, the descriptions in this chapter make your sales forecast seem realistic and even conservative.

This page intentionally blank.

CHAPTER 7:
Forecast Your Sales

The next step is developing your sales forecast. Don't fear--it isn't as hard as most people think. Think of your sales forecast as an educated guess. Forecasting takes good working knowledge of your business, which is much more important than advanced degrees or complex mathematics. It is much more art than science.

Whether you have business training or not, don't think you aren't qualified to forecast. If you can run a business, then you can forecast its sales. Most people can guess their own business' sales better than any expert device, statistical analysis, or mathematical routine. Experience counts more than any other factor.

If you've been following along with this book, you've been through some Internet sites and other information sources to know your customers and your industry. You've probably been thinking about your sales forecast while you went through that information. The research

for a good forecast is almost always harder than the final process of actually making the detailed educated guesses. You've probably already done the research.

A Simple Sales Forecast Example

When the research is already done, the mechanics of sales forecasting are relatively simple.

Break your sales down into manageable parts, and then forecast the parts. Guess your sales by line of sales, month by month, and add up the sales lines and add up the months.

Illustration 7-1 gives you an example of a simple sales forecast which estimates total dollar value for each category of sales.

Illustration 7-1: A Simple Sales Forecast

Sales	May-97	Jun-97	Jul-97	Aug-9
Retainer Consulting	$20,000	$20,000	$20,000	$20,000
Project Consulting	$30,000	$40,000	$20,000	$10,000
Market Research	$8,000	$15,000	$10,000	$5,000
Strategic Reports	$0	$0	$0	$0
Other	$0	$0	$0	$0
Total Sales	$58,000	$75,000	$50,000	$35,000

Direct Costs	May-97	Jun-97	Jul-97	Aug-9
Retainer Consulting	$2,500	$2,500	$2,500	$2,500
Project Consulting	$5,000	$6,500	$3,500	$1,500
Market Research	$6,000	$10,000	$6,000	$4,000
Strategic Reports	$0	$0	$0	$0
Other	$0	$0	$0	$0
Subtotal Direct Cost of Sales	$13,500	$19,000	$12,000	$8,000

This example of a standard sales forecast includes simple price and cost forecasts to calculate projected sales and direct cost of sales.

Break it Down for More Detail

Forecasting is usually easier when you break your forecast down into components. As an example, consider a forecast that projects $1,000 in sales for the month, compared to one that projects 100 units at $10 each for the month. In the second case, when the forecast is price x units, as soon as you know the price is going up, you also know that the resulting sales should also increase. Thinking of the forecast in components is easier.

Illustration 7-2 shows a units-based sales forecast. It takes assumptions for sales in units, then assumed average prices, and multiplies them to calculate sales dollar values. Then it takes assumptions for unit costs and uses them, along with unit sales assumptions above, to calculate direct cost of sales.

Both examples calculate sales for different product lines for the first 12 months of the business plan and then annually for the three-year period. The first year column totals the sales of the first 12 months.

Illustration 7-2: The Units-Based Sales Forecast

Unit Sales	Jan-98	Feb-98	Mar-98
Systems	45	50	75
Service	200	325	300
Software	150	200	225
Training	145	155	165
Other	1,000	1,000	1,200
Total Unit Sales	1,540	1,730	1,965

Unit Prices	Jan-98	Feb-98	Mar-98
Systems	$2,000	$2,000	$2,000
Service	$75	$69	$58
Software	$200	$200	$200
Training	$37	$35	$39
Other	$300	$300	$300

Total Sales	Jan-98	Feb-98	Mar-98
Systems	$90,000	$100,000	$150,000
Service	$15,000	$22,500	$17,500
Software	$30,000	$40,000	$45,000
Training	$5,365	$5,425	$6,435
Other	$300,000	$300,000	$360,000
Total Sales	$440,365	$467,925	$578,935

Unit Direct Costs	Jan-98	Feb-98	Mar-98
Systems	$1,000	$1,000	$1,000
Service	$60	$60	$60
Software	$100	$100	$100
Training	$22	$22	$22
Other	$150	$150	$150

Direct Costs	Jan-98	Feb-98	Mar-98
Systems	$45,000	$50,000	$75,000
Service	$12,000	$19,500	$18,000
Software	$15,000	$20,000	$22,500
Training	$3,190	$3,410	$3,630
Other	$150,000	$150,000	$180,000
Subtotal Direct Costs	$225,190	$242,910	$299,130

The sales forecast multiplies unit forecasts by price and cost forecasts to calculate projected sales and cost of sales.

Graphics as Forecasting Tools

Business charts are much more than just pretty pictures; they are an excellent tool for understanding and estimating numbers. You should always create charts to illustrate your sales forecast, then use them to evaluate the projected numbers. When you view your forecast on a business chart, does it look real? Does it make sense? It turns out that most humans sense the relative size of shapes better than they sense numbers, so we see a sales forecast differently when it shows up in a chart. Use the power of the computer to help you visualize your numbers.

For example, consider the monthly sales chart shown in Illustration 7-3. You can look at this chart and immediately see the ebbs and flows of sales during the year. Sales go up from January into March, then down from Spring into Summer, then up again in the Fall. When you look at a chart like that, you should ask yourself whether that pattern is correct. Is that the way your sales go?

The next chart, in Illustration 7-4, shows a comparison of three years of annual sales. Here again, you can sense the relative size of the numbers in the chart. If you knew the company involved, you'd be able to evaluate and discuss

Illustration 7-3: Monthly Sales Forecast Chart

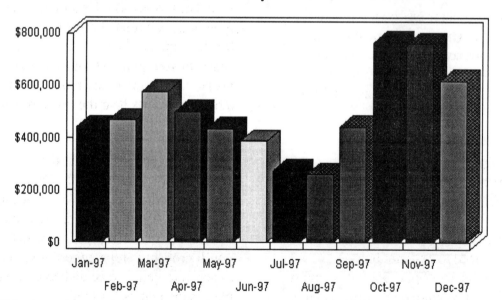

This chart shows planned sales for each month of the first 12 months.

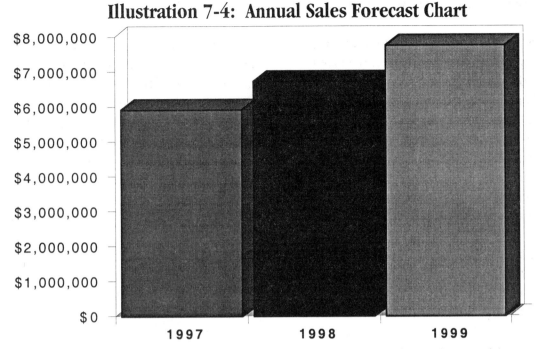

Illustration 7-4: Annual Sales Forecast Chart

This chart shows the sales forecast by product or service line, for each year of the three-year sales forecast.

this sales forecast just by looking at the chart. Of course you'd probably want to know more detail about the assumptions behind the forecast, but you'd have a very good initial sense of the numbers already.

Use Text to Explain the Forecast and Related Plans and Background

Although the charts and tables are great, you still need to explain them. A complete business plan should normally include some detailed text discussion of your sales forecast, sales strategy, sales programs, and related information. Ideally, you use the text, tables, and charts in your plan to provide some visual variety and ease of use. Put the tables and charts near the text covering the related topics.

In my standard text outline, the discussion of sales goes into Chapter 5.0, *Strategy and Implementation*. You can change that to fit whichever logic and structure you use. In practical terms, you'll probably prepare these text topics as separate items, to be gathered into the plan as the plan is finished.

Sales Strategy

Somewhere near the sales forecast you should describe your sales strategy. Sales strategies deal with how and when to close sales prospects, how to compensate sales people, how to optimize order processing and database management, how to maneuver price, delivery, and conditions.

How do you sell? Do you sell through retail, wholesale, discount, mail order, phone order? Do you maintain a sales force? How are sales people trained, and how are they compensated? Don't confuse sales strategy with your marketing strategy, which goes elsewhere. Sales should close the deals that marketing opens.

To help differentiate between marketing strategy and sales strategy, think of marketing as the broader effort of generating sales leads on a large scale, and sales as the efforts to bring those sales leads into the system as individual sales transactions. Marketing might affect image and awareness and propensity to buy, while sales involves getting the order.

Forecast Details

Your business plan text should summarize and highlight the numbers you have entered in the Sales Forecast table. Make sure you discuss important assumptions in enough detail, and that you explain the background sufficiently. Try to anticipate the questions your readers will ask. Include whatever information you think will be relevant, that your readers will need.

Sales Programs

Details are critical to implementation. Use this topic to list the specific information related to sales programs in your milestones table, with the specific persons responsible, deadlines, and budgets. How is this strategy to be implemented? Do you have concrete and specific plans? How will implementation be measured?

Business plans are about results, and generating results depends in part on how specific you are in the plan. For anything related to sales that is supposed to happen, include it here and list the person responsible, dates required, and budgets. All of that will make your business plan more real.

How Many Years?

I believe a business plan should normally project sales by month for the next 12 months, and annual sales for the following three years. This doesn't mean businesses shouldn't plan for a longer term than just three years, not by any means. It does mean, however, that the detail of monthly forecasts doesn't pay off beyond a year, except in special cases. It also means that the detail in the three-year forecasts probably doesn't make sense beyond three years.

It does mean, of course, that you still plan your business for five, 10, and even 15-year timeframes; just don't do it within the detailed context of business plan financials.

Summary

The sales forecast is hard for many people because they are unsure of how to forecast. Don't worry, if you know your business, you can give a decent educated guess of future sales. Of course it is hard, but is is also important, and if you can break the forecast down into parts and compare the future to the past, you can do it. Remember, one thing harder than forecasting is running a business without a forecast.

This page intentionally blank.

CHAPTER 8:
Your Management Team

Planning for People

A management team and bringing people together is a lot more than just resumes and venture capital. It is what makes a company work or not work.

For example: It's a sunny March Friday in Western Oregon, which is a rare; so rare, in fact, that the boss decides to have office pizza for lunch.

The controller is a former history major, Phi Beta Kappa into grad school, who discovered midway through her 30s that she really liked making numbers work. As people gather in the main room around the pizza, she announces that all should enjoy her hair that day "because I am having a rare good hair day." Everybody laughs.

The head of tech support turns the attention to the "krinkly hair" of the marketing manager. Everybody laughs again. There are jokes about the pizza and the root beer.

The product manager demonstrates ballroom dancing steps in preparation of his upcoming wedding, and somebody thinks to turn the music on hold up through the phones, as accompaniment.

The documentation manager emerges from her sunny office in the back and announces that she has a new couch in her office so people can escape from all the administration in the front.

These people seem happy. The technical support manager really likes to explain to people on the telephone; the documentation manager loves teaching and writing. The admin department includes a college student and a soccer mom, both of whom understand the accounting system very well and usually forgive it its flaws. The office manager, a former teacher, says managing this diversity is nothing compared to dealing with a classroom full of adolescents. The product manager and marketing manager both earned their business degrees while working part-time in tech support, and joined fulltime as soon as they graduated. These people like their jobs and they like each other. They work together well.

Flash back to the same company four years earlier, with a totally different staff. Back then, the controller was worried sick about the integrity of the computer system. The technical support person was tired of technical support and upset that the controller had a better computer. The sales manager spent half of her day settling disputes between the controller and the technical support person.

In other words, the jobs need to be done and the people need to match their job functions and preferences. A manufacturing company can't survive without a production manager, a software company can't live without technical support, and most companies also need office management and administration.

If we jump straight into personnel plans and resumes and business jargon related to the management team, we can inadvertently forget that there is something much more vital and alive than just looking good for investors. A company is where its employees come together most every day, for the major part of the day. If it isn't a good place to work then it won't be successful. Keep this in mind as you plan your

management and develop this part of your plan.

Cover the Bases in Text

The pesonnel management section of your plan outline will normally include an explanation of your management, management philosophy, backgrounds, organization, and functions, plus at least one table that covers your estimated personnel costs.

Summarize Your Management Chapter

The management chapter starts, like the other chapters, with a good summary. You may want to use that summary as part of a Summary memo or Loan document, so cover the main points. Consider what you'd say about your management if you only had one or two paragraphs to say it.

Make sure you cover the basic information first. That would include how many employees the company has, how many managers, and how many of the managers are founders. Is your team complete, or are there gaps still to be filled? Is your organizational structure sound, with job descriptions and logical responsibilities for all the key members?

Particularly with start-up companies, you may not have the complete team as you write the plan. In that case, be sure to point out the gaps and weaknesses, and how you intend to fill them.

Explain Your Organizational Structure

The organizational structure of a company is what you frequently see as an organizational chart, also known as an "org chart." If you have access to a graphic of an organizational chart (from a drawing program, or one of the specialized organizational charting software packages available), that works really well at this point. If not, you can just use the text to describe the organizational structure in words, without a chart.

Make sure you explain how job descriptions work and how the main company functions are divided up. Are your organizational lines drawn clearly? Is the authority properly distributed? Do you have jobs that include responsibility without authority? Do your resources seem in line with your organizational needs?

List Team Members and Their Backgrounds

List the most important members of the management team. Include summaries of their backgrounds and experience, using

them like brief resumes. Describe their functions with the company. Resumes should be attached to the back of a plan.

Discuss Your Management Gaps

You may have obvious gaps in the management, especially in start-up companies, but even in ongoing companies. For example, the manufacturing company without a production manager has some explaining to do, and the computer company without service has some problems. It is far better to define and identify a weakness than to pretend it doesn't exist. Specify where the team is weak because of gaps in coverage of key management functions. How will these weaknesses be corrected? How will the more important gaps be filled?

Other Management Team Considerations

Applicability depends on your company. Some questions that should be answered include: Do any managers or employees have "noncompete" agreements with competitors? Who is on your board of directors? What do the members contribute to the business? Who are your major stockholders? What is their role in management?

Develop Your Personnel Numbers

At this point you should normally include a personnel table to project personnel costs, including direct compensation and indirect costs. The indirect costs include vacation pay, sick pay, insurance benefits, education, and of course payroll taxes and some other costs. There are different terms for all of this, but my favorite is "personnel burden," which is a cost over and above the direct wages and salaries.

Special Treatment for Home Offices

If you are working as a sole proprietor in a home office, you should still include your own compensation as part of your business plan. What you pay yourself should be added into the profit and loss as an expense. However, in this case you don't really need to include payroll burden, because these additional expenses are irrelevant until you include additional employees.

Two Standard Personnel Variations

As with the sales forecast in the previous chapter, a good personnel plan varies according to your business and business plan needs. You may want a simple list of names, titles, or groups, each of which is assigned a monthly cost. This model is shown in Illustration 8-1.

The simpler model totals all payroll only. It is perfectly appropriate for a lot of small businesses. You can use each of the lines in the table to describe specific individuals, or groups and departments. When you have the list complete, just

Illustration 8-1: Standard Personnel Plan

	Oct-98	Nov-98	Dec-98	1998	1999
Partners	$12,000	$12,000	$12,000	$144,000	$175,000
Consultants	$0	$0	$0	$0	$50,000
Editorial/graphic	$6,000	$6,000	$6,000	$18,000	$22,000
VP Marketing	$5,000	$5,000	$5,000	$20,000	$50,000
Sales people	$0	$0	$0	$0	$30,000
Office Manager	$2,500	$2,500	$2,500	$7,500	$30,000
Secretarial	$1,750	$1,750	$1,750	$5,250	$20,000
Other	$0	$0	$0	$0	$0
Subtotal	$27,250	$27,250	$27,250	$194,750	$377,000

The standard personnel plan is a simple list of names, titles, or categories. The sum transfers into your profit and loss statement. This illustration shows the last three months and first two years of a sample plan.

add up the totals for personnel costs in your Profit and Loss (that comes in the next chapter). Multiply that total times your burden rate--say 15 or 20 percent-- to calculate your personnel burden. The burden goes into the profit and loss as a separate line.

Illustration 8-2 shows the more detailed personnel plan that divides the rows into categories, such as sales and marketing, general and administrative, and so forth. The more detailed model shown here totals the planned payroll for each of the four departments, and then calculates total payroll.

Illustration 8-2: Detailed Personnel Plan

Production	Jan-97	Feb-97	Mar-97	Apr-97	May-97
Manager	$1,000	$1,000	$1,000	$1,000	$1,000
Assistant	$3,000	$3,000	$3,000	$3,000	$3,000
Technical	$0	$0	$0	$0	$0
Technical	$0	$0	$0	$0	$0
Technical	$2,000	$2,000	$2,000	$2,000	$2,000
Fulfillment	$2,000	$2,000	$2,000	$2,000	$2,000
Fulfillment	$1,500	$1,500	$1,500	$1,500	$1,500
Other					
Subtotal	$9,500	$9,500	$9,500	$9,500	$9,500

Sales and Market	Jan-97	Feb-97	Mar-97	Apr-97	May-97
Manager	$6,000	$6,000	$6,000	$6,000	$6,000
Technical sales	$5,000	$5,000	$5,000	$5,000	$5,000
Technical sales	$3,500	$3,500	$3,500	$3,500	$3,500
Salesperson	$2,500	$2,500	$2,500	$2,500	$2,500
Salesperson	$2,500	$2,500	$2,500	$2,500	$2,500
Salesperson	$2,500	$2,500	$2,500	$2,500	$2,500
Salesperson	$2,000	$2,000	$2,000	$2,000	$2,000
Salesperson	$0	$0	$0	$0	$0
Salesperson	$0	$0	$0	$0	$0
Other	$0	$0	$0	$0	$0
Subtotal	$24,000	$24,000	$24,000	$24,000	$24,000

Administration	Jan-97	Feb-97	Mar-97	Apr-97	May-97
President	$5,500	$5,500	$5,500	$5,500	$5,500
Finance	$0	$0	$0	$0	$0
Admin Assistant	$2,000	$2,000	$2,000	$2,000	$2,000
Bookkeeping	$1,500	$1,500	$1,500	$1,500	$1,500
Clerical	$1,000	$1,000	$1,000	$1,000	$1,000
Clerical	$0	$0	$0	$0	$0
Clerical	$0	$0	$0	$0	$0
Other	$0	$0	$0	$0	$0
Subtotal	$10,000	$10,000	$10,000	$10,000	$10,000

Other	Jan-97	Feb-97	Mar-97	Apr-97	May-97
Programming	$3,000	$3,000	$3,000	$3,000	$3,000
Other technical	$0	$0	$0	$0	$0
Other	$0	$0	$0	$0	$0
Subtotal	$3,000	$3,000	$3,000	$3,000	$3,000

Total Headcount	0	0	0	0	0
Total Payroll	$46,500	$46,500	$46,500	$46,500	$46,500
Payroll Burden	$7,440	$7,440	$7,440	$7,440	$7,440
Total Payroll Exp	$53,940	$53,940	$53,940	$53,940	$53,940

The more detailed personnel plan shown here divides personnel expenditures into classifications including production, sales and marketing, general and administrative, and other.

For either the simple or detailed personnel table, you also want to calculate a payroll burden as a percentage of the total, and make sure to include the payroll burden assumption in your list of general assumptions. Payroll burden is the extra costs of payroll taxes and benefits.

The payroll assumptions in this model will also be used for the other financial projections. The Profit and Loss (also called income statement) will use personnel plan numbers.

Summary

As with your sales forecast in the previous chapter, your personnel plan is actually just an educated guess. It is hard to make this kind of guess if you aren't used to forecasting, but you can do it by breaking the assumptions down into rows and thinking it through. If you're really having trouble with it, it may help to remember that a real business plan is kept on disk and frequently revised to accommodate changes in sales, market, and finances.

CHAPTER 9:
The Bottom Line

The familiar phrase "the bottom line," often used as synonomous with the conclusion or the underlying truth, is actually taken from the standard Income statement in accounting, which subtracts costs and expenses from sales and shows profits as the bottom line of the statement.

Now that you have projected sales and cost of sales (discussed in Chapter 7), and personnel expenses (Chapter 8), you're probably starting to think about comparing expenses to your sales.

Expenses start with personnel. Then you have rent, utilities, equipment, and probably some advertising, maybe commissions, public relations, and other expenses.

What we're leading to is profits. Profits are what is left over after you start with sales, then subtract cost of sales, expenses, and taxes.

The Income statement is the same as the Profit and Loss statement. You'll also find them called "pro forma," meaning projected, as in "pro forma income" or "pro forma profit and loss." The pro forma income is the same as a standard income statement except that the standard statement shows real results from the past, while a pro forma statement is projecting the future.

Illustration 9-1 shows a simple income statement. The format and math starts with sales at the top. This example doesn't divide operating expenses into categories.

First, subtract cost of sales from sales. This gives you gross margin, an important ratio for comparisons and analysis. Acceptable gross margin levels depend on the industry. According to the 1997 Financial Statement Studies of Robert Morris Associates, an average shoe store has a gross margin of 42 percent. A hat manufacturer has a gross margin of 30 percent, and a grocery store about 20 percent.

The more detailed Profit and Loss is shown in Illustration 9-2.

Illustration 9-1: Standard Profit and Loss Statement

	May-97	Jun-97	Jul-97	Aug-97	Sep-97
Sales	$58,000	$75,000	$50,000	$35,000	$70,000
Cost of Sales	$13,500	$19,000	$12,000	$8,000	$21,500
Other	$0	$0	$0	$0	$0
Total Cost of Sales	$13,500	$19,000	$12,000	$8,000	$21,500
Gross margin	$44,500	$56,000	$38,000	$27,000	$48,500
Gross margin percent	76.72%	74.67%	76.00%	77.14%	69.29%
Operating expenses:					
Advertising/Promotion	$3,000	$3,000	$3,000	$3,000	$3,000
Public Relations	$2,500	$2,500	$2,500	$2,500	$2,500
Travel	$7,500	$7,500	$7,500	$7,500	$7,500
Miscellaneous	$500	$500	$500	$500	$500
Payroll expense	$12,000	$12,000	$12,000	$12,000	$17,000
Leased Equipment	$500	$500	$500	$500	$500
Utilities	$1,000	$1,000	$1,000	$1,000	$1,000
Insurance	$300	$300	$300	$300	$300
Depreciation	$0	$0	$0	$0	$0
Rent	$1,500	$1,500	$1,500	$1,500	$1,500
Payroll Burden	$1,680	$1,680	$1,680	$1,680	$2,380
Contract/Consultants	$0	$0	$0	$0	$0
Other	$0	$0	$0	$0	$0
Total Operating Expenses	$30,480	$30,480	$30,480	$30,480	$36,180
Profit Before Interest and T	$14,020	$25,520	$7,520	($3,480)	$12,320
Interest Expense ST	$400	$400	$400	$400	$400
Interest Expense LT	$417	$417	$417	$417	$417
Taxes Incurred	$3,301	$6,176	$1,676	($1,074)	$2,876
Net Profit	$9,903	$18,528	$5,028	($3,223)	$8,628
Net Profit/Sales	17.07%	24.70%	10.06%	-9.21%	12.33%

This illustration shows the standard income statement (profit and loss).

This example divides operating expenses into standard categories, including Sales and Marketing expenses and General and Administrative expenses. It provides a clearer picture of the business expenses and what they stand for, but for some cases the extra detail may not be relevant.

Regardless of which statement style you choose, you make very important choices as you plan your profit and loss. This is where you plan your expenses.

You are estimating expenditures across the business, from rent and overhead to marketing expenses such as advertising, sales commissions, and public relations. Decisions you make here are as important as the mathematics are simple. Your sum of expenses ultimately determines your company's profitability. This is the business plan equivalent to budgeting, as you set your sites on the levels of expenditures you expect your company will need.

Summary

Your profit and loss statement is where you budget and forecast your expenses. You also absorb the more important numbers of your sales forecast and personnel plan, to create a planned bottom line for profit. This is educated guessing. Keep it on a computer so you can revise often as the business changes.

Illustration 9-2: Detailed Profit and Loss Statement

	Jan-97	Feb-97	Mar-97	Apr-97	May-97
Sales	$440,365	$468,000	$579,000	$500,000	$435,000
Direct Cost of Sales	$225,219	$242,941	$299,163	$275,274	$233,495
Production payroll	$9,500	$9,500	$9,500	$9,500	$9,500
Other	$500	$500	$500	$500	$500
Total Cost of Sales	$235,219	$252,941	$309,163	$285,274	$243,495
Gross margin	$205,146	$215,059	$269,837	$214,726	$191,505
Gross margin percent	46.59%	45.95%	46.60%	42.95%	44.02%
Operating expenses:					
Sales and marketing expenses					
Sales/Marketing Salaries	$24,000	$24,000	$24,000	$24,000	$24,000
Ads	$15,000	$15,000	$12,000	$10,000	$15,000
Catalog	$2,000	$3,000	$2,000	$2,000	$2,000
Mailing	$3,000	$11,800	$5,500	$10,500	$10,500
Promo	$0	$0	$0	$0	$0
Shows	$0	$0	$0	$0	$0
Literature	$0	$7,000	$0	$0	$0
PR	$0	$0	$0	$1,000	$0
Seminar	$1,000	$0	$0	$5,000	$5,000
Service	$2,000	$1,000	$1,000	$500	$2,500
Training	$5,000	$5,000	$5,000	$5,000	$5,000
Total Sales and Marketi	$52,000	$66,800	$49,500	$58,000	$64,000
Sales and Marketing Pe	11.81%	14.27%	8.55%	11.60%	14.71%
General & Administrative Expenses					
G&A Salaries	$10,000	$10,000	$10,000	$10,000	$10,000
Leased Equipment	$2,500	$2,500	$2,500	$2,500	$2,500
Utilities	$750	$750	$750	$750	$750
Insurance	$500	$500	$500	$500	$500
Rent	$7,000	$7,000	$7,000	$7,000	$7,000
Depreciation	$1,000	$1,010	$1,020	$1,030	$1,040
Payroll Burden	$7,440	$7,440	$7,440	$7,440	$7,440
Other	$500	$505	$510	$515	$520
Total General and Admi	$29,690	$29,705	$29,720	$29,735	$29,750
General and Administral	6.74%	6.35%	5.13%	5.95%	6.84%
Other Operating Expenses					
Other Salaries	$3,000	$3,000	$3,000	$3,000	$3,000
Contract/Consultants	$1,000	$1,000	$1,000	$1,000	$1,000
Other	$250	$250	$250	$250	$250
Total Other Operating	$4,250	$4,250	$4,250	$4,250	$4,250
Percent of Sales	0.97%	0.91%	0.73%	0.85%	0.98%
Total Operating Expenses	$85,940	$100,755	$83,470	$91,985	$98,000
Profit Before Interest an	$119,206	$114,304	$186,367	$122,741	$93,505
Interest Expense ST	$600	$600	$1,100	$500	$500
Interest Expense LT	$1,997	$1,976	$1,955	$1,934	$1,912
Taxes Incurred	$23,322	$22,346	$36,662	$24,061	$18,219
Net Profit	$93,287	$89,382	$146,650	$96,246	$72,874
Net Profit/Sales	21.18%	19.10%	25.33%	19.25%	16.75%

This illustration shows the more detailed profit and loss analysis that divides operating expenses into categories.

This page intentionally blank.

CHAPTER 10:
Describe Your Company

After finishing the projected profit and loss, you have a sense of where your numbers are going. This is a good time to turn away from the detailed numbers and back toward the text. Explain your company and some of its underlying strategy, such as competitive edge and value proposition.

I find switching modes like this, from numbers to text and back, helps keep the process fresh as you develop your plan. Even so, this chapter still covers a table or two, either past performance or start-up costs, depending on your spevidic plan.

You're probably noticing by now that developing a business plan doesn't really happen in a straight logical order of steps. It isn't really a sequential process. For example, you looked at your market numbers first while doing the Initial Assessment, then again as you focused in more detail for the Market Analysis

topic. You probably visited those numbers again as you did the industry analysis. Now you've already projected your sales, personnel, and profits, but you'll probably have to revise those numbers as you look at your balance sheet and cash flow.

If you are starting a business, please go now to Chapter 17 dedicated to issues in starting a business. I didn't want to interrupt the flow of the plan with that discussion at this point, particularly for those who are working on an ongoing business. However, if you are starting a business, please read that chapter now and then return here.

Basic Company Information

As discussed earlier in this book, the standard business plan outline includes a chapter topic on your company, right after the Executive Summary. I pointed out then that you may not need to include this chapter if you are writing an internal plan. Any outsiders reading your plan will want to know about your company before they read about products, markets, and the rest of the story.

Summary Paragraph

Start the chapter with a good summary paragraph that you can use as part of an Investment Summary memo or a Loan application support document. Include the essential details, such as the name of the company, its legal establishment, how long it's been in existence, and what it sells to what markets.

Legal Entity and Ownership

In this paragraph, describe the ownership and legal establishment of the company. This is mainly specifying whether your company is a corporation, partnership, sole proprietorship, or some other kind of legal entity, such as a limited liability partnership. You should also explain who owns the company, and, if there is more than one owner, in what proportion.

If your business is a corporation, specify whether it is a C (the more standard type) or an S (more suitable for small business without many different owners)

corporation. Also, of course, specify whether it is privately owned or publicly traded.

Many smaller businesses, especially service businesses, are sole proprietor businesses. Some are legal partnerships. The protection of incorporating is important, but sometimes the extra legal costs and hassles of turning in corporate tax forms with double-entry bookkeeping are not worth it. Professional service businesses, such as accounting or legal or consulting firms, may be partnerships, although that mode of establishment is less common these days. If you're in doubt about how to establish a start-up company, consult a business attorney.

Locations and Facilities

Briefly describe offices and locations of your company, the nature and function of each, square footage, lease arrangements, etc.

If you have a service business, you probably don't have major manufacturing plants anywhere, but you might have Internet services, office facilities, and telephone systems that are relevant to providing service. It is conceivable that your Internet connection, as one hypothetical case, might be critical to your business.

If you're a retail store, then your location is probably a critical factor, so explain the location, traffic patterns, parking facilities, and possibly customer demographics as they relate to the specific location (your Market Analysis goes elsewhere, but if your shopping center location draws a particular kind of customer, note that here).

If you are manufacturing, then you may have different facilities for production, assembly, and various offices. You may also have manufacturing and assembly equipment, packing equipment, docks, and other facilities.

Depending on the nature of your plan, its function and purpose, you may want to include more detail about facilities as appendices attached to your plan.

For example, if your business plan is intended to help sell your company to new owners, and you feel that part of the value is the facilities and locations, then you should include all the detail you can. If you are describing a manufacturing business for bankers or investors, or anybody else trying to value your business, make sure you provide a complete list and all necessary detail about capital equipment, land, and building facilities. This kind of information can make a major difference to the value of your business.

On the other hand, if your business plan is for internal use in a small company with a single office, then this topic might be irrelevant.

Thinking Strategically About Your Company

One of the most valuable benefits of developing a business plan is thinking in depth about your company. You started that as part of the Initial Assment in Chapter 2 of this book, as you entered drafts of your objectives, mission statement, and keys to success. A standard plan also includes sections in the strategy chapter that provide deep background for strategy. This is a good point for developing those texts.

Value Proposition

Value-based marketing is a useful conceptual framework. The value proposition is benefit offered less price charged, in relative terms. It doesn't have to be in your business plan at all, but we add it here because some people find that the framework helps them develop strategy. Obviously, this has to be a quick treatment. There are textbooks written about value-based marketing, and the business literature on this topic is rich and varied.

This framework begins with defining your business offering as a value proposition. The definition encourages you to think in broad conceptual terms, with emphasis on the real benefit offered, rather than the specific tangible.

For example, the auto manufacturer, Volvo, has for years offered a value proposition based on the value of safety, at a price premium. A prestigious luxury auto, on the other hand, is offering a completely different set of benefits (luxury, elegance, prestige, for example) at a marked price premium.

Once you have a value proposition defined, then look at your business--and your business plan--in terms of how well you:

1. communicate the business proposition; and

2. fulfill your promise.

For example, if a tire manufacturer's business proposition has to do with reliable tires for families, peace of mind, and safety, then it probably shouldn't be sponsoring racing cars and advertising either performance tires or cheap tires. It should communicate its proposition with television commercials that emphasize how important the tire is to auto safety. It might also include lots of mothers and babies in cars in its advertisements, rainy roads at night, to emphasize the

dependence on tires that are safe. Like the pyramid, the framework helps you integrate your planned programs into a logical whole plan.

Competitive Edge

So what is your competitive edge? How is your company different from all others, in what way does it stand out? Is there a sustainable value there, something that you can maintain and develop over time? The classic competitive edges are based on proprietary technology protected by patents. Sometimes market share and brand acceptance are just as important, and know-how doesn't have to be protected by patent to be a competitive edge.

For example, Apple Computer for years used its proprietary operating system as a competitive edge, while Microsoft used its market share and market dominance to overcome Apple's earlier advantage.

Several manufacturers used proprietary compression to enhance video and photographic software, looking for a competitive edge. In the furniture manufacturer sample business plan, assembly technique and packaging is a competitive edge.

The competitive edge might be different for any given company, even between one company and another in the same industry.

You don't have to have the competitive edge to run a successful business--hard work, integrity, and customer satisfaction can substitute for it, to name just a few examples--but an edge will certainly give you a head start if you need to bring in new investment. Maybe it's just your customer base, as in the case with Hewlett-Packard's traditional relationship with engineers and technicians, or it's image and awareness, such as with Compaq. Maybe it is the quality control and consistency of IBM.

The most immediately understandable competitive edges are those based on proprietary technology. A patent, an algorithm, even deeply entrenched know-how, can be solid competitive edges. In services, however, the edge can be as simple as having the phone number 1 (800) SOFTWARE, which is an actual case. A successful company was built around that phone number.

Establishing Baseline Numbers

While we're focusing on the company description, let's establish some starting numbers that form the basis of your cash flow and balance sheet in the following sections. For ongoing companies, your starting balance for the future is the last balance from the past. For new companies, your plan determines the starting balances for the future.

Past Performance for Ongoing Companies

Past performance explained here is for on-going companies. If you are a start-up business, skip to the next section.

Ongoing companies need to include a summary of company history, as a topic in your text. If you are an ongoing company, then you'll need to present financial results of the recent past, and this text section is where you explain them.

Explain why your sales and profits have changed. If you've had important events like particularly bad years or good years, or new services, new locations, new partners, etc., then include that background here. Cover the founding of the company, important events, and important changes.

Your first consideration is the needs of your reader. This isn't a history assignment. Give the reader of the business plan the background information he or she needs to understand your business.

Illustration 10-1: Past Performance Table

	1994	1995	1996
Sales	$3,773,889	$4,661,902	$5,301,059
Gross	$1,189,495	$1,269,261	$1,127,568
Gross % (calcula	31.52%	27.23%	21.27%
Operating Expen	$752,083	$902,500	$1,052,917
Collection period	35	40	45
Inventory turnover	7	6	5
Balance Sheet			1996
Short-term Assets			
Cash			$55,432
Accounts receivable			$395,107
Inventory			$651,012
Other Short-term Assets			$25,000
Total Short-term Assets			$1,126,55
Long-term Assets			
Capital Assets			$350,000
Accumulated Depreciation			$50,000
Total Long-term Assets			$300,000
Total Assets			$1,426,55
Debt and Equity			
Accounts Payable			$223,897
Short-term Notes			$90,000
Other ST Liabilities			$15,000
Subtotal Short-term Liabilities			$328,897
Long-term Liabilities			$284,862
Total Liabilities			$613,759
Paid in Capital			$500,000
Retained Earnings			$238,140
Earnings	$437,411	$366,761	$74,652
Total Equity			$812,792
Total Debt and Equity			$1,426,55
Other Inputs			1996
Payment days			30
Sales on credit			$3,445,688
Receivables turnover			8.72

Important past performance items can be typed into the past performance worksheet. They are used for comparing past performance to projected future, and to establish your starting balances.

Illustration 10-1 shows a sample listing of recent financial results for an ongoing company. Generally three years is good enough. You should have these numbers as part of your standard business accounting.

For your financial analysis, as an ongoing company, you will want to make sure you have some very important highlights of your company's past financial performance, as shown in the above table.

Start-up Costs for Start-up Companies

The start-up company should include a start-up table instead of the past performance table. Illustration 10-2 is a simple example.

Start-up Expenses

The first portion of the sample start-up table estimates start-up expenses such as legal fees, stationery design, brochures, and others. Start-up expenses are only those expenses incurred before the start of the plan. If they come after the start of the plan, they belong in the profit and loss table in the appropriate month.

The table shows some common types of start-up expenses, such as legal costs, stationery, and brochures. You can delete sample expense rows, change their names, and add new rows, as you wish, to make an accurate estimate of start-up expenses.

Starting Assets

The second portion of the sample start-up table estimates the assets your business will have at start-up, including cash, inventory (except for service companies), and others.

For example, if you need $5,000 in the bank and $5,000 in inventory to start your business, type those amounts into the starting assets.

Illustration 10-2: Start-up Table

Startup Expenses	
Legal	$1,000
Stationery etc.	$3,000
Brochures	$5,000
Consultants	$5,000
Insurance	$350
Expensed equipment	$3,000
Other	$1,000
Total Start-up Expense	**$18,350**

Start-up Assets Needed	
Cash requirements	$25,000
Other Short-term Assets	$7,000
Total Short-term Assets	$32,000
Long-term Assets	
Capital Assets	$0
Total Assets	**$32,000**

Total Startup Requirements	$50,350
Left to finance:	$0

Start-up Funding Plan

Investment	
Investor 1	$20,000
Investor 2	$20,000
Other	$10,000
Total investment	**$50,000**

Short-term borrowing	
Unpaid expenses	$5,000
Short-term loans	$0
Interest-free short-term loans	$0
Subtotal Short-term Borrowing	**$5,000**
Long-term Borrowing	$0
Total Borrowing	**$5,000**

Loss at start-up	($23,000)
Total Equity	$27,000
Total Debt and Equity	**$32,000**

Use the start-up worksheet to plan your initial financing.

Start-up Funding

The third portion of the table contains your estimates for start-up funding, including investments, loans, and unpaid bills.

The total start-up requirements shown in the middle of the table is the sum of start-up expenses and start-up assets. This is the money you've decided you need--by estimating start-up expenses and start-up assets--to start the business.

Investment is money that you or your investors sink into the business for good. You don't expect to get it back. Borrowing is money loaned to the business--including loans as simple as purchases with credit cards and unpaid bills, called unpaid expenses. Loans can be unpaid expenses, short-term loans, or long-term loans. You need to invest and borrow enough money to equal the start-up expenses and start-up assets.

Loss at Start-up

The rule of accounting is that assets are equal to investment plus loans. That is the same as capital being equal to assets minus liabilities, which is also your company's net worth. In order to make your balance correct as you start your company, you must recognize a loss at start-up that you can calculate as whatever number it takes to make capital equal to assets minus liabilities. For example, if you have $5,000 in assets and $2,000 in liabilities, your capital should be $3,000. If you invested $5,000 in this case but your capital should be only $3,000, then your loss at start-up has to be $2,000. The original $5,000 investment minus the $2,000 loss at start-up gives you the correct number for capital, $3,000 (assets are equal to capital plus liabilities). Your loss at start-up should normally be equal to start-up expenses, but it will be calculated as whatever number it takes to make investment and borrowing equal to start-up assets. This makes your balance correct at the start.

To reduce the loss at start-up, you can do several things:

- reduce start-up expenses

- increase start-up assets

- decrease investment or borrowing

Remember, however, that you must show investment and borrowing to match the total of your start-up expenses and start-up assets. Every dollar of additional funding, beyond the amount required, increases your loss at start-up.

Text: Start-up Explanations

Summarize your start-up plan. Explain the list of start-up expenses, which are expenses you make before you start the business in the first month. Typical start-up expenses include legal expenses of establishment, expenses for developing logo and stationery, and for setting up an office. After the expenses you list the assets you want to have in the company as it starts. For a service company that would be cash in the bank account, and possibly short-term assets such as equipment. Service companies rarely have starting inventory. Then you show how you intend to finance both the expenses and the initial assets, which usually means investment or borrowing.

Summary

You should include a good company description, especially if you're developing a plan to be shown to people outside the company. Don't stop with just legal formation and history; include some strategic topics, such as competitive edge and value proposition.

You need one of two tables, either start-up plan or past performance, to establish a starting balance for your projected cash flow and balance sheet.

This page intentionally blank.

CHAPTER 11:
About Business Numbers

A business plan depends on both words and numbers. You can't describe a business in words alone, and the numbers don't work without the words. In this chapter, we go through the basics of how the numbers come together.

Allow me to tell a personal story about words and numbers, and why you need both to make a complete plan.

In 1974, I switched from general journalism, writing for United Press International from Mexico City, to business journalism, writing for Business International and McGraw-Hill World News. With the switch, I found myself covering business and economics instead of general news, writing for (among others) *Business Week* and *Business Latin America.* at this point. Because I thought it would be nice to have some idea what I was writing about, I went to the local graduate school at night for courses in general economics, accounting, finance, and marketing.

As I learned about macroeconomics, and how to read financial statements, I discovered that the truth in business is almost always a combination of words and numbers, and can't be explained with either one without the other. For example, when a Central American government announced a new federal budget that it said was going to both develop growth and reduce inflation, the numbers said that was a contradiction. You can't do both, you can do one or the other. You could only see that by dealing with both words and numbers.

A business plan is like that, too. You can't describe a plan without both text and tables, both words and numbers. The single most important analysis in a business plan is a cash flow plan, because cash is the most critical element in business. With the way the numbers work, however, you can't do a cash flow plan without looking at the income statement and balance sheets as well. You really can't do the income statement without looking at sales, cost of sales, personnel expenses and other expenses, so you need those too. And you'd have trouble doing a sales forecast without understanding your market, so a market analysis is recommended. And then you have the break-even as part of the initial assessment, and tables for business ratios, general assumptions, and other numbers. Step by step, the business plan becomes a collection of tables and charts around the text.

Numbers Tell the Story

Although cash is critical, people think in profits instead of cash. We all do. When you and your friends imagine a new business, you think of what it would cost to make the product, what you could sell it for, and what the profits per unit might be. We are trained to think of business as sales minus costs and expenses, which is profits.

Unfortunately, we don't spend the profits in a business. We spend cash. Profitable companies go broke because they had all their money tied up in assets and couldn't pay their expenses. Working capital is critical to business health. Unfortunately, we don't see the cash implications as clearly as we should, which is one of the best reasons for proper business planning. We have to manage cash, as well as profits.

A Simple Example

One of the best ways to understand the dilemma of cash vs. profits is to follow an otherwise-profitable company going broke because it can't meet its obligations. This is a quick and simple example. It also leads us into the relationship between income statement, balance sheet, and cash.

Start with $100, which we'll call capital. At the beginning of this exercise, your balance sheet has assets of $100--the money--and capital of $100. Assets are equal to capital plus liabilities. A summary of the simple financial statement at this point is shown in Illustration 11-1.

Illustration 11-1: Starting Numbers

Income				Balance
Sales	$0	Assets		
Cost of sales	$0		Bank Balance	$100
Profit	$0	Total		$100
		Liabilities		
		Capital		
			Paid-in	$100
			Earnings	
		Total		$100

The simple financials show a hypothetical widgets business as it starts.

If you buy a widget for $100 and sell it for $150, you should end up with $50 profit, which is what your income statement covers. Sales minus costs are profit. You should have $150 in the bank. Now your balance sheet shows the same $100 in original capital plus $50 in earnings, which are equal to the $150 you have in cash as an asset. Illustration 11-2 shows you how the financials work after the sale.

Illustration 11-2: Sell a Widget

Income				Balance
Sales	$150	Assets		
Cost of sales	$100		Bank Balance	$150
Profit	$50	Total		$150
		Liabilities		
		Capital		
			Paid-in	$100
			Earnings	$50
		Total		$150

This financial shows how the company looks after its first sale.

Buy another widget for $100 and sell it again for $150, and now you have $200 in the bank. Do it again, you have $250 in the bank. Your income statement shows sales of $450, cost of sales of $300, and profit of $150.

Illustration 11-3 shows your income statement and balance sheet at this point.

Illustration 11-3: Sell Three Widgets

Income				Balance
Sales	$450	Assets		
Cost of sales	$300		Bank Balance	$250
Profit	$150	Total		$250
		Liabilities		
		Capital		
			Paid-in	$100
			Earnings	$150
		Total		$250

At this point your business has sold 3 units and made $150 profit. In theory it has $250 in the bank.

Adding Some Realism

Now go back a step and make the situation more realistic. For example, most sales of products to businesses go on terms, with the money due in 30 days. So if you sold that widget on credit you don't have $150 in the bank. You still have $50 in your bottom line, but now you have nothing in the bank. Instead, a customer owes you $150, which is what we call "Accounts Receivable."

Compare Illustration 11-4 to Illustration 11-2. This is what really happens to the huge number of businesses that sell to other businesses.

Illustration 11-4: Selling on Terms

Income				Balance
Sales	$150	Assets		
Cost of sales	$100		Bank Balance	
Profit	$50		Accounts Receivable	$150
		Total		$150
		Liabilities		
		Capital		
			Paid-in	$100
			Earnings	$50
		Total		$150

Sales and profits are the same as in Illustration 11-2, but you sold on credit, so now you have no money in the bank.

Knowing you can buy a widget for $100 and sell it for $150, you get your Widget supplier to sell to you on the same terms you sell, net 30, instead of for cash. Now you have $100 that you owe to suppliers, which is called "Accounts Payable." You also have $100 worth of widget in inventory.

This gives you the case in Illustration 11-5, in which you are now poised to sell another widget and make more profit.

Illustration 11-5: Buying on Terms

Income			Balance
Sales	$150	Assets	
Cost of sales	$100	Bank Balance	
Profit	$50	Accounts Receivable	$150
		Inventory	$100
		Total	$250
		Liabilities	
		Accounts Payable	$100
		Total liabilities	$100
		Capital	
		Paid-in	$100
		Earnings	$50
		Total	$250

Business looked good in Illustration 11-4, so you borrowed the money to buy another widget and continue.

You have an extra $100 in assets (the widget in inventory) and an extra $100 as liabilities (Accounts Payable), so you are still in balance. Also, you still have no money.

Illustration 11-6 shows the financial picture after the same sales as in Illustration 11-3, but with sales to businesses on credit and purchase of inventory on credit.

Illustration 11-6: Numbers Mount Up

Income			Balance
Sales	$450	Assets	
Cost of sales	$300	Bank Balance	$0
Profit	$150	Accounts Receivable	$450
		Inventory	$100
		Total	$550
		Liabilities	
		Accounts Payable	$100
		Short-term debt	$200
		Total liabilities	$300
		Capital	
		Paid-in	$100
		Earnings	$150
		Total	$550

You have the same sales and profits as in Illustration11-3, but the balance sheet is more complex.

Now the case is more like what you have with real business numbers, in which you have to manage your cash very carefully, and the amounts sitting in inventory and accounts receivable are significant.

More Realism: Working Capital

Even in the case of Illustration 11-6, the example is completely unrealistic. Where are the running expenses, such as rent, salaries, telephones, or even advertising those widgets? How would they affect the cash situation? How far would we get if we couldn't pay the rent or the telephone bill while waiting for customers to pay us? Furthermore, what supplier would give us a widget on credit when we have no history and no assets? What bank would loan us money in this situation? Banks do loan against inventory and receivables, but only to a certain percentage of total value. What was missing here, all along, was working capital.

Important: *In strict accounting terms, working capital is equal to short-term assets minus short-term liabilities. In real terms, however, working capital is the glue that holds your cash flow together. Get it into the bank before you need it, or you won't survive the unexpected.*

Illustration 11-7 goes back to the beginning of this whole example and does it right, with enough capital in the beginning to finance the company.

Illustration 11-7: Working Capital

Income			Balance
Sales	$450	Assets	
Cost of sales	$300	Bank Balance	$300
Profit	$150	Accounts Receivable	$450
		Inventory	$100
		Total	$850
		Liabilities	
		Accounts Payable	$100
		Short-term debt	$200
		Total liabilities	$300
		Capital	
		Paid-in	$400
		Earnings	$150
		Total	$850

In this illustration the business has enough working capital to survive the unexpected.

Instead of starting with $100 as capital, this business looks a lot better with an opening bank balance of $400 instead of $100. With this additional capital from the start, buying on credit and borrowing against assets is more realistic.

In Illustration 11-6 the working capital of $250 just wasn't enough, but in this scenario, working capital is up to $550. Now it has a proper input of working capital at the beginning. With even the barest of business plans, we could tell that $100 wasn't enough to get this business going.

I hope the theoretical examples make the concepts clear. If you followed these illustrations, you can see some enormous implications for running a business.

Important: *Every dollar in accounts receivable means a dollar less in cash. Every dollar of inventory is a dollar less in cash. Every dollar of accounts payable is a dollar more in cash.*

A Real Case Example

Now let's look at the implications in a real case. The real case is a computer reseller (that is, computer store) in a medium-sized local market, with sales of about $6 million per year. The charts and underlying financial analysis are taken from the sample plan included with *Business Plan Pro*, named AMT.

The first graph, in Illustration 11-8, shows a representative sample business plan cash flow for 12 months, given standard assumptions for sales, costs, expenses, profits, and cash management. The sample company is profitable and growing. It sells about $6 million annually, produces about 8 percent net profit on sales, and is self supporting.

The chart shows a 12-month projection of AMT cash resources. The lighter of the two sets of bars represent the checkbook balance at the end of each month, and the other represents the cash flow, which is how much the balance changes in a month. The first set of bars should never drop below zero, because if your checkbook balance is less than zero, then you are bouncing checks. The mathematics don't care, but the banks

Illustration 11-8: As the Cash Case Starts

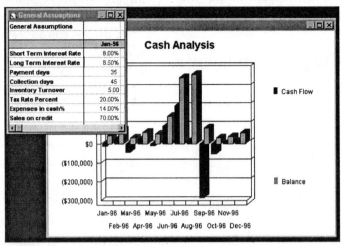

With the first take of the cash case, the business looks good and the cash plan is acceptable.

do. The cash flow bars, on the other hand, can drop below zero without major problems, as long as the balance stays above zero. For example, if a company's balance was $10,000 at the end of January, and its February cash flow is a negative $5,000, then the balance at the end of February is $5,000 and the cash flow is -$5,000. The lighter bar stays positive, but the darker one is negative.

In Illustration 11-9, only one assumption has changed: that same company now waits an extra 15 days, on average, to receive money from customers on invoices presented. The average wait, which is called "collection days." goes from 45 days to 60 days.

Nothing else changes — no new employees, no change in costs, no additional expenses.

No other changes except waiting on average an extra 15 days before receiving money owed from their customers. By the way, accountants call money owed by customers "Accounts Receivable."

Notice here the critical importance of cash, and the critical difference between cash and profits. With this single change in assumptions, the company is still as profitable as it was, down to the last dollar. **Now, however, its projected bank balance in November is more than $220,000 below zero. Therefore, the company needs more than $220,000 in additional financing.**

This is new money needed, new investment or new borrowing. The problem can't be solved by reducing expenses or increasing sales.

Illustration 11-9: Changing Collection Days Only

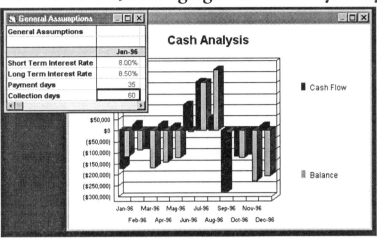

A single change, from 45 to 60 days, makes a huge difference in the cash flow.

Companies go out of business for problems like these. Even otherwise-healthy companies can go under for lack of cash. This kind of projection can kill a company if it sneaks up by surprise, but can be easily managed when there is a plan for it. This is an eloquent argument for good business planning.

In the third case, shown in Illustration 11-10, we set the collection days back to the original assumption of 45 days, but change the assumption for inventory. Where previously it kept an average of two month's worth of inventory on hand, in this changed assumption it now keeps three months of inventory on hand. Accountants call this Inventory Turnover. The changed assumption creates an inventory turnover rate of 4, instead of the previous rate of 5.

The collection days are back to 45 in this next scene, but inventory turnover went from 5 to 4, which means keeping more inventory on hand.

The implications of Illustration 11-10 are massive. This is still a profitable company, but it has a critical financial problem. You see how the cash balance bar falls to almost $310,000 below zero in November. That means that this company needs approximately $310,000 in new money, new loans or new capital investment, to make up its cash deficit, even though it is still profitable. This is hard to swallow until you see it happen in real business, but it is the truth and it will happen.

Profits are not cash.

Illustration 11-10: Changing Inventory Only

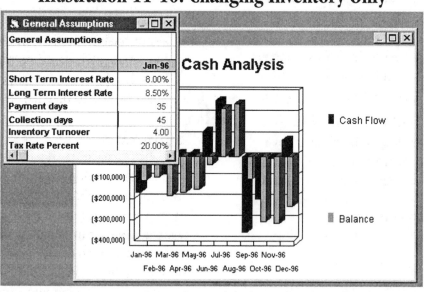

The change in inventory turnover shows the cash balance is now well below zero.

A Graphical View

As you can see from the examples, the numbers in a normal business analysis, and in a business plan, are very interrelated. In previous chapters we did the sales forecast and personnel plan, which then reappeared in the income statement, also called the profit and loss. You can see from the examples how the income statement links to the balance sheet. We'll go into cash flow and balance in following chapters, but the point here is that the assumptions and estimates in the standard business plan tables link up to each other in a complex system of relationships. You can see how these relationships work in Illustration 11-11.

Linking the Numbers

As the chart suggests and the previous examples show, there is a logical link between the business numbers in a standard analysis.

- Your sales forecast should show sales and cost of sales. The same numbers in the sales forecast are the ones you use in the profit and loss.

- As with sales, you should normally have a separate personnel table, but the numbers showing in that table should be the same numbers that show up for personnel costs in your profit and loss table.

- Your profit and loss table should show the same numbers as sales and personnel plan tables in the proper areas. It should also show interest expenses as a logical reflection of interest rates and balances of debt.

- Your cash flow has to reflect your profit and loss, plus changes in balance sheet items and non-cash expenses such as depreciation, which are on the profit and loss. The changes in the balance sheet are critical.

  For example, when you borrow money, it doesn't affect the profit or loss (except for interest expenses later on), but it makes a huge difference to your checking account balance.

- The balance sheet has to reflect the profit and loss and the cash flow.

- Your business ratios should calculate automatically, based on the numbers in sales, profit and loss, personnel, cash flow, and balance sheet.

Summary

Use the charts along with the tables to illustrate and enhance your analysis. For example, keeping the Cash Flow chart visible while changing assumptions gives you an instant picture of whether or not you have exceeded available cash resources as you plan your operations.

Illustration 11-11: Logic of Business Statements

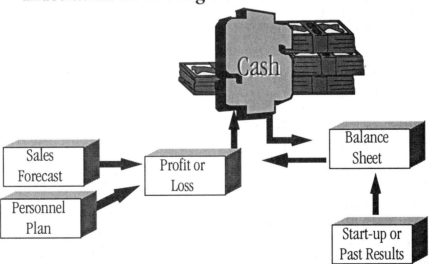

The business plan tables and charts should be linked together to reflect the practical realities of business numbers.

This page intentionally blank.

CHAPTER 12:
Cash is King

So, as we looked at business numbers in the previous chapter, we focused on the critical difference between cash and profits. This chapter looks at how to plan for cash in a business plan, understanding the critical elements that affect cash flow. You don't want to be one of those businesses that goes broke even while producing profits.

Basic Cash Planning

Let's start again with a simple example. Compared to the examples in the previous chapter, Illustration 12-1 looks at the business from a completely different point of view; money coming in and money flowing out. Sales and profits are out of the picture, (although sales influences money in and costs and expenses influence money out).

In this very simple model, your sources of money are cash sales, payments from receivables, new loan money, and new investment. Your expenditures include buying widgets in cash, paying interest, paying bills as they come due (i.e. paying accounts payable), and paying off loans.

Illustration 12-1: Basic Cash Plan

Sources of Cash	Start	Jan	Feb	Mar
Cash sales	$0	$0	$0	$0
From receivables	$0	$0	$0	$0
New loans	$0	$0	$100	$100
New investment	$400	$0	$0	$0
Total Inflow	$400	$0	$100	$100
Expenditures				
Interest payments	$0	$0	$0	$0
Purchase widgets	$0	$100	$100	$100
Pay payables	$0	$0	$0	$100
Pay loans	$0	$0	$0	$0
Total cash out	$0	$100	$100	$200
Cash Flow	$400	($100)	$0	($100)
Cash Balance	$400	$300	$300	$200

This sample shows examples of incoming cash and expenditures for our sample company.

Even at this basic level, you can see the potential complications and the need for linking the numbers up with a computer. Your estimated receipts from accounts receivable must have a logical relationship to sales and the balance of accounts receivable. Likewise, your payments of accounts payable have to relate to the balances of payables and the costs and expenses that created the payables. Vital as this is to business survival, it is not nearly as intuitive as the sales forecast, personnel plan, or income statement. The mathematics and the finance are more complex.

A More Realistic Example

The cash plan can get complicated quickly when you deal with a more realistic business example. In the following illustrations, we're going to look at the cash planning for the company whose cash balances were described in Chapter 11. This was the company whose cash flow varied widely, depending on cash assumptions.

Beginning Assumptions

With Illustrations 12-2 and 12-3 we set the starting points, which are the projected income and the starting balance.

Illustration 12-2: Sample Case Projected Income

Income Statement	Jan-99	Feb-99	Mar-99	Apr-99	May-99	Jun-99
Cash sales	$81	$103	$125	$151	$193	$146
Sales on credit	$188	$240	$292	$352	$451	$340
Total Sales	$268	$343	$417	$503	$644	$486
Direct cost of sales	$185	$250	$309	$400	$503	$368
Personnel cost of sales	$10	$10	$10	$10	$10	$10
Other cost of sales	$1	$1	$1	$1	$1	$1
Total cost of sales	$195	$260	$319	$410	$513	$378
Gross margin	$74	$83	$98	$93	$131	$108
Operating expenses						
Wages and salaries	$44	$44	$44	$44	$44	$60
Depreciation	$1	$1	$1	$1	$1	$1
Other operating expenses	$25	$40	$28	$41	$47	$35
EBIT	$3	-$2	$25	$7	$38	$12
Interest	$3	$3	$4	$5	$5	$4
Taxes	$0	-$1	$4	$0	$7	$1
Net	$1	-$4	$17	$1	$27	$7

This table shows some of the more important assumptions related to the cash plan for a sample company (numbers displayed in thousands).

We see a simple example of business income, which we'll use as a first step for planning cash. Sales hit a peak in May. The example already divides sales between cash sales and sales on credit. We also have a simplified version of wages and operating expenses so that we can focus on the cash plan instead of the income statement.

Illustration 12-3: Sample Case Starting Balance

Current assets	
Cash Balance	$55
Accounts receivable	$395
Inventory	$251
Other current assets	$25
Subtotal	$727
Capital assets	
Capital assets	$350
Accumulated depreciation	$50
Subtotal	$300
Total Assets	$1,027
Liabilities	
Current liabilities	
Accounts payable	$224
Current notes	$90
Other current liabilities	$15
Subtotal	$329
Long-term liabilities	
Subtotal	$285
Total liabilities	$614
Capital	
Paid-in capital	$500
Retained earnings	-$162
Earnings	$75
Total capital	$413
Capital and Liabilities	$1,027

This is the starting balance sheet for the cash flow example whose income statement is in Illustration 12-2.

The Process

In the following sections, I will explain the Cash Flow table, row by row, and how the numbers in your Cash Flow have a direct impact on the Balance Sheet, to help you better understand the direct link of one table to another, and how changes in one table directly affect the other.

For the purpose of discussion, we have divided a standard Cash Flow table into separate sections, Sources of Cash and Use of Cash.

Sources of Cash

Illustration 12-4 lists possible cash sources for our sample company. Most of these have balance sheet impact, and several come from the income statement. For now, we'll focus just on the cash flow. After dealing with cash, before we go on to the balance in the next chapter, we'll also look briefly at the specific cash flow implications on the balance sheet.

1. The first row, "Cash sales," is a simple estimate. It should link with your sales forecast and income statement to avoid inconsistencies. Cash sales plus sales on credit equal total sales. Normally, credit card sales are grouped into cash sales because the business gets the money

Illustration 12-4: Sample Case Sources of Cash

Sources of Cash	Jan-99	Feb-99	Mar-99	Apr-99	May-99	Jun-99
Cash sales	$81	$103	$125	$151	$193	$146
From receivables	$212	$137	$190	$284	$292	$352
From sale of inventory	$0	$0	$0	$0	$0	$0
From sale of other current assets	$0	$0	$0	$0	$0	$0
From sale of capital assets	$0	$0	$0	$0	$0	$0
From new short-term debt	$0	$100	$30	$100	$0	$0
From new other current liabilities	$0	$0	$0	$0	$0	$0
From new long-term debt	$0	$0	$100	$0	$0	$0
New capital	$0	$25	$0	$0	$300	$0
Total inflow	$293	$365	$445	$535	$785	$498

In this section of the Cash Flow table, we describe the main sources of cash, such as cash sales and monies received from accounts receivable.

in a day or two. Cash in this case means cash, check, and credit card, everything except the real sales on credit which are sales made on terms.

2. The second row, "From receivables," is an estimate of the dollar amount received from customers as payments of accounts receivable.

3. The third row, "From sale of inventory," shows special sales of inventory sold outside of the normal business. For example, sometimes a manufacturer sells excess inventory of materials or components, outside of its normal channel, for normal sales. This shouldn't include the normal sales of normal inventory, which go on the income statement as sales.

4. The fourth and fifth rows are "From sale of other current assets" and "From sale of capital assets." Selling short-term or long-term assets is another possible way to generate cash.

5. The next three rows are where you estimate amounts of money coming into the company as new borrowed money. The difference between each of the three is a matter of type of borrowing and terms. The row named "From new short-term debt" is for money you get by borrowing through normal lending institutions, as standard loans, with interest payments. The row named "From new other current liabilities" is for items like accrued taxes and accrued salaries and wages, money owed that will have to be paid, but isn't formally borrowed. Normally there are no interest expenses associated

with this row. The row named "From new long-term debt" is for new money borrowed on longer terms.

6. The last row in Sources of Cash, "New capital," is for new money coming into the company as investment.

Use of Cash

Illustration 12-5 is an example of uses of cash for our sample company.

1. The first and most obvious use of cash is to "Pay accounts payable." The accounts payable balance is money you owe. Every month, you pay off most of this.

2. The row named "Payroll etc." is for wages and salaries and other compensation-related payments you make every month to your employees and the government.

These obligations don't go into accounts payable. Instead, you pay them every month.

3. The row named "Immediate expenses" is for other expenses, aside from the wages and such in the row right above it, that you pay as incurred. They never go into payables to wait their turn.

4. The "Immediate cost of sales" row is very similar to the one above it, the difference being that these are costs of sales, instead of expenses, that are paid as incurred.

5. The next row, "Interest payments," assumes that interest is paid as incurred instead of waiting in payables to be paid later. Therefore, interest payments decrease cash. The amounts have to match the income statement.

Illustration 12-5: Sample Case Use of Cash

Use of Cash	Jan-99	Feb-99	Mar-99	Apr-99	May-99	Jun-99
Pay accounts payable	$134	$146	$229	$205	$333	$352
Payroll etc.	$54	$54	$54	$54	$54	$69
Immediate expenses	$6	$5	$5	$4	$5	$4
Immediate cost of sales	$5	$5	$4	$5	$4	$5
Interest payments	$3	$3	$4	$5	$5	$4
Principal payments short-term debt						$100
Principle payments long-term debt	$3	$3	$3	$3	$3	$3
Inventory in cash	$103	$143	$144	$251	$253	$0
New capital assets	$25		$15		$50	
Total cash out	$332	$359	$459	$527	$707	$537

This section of the Cash Flow table lists projected expenditures, such as payments on accounts payable and direct payments of wages and salaries.

6. The next two rows, "Principal payments short-term debt" and Principal payments long-term debt", are for principal payments of debt. When you pay off your loans, you lose cash. In the example, there is a regular payoff of long-term debt, and a single payoff of part of the short-term debt.

7. In the second row from the bottom, you record new "Inventory in cash." You'll have to know how much new inventory you'll be buying, so the portion of it paid in the same month is part of calculating new payables.

8. Finally, in the last row, purchases of "New capital assets" reduce cash and change the balance sheet amount for the related assets.

Calculating The Cash Balance

When you're done with both sections, add the new sources of cash and subtract the uses of cash, and you have an estimated ending Cash Balance for each month, as shown in Illustration 12-6.

Even with this detailed list, we've still missed some other items that might reduce cash. There is nothing in this sample table for purchase of short-term assets. There is nothing showing for owner's draw or dividends. There is no row for interest income, or miscellaneous income. This is just a simple example intended to point out the relationships between the different tables, and the dependencies involved in calculating a real cash flow.

Illustration 12-6: Sample Case Cash Balance

Sources of Cash	Jan-99	Feb-99	Mar-99	Apr-99	May-99	Jun-99
Cash sales	$81	$103	$125	$151	$193	$146
From receivables	$212	$137	$190	$284	$292	$352
From sale of inventory	$0	$0	$0	$0	$0	$0
From sale of other current assets	$0	$0	$0	$0	$0	$0
From sale of capital assets	$0	$0	$0	$0	$0	$0
From new short-term debt	$0	$100	$30	$100	$0	$0
From new other current liabilities	$0	$0	$0	$0	$0	$0
From new long-term debt	$0	$0	$100	$0	$0	$0
New capital	$0	$25	$0	$0	$300	$0
Total inflow	$293	$365	$445	$535	$785	$498

Use of Cash	Jan-99	Feb-99	Mar-99	Apr-99	May-99	Jun-99
Pay accounts payable	$134	$146	$229	$205	$333	$352
Payroll etc.	$54	$54	$54	$54	$54	$69
Immediate expenses	$6	$5	$5	$4	$5	$4
Immediate cost of sales	$5	$5	$4	$5	$4	$5
Interest payments	$3	$3	$4	$5	$5	$4
Principal payments short-term debt						$100
Principle payments long-term debt	$3	$3	$3	$3	$3	$3
Inventory in cash	$103	$143	$144	$251	$253	$0
New capital assets	$25		$15		$50	
Total cash out	$332	$359	$459	$527	$707	$537
Cash Flow	-$40	$6	-$14	$8	$78	-$39
Cash Balance	$16	$22	$7	$15	$93	$54

The full cash plan lets you compare your Sources of Cash with Use of Cash and see the Cash Balance.

Links with the Balance Sheet

Even though I cover the balance sheet in the next chapter, I can't talk about cash without relating the cash flow to the balance. The three most important financial statements in a plan, income statement, cash flow, and balance sheet, are all related to each other.

Illustration 12-7 shows the sample balance sheet linked to the cash flow in

the previous illustration. Most of the rows on this balance are directly affected by the cash flow, and need to change every time the cash changes. To close the circle in this chapter, let's look in detail at the balance:

1. The "Cash Balance" row is the balance in your checkbook. You calculate this with the cash flow.

Illustration 12-7: Related Balance Sheet

Assets		Jan-99	Feb-99	Mar-99	Apr-99	May-99	Jun-99
Current assets							
Cash Balance	$55	$16	$22	$7	$15	$93	$54
Accounts receivable	$395	$371	$473	$576	$644	$803	$791
Inventory	$251	$333	$445	$547	$703	$880	$648
Other current assets	$25	$25	$25	$25	$25	$25	$25
Subtotal	$727	$744	$965	$1,155	$1,387	$1,801	$1,518
Capital assets							
Capital assets	$350	$375	$375	$390	$390	$440	$440
Accumulated depreciation	$50	$51	$52	$53	$54	$55	$56
Subtotal	$300	$324	$323	$337	$336	$385	$384
Total Assets	$1,027	$1,068	$1,288	$1,492	$1,723	$2,186	$1,902

Liabilities		Jan-99	Feb-99	Mar-99	Apr-99	May-99	Jun-99
Current liabilities							
Accounts payable	$224	$268	$370	$430	$563	$702	$515
Current notes	$90	$90	$190	$220	$320	$320	$220
Other current liabilities	$15	$15	$15	$15	$15	$15	$15
Subtotal	$329	$373	$575	$665	$898	$1,037	$750
Long-term liabilities							
Subtotal	$285	$282	$279	$376	$373	$370	$367
Total liabilities	$614	$655	$854	$1,041	$1,271	$1,407	$1,117

Capital		Jan-99	Feb-99	Mar-99	Apr-99	May-99	Jun-99
Paid-in capital	$500	$500	$525	$525	$525	$825	$825
Retained earnings	-$162	-$87	-$87	-$87	-$87	-$87	-$87
Earnings	$75	$1	-$4	$13	$15	$41	$48
Total capital	$413	$413	$434	$451	$452	$779	$785
Capital and Liabilities	$1,027	$1,068	$1,288	$1,492	$1,723	$2,186	$1,902

The information on the balance sheet should follow from the income statement and the cash flow. Notice, for example, how long-term liabilities respond in March to a new loan and a regular principal payment of an existing loan.

2. "Accounts receivable" is the money owed to you by customers for sales already made. The balance increases with sales on credit, and decreases with payments of accounts receivable. For any month, the ending balance is the sum of the previous ending balance, plus new sales on credit, minus payments received.

3. Calculate the "Inventory" balance as the previous balance minus direct cost of sales plus new inventory purchases.

4. Calculate "Other current assets" as the previous balance plus new assets purchased (from the uses of cash) minus disposal of assets (from sources of cash).

5. "Capital assets" are long-term assets, usually plant and equipment. This month's balance is equal to last month's balance plus new assets purchased, minus disposal of assets.

6. "Accumulated depreciation" decreases the value of the capital assets. This month's balance is last month's balance plus new depreciation, from the income statement.

7. "Accounts payable" will be last month's balance plus additions (a subset of costs and expenses) minus payments of payables. New payables will include new inventory not paid for when purchased, plus

indirect costs of sales not paid as incurred, operating expenses not paid as incurred, and similar items.

8. "Current notes" (short-term) will be equal to last month's balance plus new borrowing minus principal payments. Interest payments are not included, because they go into the income statement and don't affect the balance. Principal payments and new borrowing should come from the cash flow.

9. "Other current liabilities" are things like accrued taxes and accrued salary, liabilities you know you have but haven't paid. These usually don't cost interest.

10. "Long-term liabilities" (debt) increases when you borrow and decreases with payment of principal. The balance is going to be last month's balance plus new borrowing as a source of cash, minus principal payments as a use. In the sample case, the March balance shows a $100 increase for a new loan, minus a $3 decrease for payment of principal, so that the $376 at the end of March is exactly $97 more than the $279 at the end of February.

11. "Paid-in capital" is money invested. The balance should be last month's balance plus new investment from sources of cash, minus dividends from uses of cash.

12. "Retained earnings" is the accumulated earnings reinvested in the company, not taken out as dividends. Normally this changes once a year when the annual statements are prepared.

13. "Earnings" are the accumulated earnings since the end of the last year. This month's balance should be equal to last month's balance plus this month's earnings. At the end of the year, with an annual adjustment, earnings still left in the business become retained earnings.

Understanding Cash Flow

Your cash plan is the most critical element of your business projections. If it is going to be useful at all, a business plan helps you develop a realistic cash estimate, based on the underlying relationships we explored in the previous chapter. Whenever you change an assumption in sales forecast, personnel plan, profit and loss, or balance sheet, it affects your cash flow.

The examples in this and the previous chapters pointed the way toward cash flow, and the way cash works. Profits are very important to cash, of course, and they work in obvious ways – the more profits, the better the cash, because profits are sales (that generate cash) minus costs and expenses (that cost cash). What is less obvious, however, is the impact of balance sheet items:

• An increase in assets decreases your cash. A decrease in assets increases cash.

• An increase in liabilities increases cash. A decrease in liabilities decreases cash.

These two principals lead eventually to the impact of receivables, inventory, and payables. As you look at your assumptions for the cash flow, keep in mind that every extra dollar of receivables or inventory as assets is a dollar that you don't have in your cash balance. Every dollar in payables is a dollar that you have in cash, too. Although this simple cash model doesn't show the critical impact as clearly as our examples in the previous chapter, the mathematics and financial principals are the same.

Summary

The cash plan is vital, the most critical analysis in the business plan. It has to manage the critical difference between cash and profits. The cash flow stands between income statement and balance sheet, and brings the two together.

This page intentionally blank.

CHAPTER 13:
Finish the Financials

If you've really followed through with the cash plan, your financials are almost done. The balance sheet should be completed by the time you have a cash flow working. Business ratios should be almost automatic too, because they draw all of their information from tables you've already finished.

The Balance Sheet

I showed you some basic balance sheets first in Chapter 11, and again in Chapter 12, because you can't deal with cash without addressing the balance. You've seen then that the balance sheet table shows the business' financial position, its assets and liabilities, at a specified time. A standard business plan includes a projected Balance Sheet table for each of the first 12 months in the plan, and for each of the three years.

The ironclad rule of Western double-entry bookkeeping and accounting is that assets are equal to capital and liabilities. This is what balance means.

If you think about it, you'll notice we used that rule as well in the Start-up costs section of Chapter 10. It comes up again with the balance sheet, as we use this rule to calculate retained earnings, which makes the balance correct.

Illustration 13-1 shows the Balance Sheet table, or pro forma Balance Sheet table. The Balance Sheet table should naturally start with either your start-up costs or your ending balance from the previous year, depending on whether your are a start-up company or an ongoing company. Then, for the first 12 months of your plan, it should give detailed projections of your assets, liabilities, and capital as your business progresses. The calculations for this come mainly from your income statement and cash flow. Between those two statements, plus the beginning balances, your Balance Sheet should be virtually done before you start.

Illustration 13-1: Sample Balance Sheet Table

Assets		Jan-99	Feb-99	Mar-99	Apr-99	May-99	Jun-99
Current assets							
Cash Balance	$55	$16	$22	$7	$15	$93	$54
Accounts receivable	$395	$371	$473	$576	$644	$803	$791
Inventory	$251	$333	$445	$547	$703	$880	$648
Other current assets	$25	$25	$25	$25	$25	$25	$25
Subtotal	$727	$744	$965	$1,155	$1,387	$1,801	$1,518
Capital assets							
Capital assets	$350	$375	$375	$390	$390	$440	$440
Accumulated depreciation	$50	$51	$52	$53	$54	$55	$56
Subtotal	$300	$324	$323	$337	$336	$385	$384
Total Assets	$1,027	$1,068	$1,288	$1,492	$1,723	$2,186	$1,902
Liabilities		Jan-99	Feb-99	Mar-99	Apr-99	May-99	Jun-99
Current liabilities							
Accounts payable	$224	$268	$370	$430	$563	$702	$515
Current notes	$90	$90	$190	$220	$320	$320	$220
Other current liabilities	$15	$15	$15	$15	$15	$15	$15
Subtotal	$329	$373	$575	$665	$898	$1,037	$750
Long-term liabilities							
Subtotal	$285	$282	$279	$376	$373	$370	$367
Total liabilities	$614	$655	$854	$1,041	$1,271	$1,407	$1,117
Capital		Jan-99	Feb-99	Mar-99	Apr-99	May-99	Jun-99
Paid-in capital	$500	$500	$525	$525	$525	$825	$825
Retained earnings	-$162	-$87	-$87	-$87	-$87	-$87	-$87
Earnings	$75	$1	-$4	$13	$15	$41	$48
Total capital	$413	$413	$434	$451	$452	$779	$785
Capital and Liabilities	$1,027	$1,068	$1,288	$1,492	$1,723	$2,186	$1,902

This illustration shows the Balance Sheet table for sample company we used in the previous chapter (numbers displayed in thousands).

Ratios

Illustration 13-2 shows the Ratios table. This table calculates several ratios that are common in financial analysis.

Ratios are often misunderstood. They aren't magic. Correct, healthy ratios vary from industry to industry, business to business, depending on the nature of the business. Chapter 5 on business information, lists sources for more information

on business ratios, including standards for your type of business. Generally, the most important insight gained from ratios is the change in a ratio over time, rather than the specific number at any given time.

While we do explain the standard financial ratios used here, there are better explanations available in financial management textbooks. Experts will almost always agree on the importance of following changes in a ratio over time, and on the wide variations of standards depending on the type of business.

Profitability Ratios

Return on equity or return on investment (ROI) is probably the most important of these ratios. A business is an investment

Illustration 13-2: The Ratios Table

Ratio Analysis

Profitability Ratios:	1998	1999	2000
Gross Margin	22.55%	26.13%	26.72%
Net Profit Margin	2.76%	5.62%	5.53%
Return on Assets	6.73%	13.76%	12.98%
Return on Equity	19.01%	43.64%	32.77%

Activity Ratios	1998	1999	2000
AR Turnover	3.75	3.75	3.75
Collection Days	65	90	90
Inventory Turnover	5.89	3.76	3.86
Accts Payable Turnover	5.90	5.90	5.90
Total Asset Turnover	2.44	2.45	2.35

Debt Ratios	1998	1999	2000
Debt to Net Worth	1.83	2.17	1.52
Short-term Liab. to Liab.	0.79	0.86	0.91

Liquidity Ratios	1998	1999	2000
Current Ratio	1.67	1.38	1.37
Quick Ratio	0.61	0.52	0.49
Net Working Capital	$881,815	$682,070	$758,509
Interest Coverage	5.45	7.10	7.10

Additional Ratios	1998	1999	2000
Assets to Sales	0.41	0.41	0.43
Debt/Assets	65%	68%	60%
Current Debt/Total Assets	51%	59%	55%
Acid Test	-0.28	-0.25	-0.31
Asset Turnover	2.44	2.45	2.35
Sales/Net Worth	6.88	7.77	5.93
Dividend Payout	$0	0.00	0.00

Most standard business plans include some standard business ratios. You should let the computer calculate them.

and it should yield profits comparable to alternative investments, unless there is additional compensation (such as salaries for the owners). In theory, at least, if ROI is low, you should sell the business and put your investment money to better use.

Return on assets and the net profit margin provide a good basis for comparison between your company and the rest of the industry. They are also good indicators of company performance from year to year.

- **Gross Margin**: sales minus cost of sales, expressed as a percentage.

- **Net Profit Margin**: net profit divided by sales, as a percentage.

- **Return on Assets**: net profit divided by the total assets.

- **Return on Equity**: also called return on investment (ROI). This ratio divides the net profit by the net worth.

Activity Ratios

These ratios are generally used to compare a company's performance to the average for its industry. Levels of acceptability tend to vary widely between different industries. Large manufacturing companies might have a very low assets turnover, but retail stores should have a high turnover.

- **AR Turnover** (accounts receivables turnover): sales on credit divided by accounts receivable. This is a measure of how well your business collects its debts.

- **Collection Days**: accounts receivable multiplied by 360, which is then divided by annual credit sales. This is another measure of debt collection and value of receivables. Generally, 30 days is exceptionally good, 60 days is bothersome, and 90 days or more is a real problem. This varies by industry.

This figure may be slightly different from your Collection Days assumption in the General Assumptions table because of the details of calculation.

- **Inventory Turnover**: cost of sales divided by the average balance of inventory. The higher the turnover, the better for cash flow and working capital requirements.

This ratio may be slightly different than your Inventory assumption in the General Assumption table because of the effect of average balances.

- **Accounts Payable Turnover**: a measure of how quickly the business pays its bills. It divides the total new accounts payable for the year by the average accounts payable balance.

- **Total Assets Turnover**: sales divided by total assets.

Debt Ratios

- **Debt to Net Worth**: total liabilities divided by total net worth.

- **Short-term Debt to Liabilities**: short-term debt divided by total liabilities. This is a measure of the depth and term of debt.

Liquidity Ratios

These are all measures of the overall financial position of a company and its ability to pay its debt. They are very important to bankers and for loan applications. The acid test (included with additional ratios in the following section) is generally considered the best measure of a company's ability to pay all its obligations without problems.

Acceptable measures vary by industry. Some industries are quite heavy on plant and equipment assets, and others (for example, service businesses) have few long-term assets.

- **Current Ratio**: short-term assets divided by short-term liabilities. This gives a view of a business' cash position and ability to meet short-term commitments.

- **Quick Ratio**: this is the same as the current ratio, except that inventories are first subtracted from short-term assets before they are divided by short-term liabilities. Many financial experts consider this a better measurement of liquidity than the current ratio, because inventory is so often not convertible to real cash in a short period of time.

- **Net Working Capital**: subtract short-term liabilities from short-term assets. This is another measure of cash position.

- **Interest Coverage**: profit before interest and taxes (operating profit) divided by total interest payments. A measure of how much a business is burdened by servicing its own debt.

Additional Ratios

- **Assets to sales**: assets divided by sales.

- **Debt/assets**: total liabilities divided by total assets.

- **Current Debt/Total Assets**: divides total assets by short-term (current) liabilities.

- **Acid Test**: short-term assets (minus accounts receivable and inventory), divided by short-term liabilities.

- **Asset Turnover**: a repetition of the same ratio in activity ratios above.

- **Sales/Net Worth**: total sales divided by net worth.

- **Dividend Payout**: dividends divided by net profit.

Break-Even Analysis

You prepared a preliminary break-even analysis in Chapter 2. Now it's time to go back to that and review the numbers. Illustration 13-3 shows (again) the standard break-even analysis included in a standard business plan.

This is a monthly break-even analysis. It assumes monthly fixed costs, and per-unit sales price and variable costs. It uses the standard break-even formulas detailed below, but suggests some modified assumptions. Where standard fixed costs are supposed to be costs that would be sustained even if the business stopped, we suggest you use operating expenses instead. I suggest this change in standard financial analysis because you are better off knowing break-even points on real operations, rather than on some theoretical calculation of fixed expenses.

The units break-even point, which is calculated in the financial worksheet, is:

$$\frac{\text{Fixed Cost}}{\text{Unit Price - Unit Variable Costs}}$$

Illustration 13-3: Break-even Assumptions

Break Even Analysis:	
Monthly Units Break-even	1,222
Monthly Sales Break-even	$397,266
Assumptions:	
Average Per-Unit Revenue	$325.00
Average Per-Unit Cost	$248.07
Fixed Cost	$94,035

This section of the model calculates technical break-even points, based on the assumptions for unit prices, variable costs, and fixed costs.

The sales break-even point is from the formula:

$$\frac{\text{Fixed Cost}}{(1 - (\text{Unit variable Costs/Unit Price}))}$$

The Break-even Chart

The break-even analysis depends on assumptions for fixed costs, unit price, and unit variable costs. These are rarely exact assumptions. This is not a true picture of fixed costs by any means, but is quite useful for determining a break-even point.

Break-even points can be determined for any month or year, covered in the main numbers worksheet because each column has a different fixed cost. This

Illustration 13-4: Break-even Chart

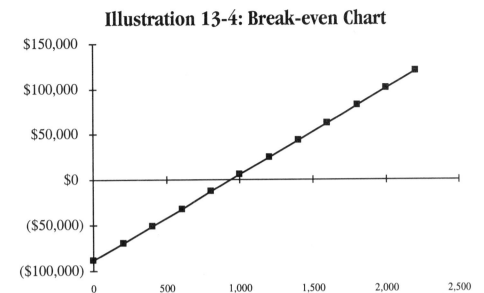

This illustration shows the break-even analysis that compares unit sales to profits. It uses data from the table.

analysis is included in the chart in Illustration 13-4, which shows a general break-even analysis for assumed fixed costs of $94,035, average per-unit revenue of $325, and average per-unit variable cost of $248. This chart is produced automatically by the software.

The line on the chart shows profits increasing and crossing the break-even line at approximately 1,200 units. Use the break-even worksheet and chart to experiment with break-even points for your company.

Refine and Polish the Financials

Your financial tables are interrelated. The sales and personnel forecasts and assumptions affect the profit and loss, the profit affects cash, and the cash and balance sheet work together.

Summary

Financial analysis is rarely a true step-by-step process. You will probably have to go back through your tables to review the assumptions for realism and accuracy. As you revise assumptions, make sure you constantly check back to keep your cash flow positive.

This page intentionally blank.

CHAPTER 14:
Strategy and Tactics

With most of the financials now done, it's time to turn to strategy and tactics. You've been developing strategy throughout, I know, because you can't do the numbers without thinking about the strategy. However, now you want to explain your strategy and develop the implementation. If you refer back to the text outline we discussed in Chapter 3, you probably have several topics still blank in your plan document. But not in your mind. Its time to write your thoughts on strategy and tactics into your text outline.

Define Overall Strategy

Think of strategy as focus. Of the whole range of possible market segments, and the whole range of services and possible sales and marketing activities, which are your main priorities? Avoid making long lists of priorities. More than three or four points makes them more like a laundry list or to-do list than a strategic focus.

The Strategy Pyramid

Imagine a pyramid made of three levels. The top of the pyramid is a single box, which contains a strategy. Strategy is an area of resource focus. In the middle level, you have three or so boxes which contain tactics. In the third level, you have five or six boxes that stand for programs. It would look something like Illustration 14-1.

Illustration 14-1: The Strategy Pyramid

Don't get lost in defining strategy and tactics. Make the strategic view work logically.

Your definitions don't have to be exact. A strategy is a main focus, which might be on a specific target market, product opportunity, positioning statement, or some other important or fundamental element.

Tactics are there to implement strategies. For example, if a computer store's strategy is to build long-term relationships with business customers, its tactics might include increasing networking offerings, training, and support.

Programs are specific business activities, each of which has concrete dates and responsibilities, and probably a budget. In the computer store example, programs for the strategy might include upgrade mailings, seminars, installation services, network training, and others, each of which is built on specifics.

You don't necessarily do a complete business strategy in a single pyramid. Each fundamental business strategy might be a different pyramid.

One important benefit of the pyramid method is integration and alignment. If your strategy is to focus on one thing, you should be able to trace that strategy into its tactics and, most important, into your actual spending and activity priorities. Flip back and forth between your pyramid strategy and your specific programs, and ask yourself: do your programs match the emphasis you put on strategy?

The Value Proposition

Value-based marketing is another conceptual framework. Like the pyramid described in the previous topic, it doesn't have to be in your business plan at all, but we add it here because some people find that the framework helps them develop their strategy. Obviously, this has to be a quick treatment. There are textbooks written about value-based marketing, and the business literature on this topic is rich and varied.

This framework begins with defining your business offering as a value proposition. The value proposition is benefit offered minus price charged, in relative terms. The definition encourages you to think in broad conceptual terms, with emphasis on the real benefit offered, rather than the specific tangible. For example, a national fast food chain probably offers the value of convenience and reliability, probably at a slight price premium (at least when compared to the weaker chains). A prestigious local restaurant, on the other hand, is offering a completely different set of benefits (luxury, elegance, prestige, for example) at a marked price premium. A graphic designer is probably selling benefits related to communication and advertising, not just drawings.

Once you have a value proposition defined, then look at your business--and your business plan--in terms of how well you:

1. communicate the business proposition; and
2. fulfill your promise.

For example, if a computer store's business proposition has to do with reliable service for small business, peace of mind, and long-term relationships, then it probably shouldn't be taking out full-page newspaper advertisements promising the lowest prices in town on brand-name hardware. It probably should communicate that proposition with sales literature that emphasizes how the computer store will become a strategic ally of its clients. It might also think twice about how it handles overdue bills from customers, who might really be holding out for more service or better support.

Like the pyramid, the framework helps you integrate your planned programs into a logical whole plan.

Define Marketing Strategy

Your marketing strategy normally involves target market focus, emphasis on certain services or media, or ways to position your company and your service uniquely.

Your marketing strategy depends a great deal on which market segments you've chosen as target market groups. You covered this in detail in Chapter 4. You may also have developed strategy using the pyramid or value proposition. Obviously, you want to make sure to preserve the same basic focus and themes.

Aside from the target market strategy, your marketing strategy might also include the positioning statement, pricing, promotion, and whatever else you want to add. You might also want to look at media strategy, business development, or other factors. Strategy is creative, and hard to predict. Some of the material below will give you more ideas.

Product Positioning

Product positioning statements can be a good way to define your marketing strategy. The positioning statements should include a strategic focus on the most important target market, that market's most important market need, how your product meets that need, what is the main competition, and how your product is better than the competition.

Consider this simple template:

For [target market description] who [target market need], [this product] [how it meets the need]. Unlike [key competition], it [most important distinguishing feature].

For example, the positioning statement for the original *Business Plan Pro*, in 1994, was: "For the businessperson who is starting a new company, launching new products or seeking funding or partners, *Business Plan Pro* is software that produces professional business plans quickly and easily. Unlike [name omitted], *Business Plan Pro* does a real business plan, with real insights, not just cookie-cutter fill-in-the-blanks templates."

Pricing Tactics

You ought to provide detail on product pricing, and relate pricing to strategy. Your value proposition, for example, will normally include implications about relative pricing, and therefore, you should check whether your detailed product-by-product pricing matches the implied pricing in the value proposition. Pricing is also supposed to be intimately related to the positioning statement in the previous topic, since pricing is probably the most important factor in product positioning.

Promotion Tactics

Think of promotion in a broader sense than simply sales promotion. Think of how you spread the word about your business to your future customers. Think of it in the broader context, including the whole range of advertising, public relations, events, direct mail, seminars, and sales literature.

Think strategically. What, in general, is your strategy about communicating with people? Do you look for expensive ads in mass media, or targeted marketing in specialized publications, or even more targeted, with direct mail? Do you have a way to leverage the news media, or reviewers? Do you advertise more effectively through public relations events, trade shows, newspaper, or radio? What about telemarketing, the World Wide Web, or even multilevel marketing?

Are you satisfied with how this is working for you now, or is it a problem area that needs to be addressed? Are you meeting your needs, and in line with your opportunities?

How does your promotion strategy fit with the rest of your strategy? Check for alignment between what you say here and what you say in your strategy pyramid, and your value proposition? As you described market trends and target market segments, did you see ways to improve your promotion strategy?

Define Sales Strategy

Describe sales strategy as different from marketing strategy. To help differentiate between marketing strategy and sales strategy, think of marketing as the broader effort of generating sales leads on a large scale, and sales as the efforts to bring those sales leads into the system as individual sales transactions. Marketing might affect image and awareness and propensity to buy, while Sales should close the deals and get the order that marketing opens.

Sales tactics deal with how and when to close sales prospects, how to compensate sales people, how to optimize order processing and database management, how to maneuver price, delivery, and conditions.

As with your marketing strategy, your sales strategy depends a great deal on which market segments you've chosen as target market groups. Obviously, you don't sell major deals to large companies the same way you sell cereal boxes off grocery store shelves. Think about how you sell in your business. What is your strategy for optimizing your way of selling?

Implementation Milestones

At this point you should be able to build some implementation into your business plan. You've been through the main thinking and analysis. It is time to put some bite into your plan and management, by listing specific actions to be taken. Each action is called a milestone.

Make your plan real. Give it as many milestones as you can think of to make it more concrete. Then make sure that all your people know that you will be following the plan, and tracking results. Details are good.

Business plan milestones, which you should develop as a business table, are critical. This is where a business plan becomes a real plan, with specific and measurable activities, instead of just a document. Include as many specific programs as possible. For each program, give each milestone a name, a person responsible, a milestone date, and a budget.

In the sample table, you see columns reserved for evaluating the actual results and the difference between plan and actual results, for each program. You also have a place to track actual spending and milestone dates, and you can also sort the table by person responsible, milestone date, and budget, and by department.

Specifics are the key to business plan implementation. Unless you include specific dates and budget responsibilities, you can't follow up with tracking and plan-vs.-actual analysis. If you don't follow up, your plan will not be implemented.

The value of a plan is measured in its implementation.

The Milestones table should be the most important section of the entire business plan. Milestones are used to fix specific dates and objectives for all of the business activities included in the plan. This is where what might be time wasted in theoretical planning and long-term strategy becomes time invested in concrete planning and implementation.

Each marketing and sales-related program you plan should be listed in the

table and explained in the related text, along with relevant details. You want to cement your sales strategy with programs that make it real. How is this strategy to be implemented? Do you have concrete and specific plans? How will implementation be measured?

The milestones are the key to implementation planning. Illustration 14-2 shows a sample plan Milestones table.

Manage Your Summaries

Each of your business plan chapters should begin with a summary paragraph that describes all the high points of the chapter. A good strategy and implementation chapter probably includes several summaries, one for strategy overall, one for marketing strategy, and one for sales strategy. As

Illustration 14-2: Milestones Table

Milestone	Mngr	Date	Dept.	Budget	Act date	Act $
Corporate Identity	TJ	12/17/95	Marketing	$10,000	1/15/96	$12,004
Seminar implementation	IR	1/10/96	Sales	$1,000	12/27/95	$5,000
Business Plan Review	RJ	1/10/96	GM	$0	1/23/96	$500
Upgrade mailer	IR	1/16/96	Sales	$5,000	2/12/96	$12,500
New corporate brochure	TJ	1/16/96	Marketing	$5,000	1/15/96	$5,000
Delivery vans	SD	1/25/96	Service	$12,500	2/26/96	$3,500
Direct mail	IR	2/16/96	Marketing	$3,500	2/25/96	$2,500
Advertising	RJ	2/16/96	GM	$115,000	3/6/96	$100,000
X4 Prototype	SG	2/25/96	Product	$2,500	2/25/96	$0
Service revamp	SD	2/25/96	Product	$2,500	2/25/96	$2,500
6 Presentations	IR	2/25/96	Sales	$0	1/10/96	$1,000
X4 Testing	SG	3/6/96	Product	$1,000	1/16/96	$0
3 Accounts	SD	3/17/96	Sales	$0	3/17/96	$2,500
L30 Prototype	PR	3/26/96	Product	$2,500	4/11/96	$15,000
Tech95 Expo	TB	4/12/96	Marketing	$15,000	1/25/96	$1,000
VP S&M hired	JK	6/11/96	Sales	$1,000	7/25/96	$5,000

These are the milestones, the heart and core of the business plan. The sample here is taken from the AMT, Inc. business plan, a published sample plan.

you develop these summaries, keep in mind that many business plan readers will read only the summaries that begin each chapter. You should make sure to include all the important points that you need to make even for browsers who don't read every word.

One of the best tactics in preparing a business plan is to write your chapter summaries well enough to use them by themselves as the core of a summary document. In seeking investment, for example, you will need to have a summary document that describes the complete plan in just a few pages. You should be able to pick out your summary paragraphs and use them to create the summary document.

The Executive Summary is the most important. It is the doorway to the rest of the plan. Get it right or your target readers will go no further. The best length is a single page. Emphasize the main points of your plan and keep it brief.

The Long-Term Plan

While you're involved with summaries, consider adding a discussion of long-term plans. How do you expect your company to change over the next five, 10, or 20 years? What are the important drivers of change? What is your

company doing to position itself to manage and even thrive on future growth?

I don't recommend including financial details beyond three years in a business plan. At the most, a brief summary of a five-year plan in text is sufficient. However, this is not because I don't believe in long-term planning. Far from it. Business should indeed plan for longer than three years, but the long-term plans running five years, 10 years, or more, work better in different formats. They are much less dependent on specific information, and specific business numbers.

Summary

Make it consistent and make it realistic. A mediocre strategy implemented well and with consistency will always beat a brilliant strategy that was never implemented. Check your plan for consistency throughout. Does your spending, in the details, reflect your strategy? Do your numbers, including your sales forecast, expense forecast, and personnel plan, reflect your strategy? Is your strategy a reflection of your company's strengths and weaknesses?

This page intentionally blank.

CHAPTER 15:
Print and Publish

So you're about ready to print your plan. Please make sure to run it through a final critical edit. Then make sure to publish it so that commitments made by managers are clearly known and acknowleged. Also make it clear that you will be tracking results, and comparing your actual results to the planned results, and discussing the difference.

Final Edit

Always run a business plan through a final edit. Have you run your spellcheck software? Have you read it over again? Do you have some friends who can read it for you? Sometimes you don't see the errors that others would see, because you are too close to it.

Check the numbers in your charts and tables. Make sure they match each other, and go back and check the references to numbers in the text. People often change numbers after writing objectives, which results in conflicting information. Your objectives text, for example, might set

sales objectives of $500,000, but your plan tables show sales projections of $400,000. The computer can't check those kinds of errors automatically, so watch for them.

Publishing = Management

Don't forget the process of publishing within your own company. In this case, publishing means distributing the plan where all the managers can see it. People who make commitments as part of the plan need to see those commitments on record. They need to know that the plan will be tracked. The difference between planned results will be calculated and discussed.

Related Documents

In the process of finding investment financing for a new business or a small business, people normally use a two-to-four-page summary memo. This contains the highlights of a business plan, organized so that potential investors can understand the main points quickly, then decide whether or not they want to know more.

When looking for loans for your business, you will probably want to prepare a slightly different two-to-four-page document, called a loan application summary.

Summary

As you finish your plan, review it from the point of view of the business purpose. Does it cover what you need it to cover? Is it going to achieve the purpose you planned for it? Are there topics that the plan's audience will ask about that you haven't covered? Think of the three most important questions you would expect to get from your intended reader. Have you answered them?

CHAPTER 16:
Planning for Implementation

Some plans are more likely to be implemented than others. Successful implementation starts with a good plan, one that is full of specific information on milestones, managers, responsibilities, dates and budgets. Beyond the plan itself, however, there are other factors also critical to implementation. Are you going to track results, comparing the planned results to the actual results? Are you going to follow up with your management team, *making revisions and checking on performance?*

Start With a Good Plan

Illustration 16-1 shows a view of what it takes to develop and implement a business plan. I call this "planning for implementation." There are some important factors beyond the plan that are also critical:

Illustration 16-1: Implementation Isn't Automatic

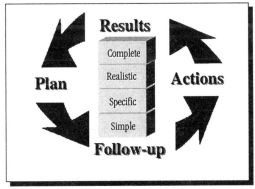

A business plan will be hard to implement unless it is simple, specific, realistic and complete. Even if it is all these things, a good plan will need someone to follow up and check on it.

1. Is the plan simple? Is it easy to understand and to act on? Does it communicate its contents easily and practically?

2. Is the plan specific? Are its objectives concrete and measurable? Does it include specific actions and activities, each with specific dates of completion, specific persons responsible and specific budgets?

3. Is the plan realistic? Are the sales goals, expense budgets, and milestone dates realistic? Nothing stifles implementation like unrealistic goals.

4. Is the plan complete? Does it include all the necessary elements? Requirements of a business plan vary, depending on the context. There is no guarantee, however, that the plan will work if it doesn't cover the main bases.

Track and Follow-Up

Ironically, a good plan alone isn't enough. Illustration 16-1 indicates other elements that are also critical. Even a good plan means virtually nothing if somebody doesn't follow-up on its concrete and specific milestones or results. A plan won't be implemented unless responsibilities are assigned to specific people, milestones are established and agreed upon, and the people responsible know that somebody will follow-up to check on results.

Keep Your Plan Alive

Remember that a useful business plan is a live document. As you review implementation results with the people responsible, you will, of course, find the need to revise your plan and set new goals and course corrections. One of the main advantages of creating a plan on a computer is that you can easily change it. Keep track of the original plan and manage changes carefully. Although changes should be made only with good reason, don't be afraid to update your plan and keep it alive.

If you're going to implement and track a business plan, you have to follow actual results and make corrections. The actual results area is perfectly set up for making course corrections. Month by month, as you record your actual results, make changes in your plan in the future months of the actual tables, to preserve the plan tables.

A Simple Case Example

The following example shows how a hypothetical company keeps its business plan alive.

Illustration 16-2: Beginning Sales Plan

Unit Sales	Jan	Feb	Mar
Systems	85	115	145
Service	200	200	200
Software	150	200	250
Training	145	155	165
Other	160	176	192
Total Unit Sales	740	846	952

Unit Prices	Jan	Feb	Mar
Systems	$2,000.00	$2,000.00	$2,000.00
Service	$75	$69	$58
Software	$200	$200	$200
Training	$37	$35	$39
Other	$300	$300	$300

Sales	Jan	Feb	Mar
Systems	$170,000	$230,000	$290,000
Service	$15,000	$13,846	$11,667
Software	$30,000	$40,000	$50,000
Training	$5,365	$5,500	$6,500
Other	$48,000	$52,800	$57,600
Total Sales	$268,365	$342,146	$415,767

To set the scene, this illustration shows the cash plan as the business plan is finished.

The Starting Plan

The example begins in Illustration 16-2 with the sales forecast portion of a finished business plan.

Recording Actual Results

In Illustration 16-3, we see the actual results for the same company for the first three months of the plan. These results should be typed into the appropriate place in the plan, by using the **Tables**

menu, select the **Actual** mode, and then select the Sales Forecast table.

For those with units-based sales forecasts, the Actual Results view doesn't multiply price by units to calculate sales, like the plan view does. You must type in your own sales results in dollar (or other currency) sales as well as in units sales. The summary rows and annual totals columns retain their formulas and continue to summarize the rest of the data. The software calculates variances for costs, units, and sales.

Illustration 16-3: Actual Sales Results

Unit Sales	Jan	Feb	Mar
Systems	63	74	108
Service	168	171	174
Software	174	235	289
Training	156	171	183
Other	162	151	220
Total Unit Sales	723	802	974

Unit Prices			
Systems	$1,782.57	$1,801.20	$1,791.14
Service	$102.52	$104.36	$90.04
Software	$223.57	$185.39	$276.77
Training	$48.35	$38.77	$46.17
Other	$1,360.65	$1,704.14	$1,574.44

Sales			
Systems	$112,302	$133,289	$193,443
Service	$17,223	$17,846	$15,667
Software	$38,901	$43,567	$79,987
Training	$7,543	$6,629	$8,449
Other	$44,456	$55,994	$48,832
Total Sales	$220,425	$257,325	$346,378

The actual cash flow at the end of March shows actual cash flow numbers plus adjustments and course corrections.

Plan vs. Actual

After the actual results are typed in, the variance area (another menu setting) shows you the plan-vs.-actual results, as shown in Illustration 16-4. As you look at the variance (plan vs. actual) for the sales forecast for the first three months, you should see several important trends.

1. Unit sales of systems are disappointing, well below expectations.

2. The average revenue for systems sales is also disappointing.

3. Unit sales for service are disappointing, but dollar sales are way up.

4. Sales are well above expectations for software and training.

Adjusting the Plan

Illustration 16-5 shows how this company makes its course corrections on-line, using the actual results area. Compare the difference in the April and

Illustration 16-4: Sales Variance

Unit Sales	Jan	Feb	Mar
Systems	(22)	(41)	(37)
Service	(32)	(29)	(26)
Software	24	35	39
Training	11	16	18
Other	2	(25)	28
Total Unit Sales	(17)	(44)	22

Unit Prices			
Systems	($217.43)	($198.80)	($208.86)
Service	$27.52	$36.90	$30.49
Software	$23.57	($14.61)	$76.77
Training	$11.35	$3.28	$6.78
Other	($8.77)	$70.82	($78.04)

Sales			
Systems	($57,698)	($96,711)	($96,557)
Service	$2,223	$4,302	$3,789
Software	$8,901	$3,567	$29,987
Training	$2,178	$1,129	$1,949
Other	($821)	$3,194	($8,768)
Total Sales	($45,217)	($84,519)	($69,600)

The Variance setting automatically shows plan vs. actual results for the different tables in the menu. This discussion focuses on the sales forecast variance.

May columns in Illustration 16-2, the original plan, and Illustration 16-5, the actual results area.

Use the actual results area to plan ahead, typing in revised plan numbers even months ahead of the actual results. If you know by March that your sales will be different than planned in April, estimate the revised forecast in the Actual area, as a correction to future results. When the actual results are available, you'll type over your revised plan numbers with

actual results. The actual results area becomes a plan area for course corrections.

Notice how the forecast has been revised for April and May. Since we know systems sales will be down, we should plan on that. We make a revised forecast and run it in the actuals area.

Important: *Even though not shown here, the same revision affects projected profits, balance sheet, and--most important--cash.*

Catching Trends As They Develop

Illustration 16-6 shows the plan vs. actual cash for the same sample plan shown in the previous illustrations. You can see in that illustration how much the cash flow changed as the sales came out different from plan.

In this illustration, you can see that the company had to make significant adjustments to its short-term credit management, in order to compensate for changed plans. It postponed payments of short-term debt on its credit line, and planned on additional adjustments with the short-term credit line.

This points out the importance of keeping a live plan and making adjustments. The projected cash flow in the revised scenario is acceptable to the bank, if planned in advance.

Illustration 16-5: Revised Plan in Actual Results Area

Unit Sales	Jan	Feb	Mar	Apr	May
Systems	63	74	108	150	200
Service	168	171	174	175	225
Software	174	235	289	375	450
Training	156	171	183	200	250
Other	162	151	220	240	200
Total Unit Sales	723	802	974	1,140	1,325

Unit Prices					
Systems	$1,782.57	$1,801.20	$1,791.14	$1,775.00	$1,775.00
Service	$102.52	$106.13	$88.83	$90.00	$90.00
Software	$223.57	$185.39	$276.77	$275.00	$275.00
Training	$48.35	$38.77	$46.17	$50.00	$50.00
Other	$291.23	$370.82	$221.96	$300.00	$300.00

Sales					
Systems	$112,302	$133,289	$193,443	$266,250	$355,000
Service	$17,223	$18,148	$15,456	$15,750	$20,250
Software	$38,901	$43,567	$79,987	$103,125	$123,750
Training	$7,543	$6,629	$8,449	$10,000	$12,500
Other	$47,179	$55,994	$48,832	$72,000	$60,000
Total Sales	$223,148	$257,627	$346,167	$467,125	$571,500

The illustration shows revisions in the April and May columns, even before they happen, to reflect the changes shown in the January-March period.

Prescription for Live Planning

1. After your plan starts, type actual results into the balance sheet, sales forecast, profit and loss, and cash plan. Watch what the plan-vs.-actual worksheets tell you.

2. Note when actual results indicate that you need to make changes.

3. Stay in the Actual mode, leave the plan mode alone, and make adjustments to future months of your Actual cash plan. After all, it is already more accurate than the original plan, because it has actual results for the months already completed.

4. As each month closes, type your actual results over your revised plan numbers that were typed into the Actual area.

Plan vs. Actual (Variance) Analysis

Plan-vs.-actual analysis is called variance analysis by professionals. It is critical to the success of a business plan. Tracking variances is the best way

Illustration 16-6: Plan vs. Actual Cash Flow

	Jan	Feb	Mar	Apr	May
Net Profit	$6,778	($24,902)	$8,431	$36,752	$43,097
Plus:					
Depreciation	$1,000	$1,010	$1,020	$1,030	$1,040
Change in Accounts Payable	($22,692)	$93,431	$58,509	$109,308	$122,353
Current Borrowing (repayment)	$0	$100,000	$30,000	($50,000)	$45,000
Increase (decrease) Other Liabilities	$0	$0	$0	$0	$0
Long-term Borrowing (repayment)	($2,942)	($2,962)	$97,017	($3,005)	($3,026)
Capital Input	$0	$25,000		$0	$300,000
Subtotal	($17,856)	$191,576	$194,977	$94,086	$508,465
Less:	Jan	Feb	Mar	Apr	May
Change in Accounts Receivable	($164,011)	$35,707	$91,693	$89,650	$115,398
Change in Inventory	$7,391	$60,936	$109,654	$138,607	$154,543
Change in Other ST Assets	$0	$0	$0	$0	$0
Capital Expenditure	$25,000	$0	$15,000	$0	$50,000
Dividends	$0	$0	$0	$0	$0
Subtotal	($131,620)	$96,643	$216,347	$228,257	$319,941
Net Cash Flow	$113,764	$94,934	($21,370)	($134,171)	$188,524
Cash Balance	$169,196	$264,130	$242,759	$108,588	$297,112

The plan vs. actual cash flow shows how much can change, in the real world, despite good planning. A company needs to adjust to change by keeping its plan live.

of following through on the plan to assure implementation.

Recording Actual Results

Following the example in this chapter, Illustration 16-7 shows a portion of the profit and loss plan for the sample company, as it stood in the plan. Illustration 16-8 shows the actual results recorded in that portion of profit and loss, after the end of March, and Illustration 16-9 shows the variance.

Practical Follow-Up

Looking back at Illustration 16-8, the actual results illustration means little without comparison to the original budget in Illustration 16-7. The format is the same for both, and the numbers are in the same order of magnitude.

Important: *Unfortunately, many businesses also forget to compare the original to the actual. Especially if business is going well— the operation shows a profit, and cash flow is satisfactory—comparisons with the original budget are made poorly or not at all.*

Illustration 16-7: A Portion of Planned Profit and Loss

	Jan	Feb	Mar	Apr	May
Sales	$268,365	$342,146	$415,767	$501,731	$643,826
Direct Cost of Sales	$184,510	$249,061	$307,612	$398,087	$503,238
Production payroll	$9,500	$9,500	$9,500	$9,500	$9,500
Other	$500	$500	$500	$500	$500
Total Cost of Sales	$194,510	$259,061	$317,612	$408,087	$513,238
Gross Margin	$73,856	$83,086	$98,155	$93,644	$130,589
Gross Margin %	27.52%	24.28%	23.61%	18.66%	20.28%
Operating expenses:					
Sales and Marketing Expenses					
Sales and Marketing Payroll	$24,000	$24,000	$24,000	$24,000	$24,000
Ads	$5,000	$5,000	$7,000	$10,000	$15,000
Catalog	$2,000	$3,000	$2,000	$2,000	$2,000
Mailing	$3,000	$11,800	$5,500	$10,500	$10,500
Promo	$0	$0	$0	$0	$0
Shows	$0	$0	$0	$0	$0
Literature	$0	$7,000	$0	$0	$0
PR	$0	$0	$0	$1,000	$0
Seminar	$1,000	$0	$0	$5,000	$5,000
Service	$2,000	$1,000	$1,000	$500	$2,500
Training	$450	$450	$450	$450	$450
Total Sales and Marketing Expe	$37,450	$52,250	$39,950	$53,450	$59,450

This table shows the gross margin and sales and marketing expense area of the original plan.

Illustration 16-8: Portion of Actual Profit and Loss Results

	Jan	Feb	Mar	Apr	May
Sales	$223,148	$257,627	$346,167	$467,125	$571,500
Direct Cost of Sales	$141,394	$176,275	$240,051	$321,100	$411,250
Production payroll	$9,308	$9,224	$9,759	$9,500	$9,500
Other	$33	$782	$436	$500	$500
Total Cost of Sales	$150,735	$186,281	$250,246	$331,100	$421,250
Gross Margin	$72,413	$71,346	$95,921	$136,025	$150,250
Gross Margin %	32.45%	27.69%	27.71%	29.12%	26.29%
Operating expenses:					
Expenses					
Payroll	$23,456	$24,529	$23,871	$24,000	$24,000
Ads	$0	$22,674	$7,896	$10,000	$15,000
Catalog	$2,200	$3,100	$2,095	$2,000	$2,000
Mailing	$1,873	$12,075	$6,621	$10,500	$10,500
Promo	$0	$0	$0	$0	$0
Shows	$0	$0	$0	$0	$0
Literature	$0	$0	$6,401	$0	$0
PR	$0	$0	$0	$1,000	$0
Seminar	$1,000	$0	$0	$5,000	$5,000
Service	$0	$3,023	$1,023	$500	$2,500
Training	$0	$1,000	$500	$450	$450
Total Expenses	$28,529	$66,401	$48,407	$53,450	$59,450

The illustration shows actual results on the actual worksheet. Note how actual sales, costs, and expenses are different from planned results.

Illustration 16-9 shows the variance, the difference between planned and actual expenses. The actual results are subtracted from the budget numbers, leaving negative numbers when the actual spending was more than budget, or when the sales or profits was less than budget. Those, of course, are the variances.

Variances are calculated differently in different portions of the plan.

- In expense rows, variance becomes the planned amount minus the actual amount. Lower expenses are a positive variance.

- In the profits and sales areas, variance becomes actual amount minus planned amount. In these cases, higher sales are a positive variance.

Illustration 16-9: A Portion of Profit and Loss Variance

	Jan	Feb	Mar	Apr	May
Sales	($45,217)	($84,519)	($69,600)	($34,606)	($72,326)
Direct Cost of Sales	$43,116	$72,786	$67,561	$76,987	$91,988
Production payroll	$192	$276	($259)	$0	$0
Other	$467	($282)	$64	$0	$0
	------------	------------	------------	------------	------------
Total Cost of Sales	$43,775	$72,780	$67,366	$76,987	$91,988
Gross Margin	($88,991)	($157,299)	($136,966)	($111,593)	($164,314)
Gross Margin %	196.81%	186.11%	196.79%	322.47%	227.18%
Operating expenses:					
Expenses					
Payroll	$544	($529)	$129	$0	$0
Ads	$5,000	($17,674)	($896)	$0	$0
Catalog	($200)	($100)	($95)	$0	$0
Mailing	$1,127	($275)	($1,121)	$0	$0
Promo	$0	$0	$0	$0	$0
Shows	$0	$0	$0	$0	$0
Literature	$0	$7,000	($6,401)	$0	$0
PR	$0	$0	$0	$0	$0
Seminar	$0	$0	$0	$0	$0
Service	$2,000	($2,023)	($23)	$0	$0
Training	$450	($550)	($50)	$0	$0
	------------	------------	------------	------------	------------
Total Expenses	$8,921	($14,151)	($8,457)	$0	$0

The illustration shows a portion of the *Profit and Loss Variance. March results showed sales below plan and costs above plan, for a large negative variance. Sales and Marketing expenses were also above plan in March, causing another negative variance.*

Understanding Variance Analysis

Variance is the frequently-forgotten other half of budgeting. Without ways of tracking results and seeing the difference between budgeted and actual results, budgeting is little more than an academic exercise. Variance is the difference between budgeted and actual: for example, between actual costs and

budgeted costs. Variance analysis looks after the fact at what caused a difference. Good management looks at what that difference means to the business.

Many businesses, especially the small, entrepreneurial kinds, ignore or forget the other half of the budgeting. Budgets are too often proposed, discussed, accepted, and forgotten. Without an eventual comparison between budget and actual results, budgeting is little more than an academic exercise.

Variance analysis ranges from simple and straightforward to sophisticated and complex. Some cost-accounting systems separate variances into many types and categories. Sometimes a single result can be broken down into many different variances, both positive and negative. The most sophisticated systems separate unit and price factors on materials, hours worked, cost per hour on direct labor, and fixed and variable overhead variances. Though difficult, this kind of analysis can be invaluable in a complex business.

Look for Specifics

This presentation of variances shows how important good analysis is. In theory, the positive variances are good news because they mean spending less than budgeted. The negative variance means spending more than the budget. So the $15,000 variance in advertising in January means $15,000 less than planned was spent, and the $7,000 positive variance for literature in February means $7,000 less than planned was spent. The negative variance for advertising in February and March, and the negative variance for

literature in March, mean that more than what was planned was spent for those items.

Evaluating these variances takes thought. Positive variances aren't always good news. For example, the positive variance of $15,000 in advertising means that money wasn't spent, but it also means that advertising wasn't placed. Systems sales are way below expectations for this same period--could the advertising missed in January be a possible cause? For literature, the positive $7,000 in February may be evidence of a missed deadline for literature that wasn't actually completed until March. If so, at least it appears that the costs on completion were $4,325, considerably less than the $7,000 planned. Among the larger single variances for an expense item in a month shown on the illustration was the positive $7,000 variance for the new literature expenses in February. Is this good news or bad news?

Every variance should stimulate questions. Why did one project cost more or less? Were objectives met? Is a positive variance a cost saving or a failure to implement? Is a negative variance a change in plans or a management failure or an unrealistic budget?

The variance table should always provide management with significant information. Without this data, some of these important questions might go unasked.

More on Variance

Variance analysis can be very complex. There can be very significant differences between higher or lower sales because of different unit volumes, or because of different average prices. For purposes of example, Illustration 16-10 shows the full sales table (including costs) in variance mode, for the sales forecast used as an example in this chapter.

The units variance shows that the sales of systems were disappointing. In the expenses, we see that advertising and mailing costs were below plan. Could there be a correlation between the saved expenses in mailing, and the lower-than-planned sales? Yes, of course there could. The mailing cost was much less than planned, but as a result the planned sales never came. The positive expense variance is not good for the company.

In systems, the comparison between units variance and sales variance yields no surprises. The lower-than-expected unit sales also had lower-than-expected sales values. Compare that to service, in which lower units yielded higher sales

(indicating much higher prices than planned). Is this an indication of a new profit opportunity, or a new trend? This clearly depends on the specifics of your business.

Illustration 16-10: Sales Forecast Variance

Unit Sales	Jan	Feb	Mar
Systems	(22)	(41)	(37)
Service	(32)	(29)	(26)
Software	24	35	39
Training	11	16	18
Other	2	(25)	28
Total Unit Sales	(17)	(44)	22

Unit Prices			
Systems	($217.43)	($198.80)	($208.86)
Service	$27.52	$36.90	$30.49
Software	$23.57	($14.61)	$76.77
Training	$11.35	$3.28	$6.78
Other	($8.77)	$70.82	($78.04)

Sales			
Systems	($57,698)	($96,711)	($96,557)
Service	$2,223	$4,302	$3,789
Software	$8,901	$3,567	$29,987
Training	$2,178	$1,129	$1,949
Other	($821)	$3,194	($8,768)
Total Sales	($45,217)	($84,519)	($69,600)

Direct Unit Costs			
Systems	$65.95	$10.99	$42.67
Service	($2.75)	($4.71)	$7.77
Software	$16.87	$25.97	$4.44
Training	$4.59	($0.15)	$1.95
Other	$3.66	($17.29)	$13.19

Direct Cost of Sales			
Systems	$41,555	$70,513	$67,508
Service	$498	$935	$2,912
Software	$55	$1,902	($3,398)
Training	$595	($204)	$158
Other	$413	($361)	$381
Subtotal Direct Cost	$43,116	$72,786	$67,561

The illustration shows the sales variance for the same example set used in other illustrations in this section.

It is often hard to tell what caused differences in costs. If spending schedules aren't met, variance might be caused simply by lower unit volume. Management probably wants to know the results per unit, and the actual price, and the detailed feedback on the marketing programs.

Measure a Plan by its Implementation

The quality of a business plan is measured, not by the quality of its ideas, its analysis, or presentation, but only by the implementation it causes. It is true, of course, that some business plans are developed only as selling documents to generate financial resources. For these plans, their worth is measured by their effectiveness in selling a business opportunity to a prospective investor. For plans created to help run a business, their worth is measured by how much they help run a business – or, in other words, their implementation.

Summary

Variance analysis is vital to good management. You have to track and follow up on budgets, mainly through variance analysis, or the budgets are useless.

Although variance analysis can be very complex, the main guide is common sense. In general, going under budget is a positive variance, and over budget is a negative variance. But the real test of management should be whether or not the result was good for business.

This page intentionally blank.

CHAPTER 17:
Starting a Business

I'll always remember a talk I had with a man who had spent 15 years trying to make his sailboat manufacturing business work, achieving not much more than aging and more debt. "If I can tell you only one thing," he said, "it is that you should never take money from friends and family. If you do, then you can never get out. Businesses sometimes fail, and you need to be able to close it down and walk away. I wasn't able to do that."

If I could make only one point with budding entrepreneurs, it would be that you should know what money you need and understand that it is at risk. Don't bet money you can't afford to lose. Know how much you are betting.

Customers First

A business plan is not the most important single requirement for starting a business. Many other things are much more important. For example:

- **Customers**: The first thing you really need to start a business, maybe even the only thing you really need, is customers. It all starts with at least one customer.

- *Customer needs*: Your business must fulfill some type of customer need in order to be successful. Sometimes customer needs can be intangible, like security or prestige. Some customer needs seem frivolous, but they still matter. Make sure there is a market for your service or product. Your business will fail if it doesn't address a customer need.

Myths on Starting a Business

It is dangerous to fall in love with the idea of starting your own business without understanding the realities. There are several myths about owning and operating a business that should be avoided at all costs. These common myths cause a lot of problems:

1. The myth of "being your own boss:" You are not your own boss when you own a business. Your customers are your boss. Your bank is your boss. Your fixed costs are your boss.

2. The myth of "independence": Owning a business doesn't make you independent – not needing money makes you independent. As long as you need money, you can't be independent.

The folklore of business start-ups generally underestimates the risks. Imagine yourself missing mortgage payments when you can't cover your business costs, and facing employees when you can't make payroll. Those negative images are also part of business ownership.

The Business Plan for Start-ups

Your business plan is very important even at the early start-up stage. Even before you purchase business stationery or telephones, or rent a location, you should do a business plan. Pay special attention to the general business evaluation and review the elements of starting a business plan in Chapter 2, *Initial*

Assessment. The Mission Statement, Keys to Success, Market Analysis, and Break-Even Analysis give you a critical head start toward understanding your business.

Realistic Start-up Costs

Start-up expenses are those expenses incurred <u>before</u> the business is running. Many people underestimate start-up costs and start their business in a haphazard, unplanned way. This can work, but is usually a harder way to do it. Customers are wary of brand new businesses with makeshift logistics.

Use a start-up worksheet to plan your initial financing. You'll need this information to set up initial business balances and to estimate start-up expenses such as legal fees, stationery design, brochures, and others. Don't underestimate costs.

Illustration 17-1 reproduces a typical Start-up table for a home office or service business – in this case a resume writing service. The assumptions used in this illustration show how even simple, service-based businesses need some start-up money.

Illustration 17-1: Start-Up Costs

Startup Expenses	
Legal	$50
Stationery etc.	$100
Brochures	$450
Consultants	$100
Insurance	$50
Rent	$0
Research and development	$0
Expensed equipment	$500
Other	$500
Total Start-up Expense	**$1,750**
Start-up Assets Needed	
Cash Requirements	$500
Start-up Inventory	$250
Other Short-term Assets	$25
Total Short-term Assets	$775
Long-term Assets	
Capital Assets	$0
Total Assets	**$775**
Total Startup Requirements:	**$2,525**
Start-up Funding Plan	
Investment	
Investor 1	$2,525
Investor 2	$0
Investor 3	$0
Total investment	**$2,525**
Short-term Borrowing	
Unpaid expenses	$0
Short-term loans	$0
Interest-free short-term loans	$0
Subtotal Short-term Borrowing	$0
Long-term Borrowing	$0
Total Borrowing	**$0**
Loss at start-up	($1,750)
Total Equity	$775
Total Debt and Equity	$775
Left to finance:	**$0**

Start-up table for a hypothetical home office resumé service.

Understand the Risks

I've spent many years as an entrepreneur and working with entrepreneurs. I understand and sympathize with the urge to create something, to build your own and make it work. However, I've also seen the disaster of the business start-up that absorbs more money than it should, and the optimistic owners who keep dumping more money into a lost cause, digging themselves deeper into a hole instead of getting out of it.

The following illustrations outline the start-up costs for three different companies. The first, Illustration 17-2, shows actual numbers for a successful service company. Illustration 17-3 shows a successful product company, and Illustration 17-4 shows a failed product company.

Illustration 17-5 is a chart of all three of these hypothetical start-up companies. It shows simple lines indicating the cumulative balance for each business. This cumulative balance stands for how much money is spent or received, and how much money is at risk.

Both the successful and the failed product company launches look the same in the beginning. The successful launch turns upward and generates money, but the unsuccessful launch never does. The service company, in contrast, generates less money but also risks less money.

Illustration 17-2: Successful Service Start-Up

II. Successful Service Example

Start-up Expenses	Jan	Feb	Mar	Apr	May	Jun	Jul	Aug	Sep	Oct	Nov	Dec
Start up	$2,500											
Product release PR		$500	$500	$0	$0							
Subtotal	$2,500	$500	$500	$0	$0	$0	$0	$0	$0	$0	$0	$0
Revenues												
Sales			$1,000	$3,500	$6,000	$8,500	$11,000	$13,500	$16,000	$18,500	$21,000	$23,500
Cost of sales	$0		$50	$175	$300	$425	$550	$675	$800	$925	$1,050	$1,175
Operating Expenses	$1,500	$1,500	$1,750	$2,375	$3,000	$3,625	$4,250	$4,875	$5,500	$6,125	$6,750	$7,375
Accounts receivable				$1,000	$3,500	$6,000	$8,500	$11,000	$13,500	$16,000	18,500	$21,000
Receipts	$0	$0		$1,000	$3,500	$6,000	$8,500	$11,000	$13,500	$16,000	$18,500	$21,000
Net cash	($4,000)	($2,000)	($2,300)	($1,550)	$200	$1,950	$3,700	$5,450	$7,200	$8,950	$10,700	$12,450
Cumulative cash	($4,000)	($6,000)	($8,300)	($9,850)	($9,650)	($7,700)	($4,000)	$1,450	$8,650	$17,600	$28,300	$40,750

A table comparison of start-up numbers for two product businesses and one service start-up business.

Illustration 17-3: Successful Product Start-up

I. Successful Product Example

Start-up Expenses	Jan	Feb	Mar	Apr	May	Jun	Jul	Aug	Sep	Oct	Nov	Dec
Start-up	$4,500											
Product work		$5,000	$5,000									
Packaging work			$5,000	$5,000								
Product release PR			$5,000	$5,000	$5,000							
Initial inventory build				$10,000								
Subtotal	$4,500	$5,000	$15,000	$20,000	$5,000	$0	$0	$0	$0	$0	$0	$0
Revenues												
Sales					$50,000	$75,000	$100,000	$125,000	$150,000	$150,000	$150,000	$150,000
Cost of sales	$0				$10,000	$15,000	$20,000	$25,000	$30,000	$30,000	$30,000	$30,000
Operating expenses	$5,000	$5,000	$5,000	$10,000	$10,000	$20,000	$20,000	$20,000	$20,000	$20,000	$20,000	$20,000
Accounts receivable	$0	$0	$0	$0	$50,000	$125,000	$175,000	$225,000	$275,000	$300,000	$300,000	$300,000
Receipts	$0	$0	$0	$0	$0	$0	$50,000	$75,000	$100,000	$125,000	$150,000	$150,000
Net Cash	($9,500)	($10,000)	($20,000)	($30,000)	($25,000)	($35,000)	$10,000	$30,000	$50,000	$75,000	$100,000	$100,000
Cumulative Cash	($9,500)	($19,500)	($39,500)	($69,500)	($94,500)	($129,500)	($119,500)	($89,500)	($39,500)	$35,500	$135,500	$235,500

Illustration 17-4: Failed Product Start-Up

III. Failed Product Example

Start-up Expenses	Jan	Feb	Mar	Apr	May	Jun	Jul	Aug	Sep	Oct	Nov	Dec
Start-up	$4,500											
Product work		$5,000	$5,000									
Packaging work			$5,000	$5,000								
Product release			$5,000	$5,000	$5,000							
Initial inventory build				$10,000								
Subtotal	$4,500	$5,000	$15,000	$20,000	$5,000	$0	$0	$0	$0	$0	$0	$0

Revenues												
Sales					$25,000	$27,500	$30,000	$32,500	$35,000	$37,500	$40,000	$42,500
Cost of sales	$0				$5,000	$5,500	$6,000	$6,500	$7,000	$7,500	$8,000	$8,500
Gross Margin	$0	$0	$0	$0	$20,000	$22,000	$24,000	$26,000	$28,000	$30,000	$32,000	$34,000
Operating Expenses	$5,000	$5,000	$5,000	$10,000	$10,000	$20,000	$20,000	$20,000	$20,000	$20,000	$20,000	$20,000
Earnings	($5,000)	($5,000)	($5,000)	($10,000)	$10,000	$2,000	$4,000	$6,000	$8,000	$10,000	$12,000	$14,000
Accounts receivable	$0	$0	$0	$0	$25,000	$52,500	$57,500	$62,500	$67,500	$72,500	$77,500	$47,500
Receipts	$0	$0	$0	$0	$0	$0	$25,000	$27,500	$30,000	$32,500	$35,000	$72,500
Net cash	($9,500)	($10,000)	($20,000)	($30,000)	($20,000)	($25,500)	($1,000)	$1,000	$3,000	$5,000	$7,000	$44,000
Cumulative cash	($9,500)	($19,500)	($39,500)	($69,500)	($89,500)	($115,000)	($116,000)	($115,000)	($112,000)	($107,000)	($100,000)	($56,000)

Illustration 17-5: The Start-up Curve and Risk

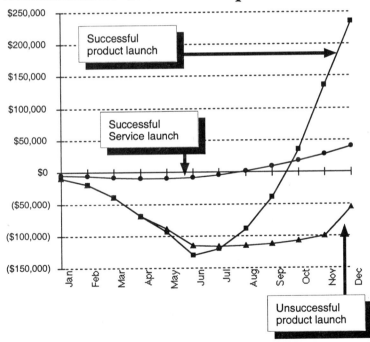

The lines show the cumulative cash positions for a hypothetical start-up product company and a start-up service company. The product company risks more than the service company.

The chart in Illustration 17-5 makes two extremely important points about the money at risk in different kinds of businesses:

- Product businesses usually require more investment than service businesses.

- "Bootstrapping" (starting the business without start-up capital) is much harder for product businesses than service businesses.

Incorporation and Legal Advice

To incorporate or not to incorporate

Generally, many start-up businesses don't have to be corporations, or partnerships, or anything else quite so formal. In most of the United States, the simplest legal way to start a company is to register a company name as a "Fictitious business name," also called a DBA ("Doing Business As"). Depending on your state, you can usually obtain this through the county government, and the cost is no more than a small registration fee plus a required newspaper ad, for a total of less than $100 in most states.

See an Attorney

Do-it-yourself legal advice is not recommended. The trade-offs involved in incorporation vs. partnership vs. other forms of business are significant. Small problems developed at the early stages of a new business can become horrendous problems later on. The cost of simple legal advice in this regard is almost always worth it. Starting a company should not involve a major legal bill except in special cases. Don't skimp on legal costs.

The pros and cons of different business formations are worth understanding. They vary by state – this is not a good area for guesswork.

Summary

Don't go into a business based on the folklore and myths. There are plenty of good reasons to do it. And as you start a company, plan ahead. Give yourself the benefit of a real estimate of start-up costs, and if you can't afford to lose the money, then don't put it at risk. If you can't convince somebody else to put up the money, think again about the business you want to start.

CHAPTER 18:
Getting Financed

Contrary to popular belief, business plans do not generate business financing. True, there are many kinds of financing options that require a business plan, but nobody invests in a business plan. Investors need a business plan as a document that communicates ideas and information, but they invest in a company, in a product, and in people.

Myths of Small Business Financing

- Venture capital financing is very rare. I'll explain more later, but start with the assumption that only a very few high-growth plans with high-power management teams are venture opportunities.

- Banks don't finance business start-ups. I'll have more on that later, too. Banks aren't supposed to invest depositors' money in new businesses.

- Business plans don't sell investors.

Where to Look for Money

In Chapter 3, *Pick Your Plan*, I said the plan matches the needs of the company. So does the process of looking for money. Where you look for money, and how you look for money, depends on your company and the kind of money you need. There is an enormous difference, for example, between a high-growth Internet-related company looking for second-round venture funding and a local retail store looking to finance a branch store. In the following sections of this chapter, I want to talk more specifically about the types of investment and lending available, but first let's consider what type you might need.

Venture Capital

The business of venture capital is frequently misunderstood. Many start-up companies resent venture capital companies for failing to invest in new ventures or risky ventures. People talk about venture capitalists as sharks – because of their supposedly predatory business practices – or sheep – because they supposedly think like a flock, all wanting the same kinds of deals.

This is not the case. The venture capital business is a business, and the people we call venture capitalists are business people who are charged with investing other people's money. They have a professional responsibility to reduce risk as much as possible. They should not take more risk than is absolutely necessary to produce the risk/return ratios that the sources of their capital ask of them.

Venture capital shouldn't be thought of as a source of funding for any but a very few exceptional start-up businesses. Venture capital can't afford to invest in start-ups unless there is a rare combination of product opportunity, market opportunity, and proven management. A venture capital investment has to have a reasonable chance of producing a tenfold increase in business value within three years. It needs to focus on newer products and markets that can reasonably project increasing sales by huge multiples over a short period of time. It needs to work with proven managers who have dealt with successful start-ups in the past.

If you are a potential venture capital investment, you probably know it al-

ready. You have management team members who've been through that already. You can convince yourself and a room full of intelligent people that your company can grow ten times over in three years.

If you have to ask whether your new company is a possible venture capital opportunity, it probably isn't. People in new growth industries, such as multimedia communications, biotechnology, or the far reaches of high technology products, generally know about venture capital and venture capital opportunities.

If you are looking for names and addresses of venture capitalists, and you own *Business Plan Pro*, start with the database of venture capitalists and small business investment companies included on the *Business Plan Pro* CD-ROM. There is more on that at the end of this chapter. You can also look for links on any of the Palo Alto Software Web sites: **www.palo-alto.com**, **www.bizplans.com**, and **www.bplans.com**. We keep these updated and they are likely to have more specific information.

Otherwise, start with the Internet, with the net search engines I discussed in Chapters 4 and 5. You'll get at least 50 venture capital firms showing up when you search **www.yahoo.com** for "venture capital."

The names and addresses of venture capitalists are also available in a couple of annual directories:

The *Western Association of Venture Capitalists* publishes an annual directory. This organization includes most of the California venture capitalists based in Menlo Park, CA, which is the headquarters of an amazing percentage of the nation's venture capital companies.

Pratt's Guide to Venture Capital Sources is an annual directory available for $225 (at the time of this printing; prices may change) plus shipping. Contact Venture Economics, 40 W. 57th St., 11th Floor, New York, NY 10019 (212) 765-5311.

"Sort-of" Venture Capital: Angels and Others

Venture capital is not the only source of investment for start-up businesses or small businesses. Many companies are financed by smaller investors in what is called "private placement." For example, in some areas there are groups of potential investors who meet occasionally to hear proposals. There are also wealthy individuals who occasionally invest in new companies. In the lore of business start-ups, groups of investors are often referred to as "doctors and dentists," and individual investors are often called "angels." Many entrepreneurs turn to friends and family for investment.

Your next question of course is how to find the "doctors, dentists, and angels" that might want to invest in your business. The discussion in Chapter 5 includes some government agencies, business development centers, business incubators and similar organizations that will be tied into the investment communities in your area. Turn first to the local Small Business Development Center (SBDC), which is most likely associated with your local community college, or the Small Business Administration (SBA) offices in your area. Names and Web site addresses are in Chapter 5.

You may want to try some secondary listing services and online sourcing businesses. Although I haven't had specific dealings with any of them, and can't actually recommend any from experience, I do know the owners and operators of the *American Venture Capital Exchange*, and I know that they have been working to provide fair and respectful matching services between investors and companies needing investment. However, I haven't actually used the service. I've just dealt with the people (they have occasionally included literature in Palo Alto Software boxes). They offer an online database of financing sources, and a forum to list businesses seeking financing. Their Web site is **www.avce.com**; phone 800-292-1993, fax is (503) 221-9987; and e-mail is avce@aol.com.

I have listed several consultants with whom I've had dealings, including people I worked with while consulting for Apple and other companies, on my personal Web site at **www.timberry.com**. For legal reasons, I have to insist that my recommendation is at your risk, not mine, and I can't be responsible for third parties. I should also note that my recommendation has never and will never be sold for money or compensation of any kind, even in trade.

At your own risk, the following are some of the online services available through bulletin boards and similar sources. Deal with them carefully:

- Business Opportunities On-Line. Telephone (310) 477-0408.

- Texas Capital Network, 8920 Business Park Drive, Austin, TX 78759-7405, Telephone (512) 794-9398.

- The Investment Exchange, Telephone (416) 512-9957.

- Seed Capital Network, 8905 Kingston Pike Suite 12, Knoxville, TN 37923, Telephone (615) 573-4655.

Warning: Be very careful in dealing with anybody who offers to help you find financing as a service for money. These are shark infested waters. We are aware of some legitimate providers of business plan consulting, small business finance consulting

and related assistance, but the legitimate providers are harder to find than the sharks. In general, you should never pay money in advance for investment finding services, and a request for money in advance should be a warning signal. There are more fakes and frauds in the business of finding investment than there are legitimate finders. Be careful!

Illustration 18-1: The Money Eater

Beware of experts asking money in advance for finding investment.

Commercial Lenders

Banks are even less likely than venture capitalists to invest in or loan money to start-up businesses. They are, however, the most likely source of financing for most small businesses.

Start-up entrepreneurs and small business owners are too quick to criticize banks for failing to finance new businesses. Banks are not supposed to invest in businesses, and are strictly limited in this respect by federal banking laws. The government prevents banks from investment in businesses because society, in general, doesn't want banks taking savings from depositors and investing in risky business ventures; obviously, when (and if) those business ventures fail, bank depositors' money is at risk. Would you want your bank to invest in new businesses (other than your own, of course)?

Furthermore, banks should not be loaning money to start-up companies either, for many of the same reasons. Federal regulators want banks to keep money safe, in very conservative loans, backed by solid collateral. Start-up businesses are not safe enough for bank regulators, and they don't have enough collateral.

Why then do we say that banks are the most likely source of small business financing? Because small business owners borrow from banks. A business that has been around for a few years generates enough stability and assets to serve as collateral. Banks commonly make loans to small businesses backed by the business' inventory or accounts receivable. Normally there are formulas that determine how much can be loaned, depending on how much is in inventory and in accounts receivable.

A great deal of small business financing is accomplished through bank loans based on the business owner's personal collateral, such as home ownership. Some would say that home equity is the greatest source of small business financing.

The Small Business Administration (SBA)

The SBA makes loans to small businesses and even to start-up businesses. SBA loans are almost always applied for and administered by local banks. You normally deal with a local bank throughout the process.

For start-up loans, the SBA will normally require that at least one third of the required capital be supplied by the new business owner. Furthermore, the rest of the amount must be guaranteed by reasonable business or personal assets.

The SBA works with "certified lenders," which are banks. It takes a certified lender as little as one week to get approval from the SBA. If your own bank isn't a certified lender, you should ask your banker to recommend a local bank that is.

Chapter 5 lists the Web sites and some addresses and telephone numbers for SBA offices.

Other Lenders

Aside from standard bank loans, an established small business can also turn to accounts receivable specialists to borrow against its accounts receivables.

The most common accounts receivable financing is used to support cash flow when working capital is hung up in accounts receivable. For example, if your business sells to distributors that take 60 days to pay, and the outstanding invoices waiting for payment (but not late) come to $100,000, your company can probably borrow more than $50,000. Interest rates and fees may be relatively high, but this is still often a good source of small business financing. In most cases, the lender doesn't take the risk of payment — if your customer doesn't pay you, you have to pay the money back anyhow. These lenders will often review your debtors, and choose to finance some or all of the invoices outstanding.

- One such lender is Concord Growth Capital of Palo Alto, CA, (415) 493-0921. I have had personal experience with this company, which is a well-run, legitimate business. I was a customer for several years when I was more consulting oriented and based nearby. Here again, for legal reasons, I have to remind you that I can't be responsible for recommendations. I do it as a help, but you should proceed at your own risk.

- Another is American Classic Financial Inc., (215) 238-0220, Fax (215) 238-0834. We have had no experience whatsoever with this company, but include it here as a service only. Proceed with caution.

Another related business practice is called factoring. So-called factors actually purchase obligations, so if a customer owes you $100,000 you can sell the related paperwork to the factor for some percentage of the total amount. In this case, the factor takes the risk of payment, so discounts are obviously quite steep. You can ask your banker for additional information about factoring in your area.

Words of Warning

Don't take private placement, angels, and friends and family as good sources of investment capital just because they are described here or taken seriously in some other source of information. Some investors are a good source of capital, and some aren't. These less established sources of investment may be necessary, but they should be handled with <u>extreme caution</u>.

Never, NEVER spend somebody else's money without first doing the legal work properly. Have the papers done by professionals, and make sure they're signed.

Never, NEVER spend money that has been promised but not delivered. It is amazing how often companies get investment commitments and contract for expenses, and then the investment falls through.

Avoid turning to friends and family for investment. The worst possible time to not have the support of friends and family is when your business is in trouble. When the business is financed by friends and family, you risk losing friends, family, and your business at the same time. We know an entrepreneur who stuck with a losing business for six years longer than he should have, because he started it with money from friends and family.

The Process of Submitting a Plan

The information you submit to investors or lenders depends a great deal on what your objective is. Sometimes you'll need to submit a complete business plan, sometimes a summary memo, sometimes a loan support document. In most cases, even if you submit a short summary, you have to have the complete business plan ready to go as soon as the investors or lenders ask for it.

If you're looking for an investor, you normally need a short summary document and a cover letter. Many entrepre-

neurs use mail merge programs to submit these summary memos to multiple potential investors.

If you need a lender, whether you're looking for lease financing, receivables, or a bank loan, you'll want to submit a loan summary document.

When the search has provided you with a list of useful names, you can print your investor summary or loan summary documents and send a copy to each of the investors, along with a brief cover letter.

Summary

Most businesses are financed by home equity or personal savings as they start. Only a few can attract outside investment. Venture capital deals are extremely rare. As your business grows, you'll begin to have access to more financing and particularly to borrowing money through banks, whether or not they have SBA assistance. Borrowing will always depend on collateral and guarantees, not on business plans or ideas.

This page intentionally blank.

Sample Plan: **Acme Consulting**

This sample business plan has been made available to users of Business Plan Pro™, business plan software published by Palo Alto Software. It is based on a real business plan of an existing company. Names and numbers have been changed, and substantial portions of text may have been omitted to preserve confidential information.

You are welcome to use this plan as a starting point to create your own, but you do not have permission to reproduce, publish, distribute, or even copy this plan as it exists here.

Requests for reprints, academic use, and other dissemination of this sample plan should be addressed to the marketing department of Palo Alto Software.

Confidentiality Agreement

The undersigned reader acknowledges that the information provided by Acme Consulting in this business plan is confidential; therefore, reader agrees not to disclose it without the express written permission of Acme Consulting.

It is acknowledged by reader that information to be furnished in this business plan is in all respects confidential in nature, other than information which is in the public domain through other means and that any disclosure or use of same by reader, may cause serious harm or damage to Acme Consulting.

Upon request, this document is to be immediately returned to Acme Consulting.

_____   _____

Signature   Date

_____

Name (typed or printed)

This is a business plan. It does not imply an offering of securities.

Table Of Contents

1.0 Executive Summary

Acme Consulting will be formed as a consulting company specializing in marketing of high-technology products in international markets. Its founders are former marketers of consulting services, personal computers, and market research, all in international markets. They are founding Acme to formalize the consulting services they offer.

Business Plan Highlights

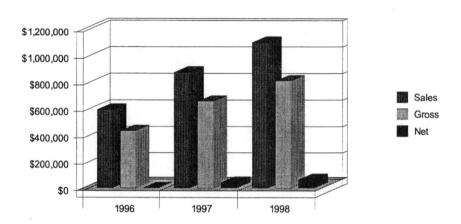

1.1 Objectives

1. Sales of $350,000 in 1995 and $1 million by 1997..

2. Gross margin higher than 80%.

3. Net income more than 10% of sales by the third year.

1.2 Mission

Acme Consulting offers high-tech manufacturers a reliable, high-quality alternative to in-house resources for business development, market development, and channel development on an international scale. A true alternative to in-house resources offers a very high level of practical experience, know-how, contacts, and confidentiality. Clients must know that working with Acme is a more professional, less risky way to develop new areas even than working completely in-house with their own people. Acme must also be able to maintain financial balance, charging a high value for its services, and delivering an even higher value to its clients. Initial focus will be development in the European and Latin American markets, or for European clients in the United States market.

1.3 Keys to Success

1. Excellence in fulfilling the promise--completely confidential, reliable, trustworthy expertise and information.

2. Developing visibility to generate new business leads.

3. Leveraging from a single pool of expertise into multiple revenue generation opportunities: retainer consulting, project consulting, market research, and market research published reports.

2.0 Company Summary

Acme Consulting is a new company providing high-level expertise in international high-tech business development, channel development, distribution strategies, and marketing of high-tech products. It will focus initially on providing two kinds of international triangles:

- Providing United States clients with development for European and Latin American markets.

- Providing European clients with development for the United States and Latin American markets.

As it grows it will take on people and consulting work in related markets, such as the rest of Latin America, the Far East, and similar markets. It will also look for additional leverage by taking brokerage positions and representation positions to create percentage holdings in product results.

2.1 Company Ownership

Acme Consulting will be created as a California C corporation based in Santa Clara County, owned by its principal investors and principal operators. As of this writing, it has not been chartered yet and is still considering alternatives of legal formation.

2.2 Start-up Summary

Total start-up expense (including legal costs, logo design, stationery and related expenses) come to $73,000. Start-up assets required include $3,000 in short-term assets (office furniture, etc.) and $1,000,000 in initial cash to handle the first few months of consulting operations as sales and accounts receivable play through the cash flow. The details are included in Table 2-2.

Start-Up Financing

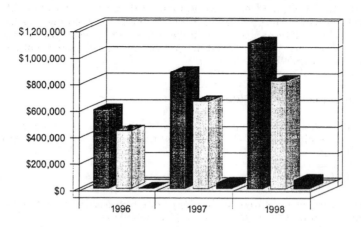

Table 2.2: Start-up Costs

Start-up Expenses	
Legal	$1,000
Stationery etc.	$3,000
Brochures	$5,000
Consultants	$5,000
Insurance	$350
Expensed equipment	$3,000
Other	$1,000
Total Start-up Expense	$18,350
Start-up Assets Needed	
Cash Requirements	$25,000
Other Short-term Assets	$7,000
Total Short-term Assets	$32,000
Long-term Assets	$0
Total Assets	$32,000
Total Start-up Requirements:	$50,350
Left to finance:	$0
Start-up Funding Plan	
Investment	
Investor 1	$20,000
Investor 2	$20,000
Other	$10,000
Total investment	$50,000
Short-term Liabilities	
Unpaid Expenses	$5,000
Short-term Loans	$0
Interest-free Short-term Loans	$0
Subtotal Short-term Liabilities	$5,000
Long-term Liabilities	$0
Total Liabilities	$5,000
Loss at Start-up	($23,000)
Total Capital	$27,000
Total Capital and Liabilities	$32,000
Checkline	$0

2.3 Company Services

Acme offers expertise in channel distribution, channel development, and market development, sold and packaged in various ways that allow clients to choose their preferred relationship: these include retainer consulting relationships, project-based consulting, relationship and alliance brokering, sales representation and market representation, project-based market research, published market research, and information forum events.

2.4 Company Locations and Facilities

The initial office will be established in A-quality office space in the Santa Clara County "Silicon Valley" area of California, the heart of the U.S. high tech industry.

3.0 Services

Acme offers the expertise a high-technology company needs to develop new product distribution and new market segments in new markets. This can be taken as high-level retainer consulting, market research reports, or project-based consulting.

3.1 Service Description

1. Retainer consulting: We represent a client company as an extension of its business development and market development functions. This begins with complete understanding of the client company's situation, objectives, and constraints. We then represent the client company quietly and confidentially, sifting through new market developments and new opportunities as is appropriate to the client, representing the client in initial talks with possible allies, vendors, and channels.

2. Project consulting: Proposed and billed on a per-project and per-milestone basis, project consulting offers a client company a way to harness our specific qualities and use our expertise to solve specific problems, develop and/or implement plans, and develop specific information.

3. Market research: Group studies available to selected clients at $5,000 per unit. A group study is a packaged and published complete study of a specific market, channel, or topic. Examples might be studies of developing consumer channels in Japan or Mexico, or implications of changing margins in software.

3.2 Competitive Comparison

The competition comes in several forms:

1. The most significant competition is no consulting at all, companies choosing to do business development, channel development and market research in-house. Their own managers do this on their own, as part of their regular business functions. Our key advantage in competition with in-house development is that managers are already overloaded with responsibilities, they don't have time for additional responsibilities in new market development or new channel development. Also, Acme can approach alliances, vendors, and channels on a confidential basis, gathering information and making initial contacts in ways that the corporate managers can't.

2. The high-level prestige management consulting: McKinsey, Bain, Arthur Anderson, Boston Consulting Group, etc. These are essentially generalists who take their name-brand management consulting into specialty areas. Their other very important weakness is the management structure that has the partners selling new jobs, and inexperienced associates delivering the work. We compete against them as experts in our specific fields, and with the guarantee that our clients will have the top-level people doing the actual work.

3. The third general kind of competitor is the international market research company: International Data Corporation (IDC), Dataquest, Stanford Research Institute, etc. These companies are formidable competitors for published market research and market forums, but cannot provide the kind of high-level consulting that Acme will provide.

4. The fourth kind of competition is the market-specific smaller house. For example: Nomura Research in Japan, Select S.A. de C.V. in Mexico (now affiliated with IDC).

5. Sales representation, brokering, and deal catalysts are an ad-hoc business form that will be defined in detail by the specific nature of each individual case.

3.3 Sales Literature

The business will begin with a general corporate brochure establishing the positioning. This brochure will be developed as part of the start-up expenses.

Literature and mailings for the initial market forums will be very important.

3.4 Sourcing

1. The key fulfillment and delivery will be provided by the principals of the business. The real core value is professional expertise, provided by a combination of experience, hard work, and education (in that order).

2. We will turn to qualified professionals for freelance back-up in market research and presentation and report development, which are areas that we can afford to sub-contract without risking the core values provided to the clients.

3.5 Technology

Acme Consulting will maintain the latest Windows and Macintosh capabilities including:

1. Complete e-mail facilities on the Internet, Compuserve, America-Online, and Applelink, for working with clients directly through e-mail delivery of drafts and information.

2. Complete presentation facilities for preparation and delivery of multimedia presentations on Macintosh or Windows machines, in formats including on-disk presentation, live presentation, or video presentation.

3. Complete desktop publishing facilities for delivery of regular retainer reports, project output reports, marketing materials, and market research reports.

3.6 Future Services

In the future, Acme will broaden the coverage by expanding into coverage of additional markets (e.g., all of Latin America, Far East, Western Europe) and additional product areas (e.g., telecommunications and technology integration).

We are also studying the possibility of newsletter or electronic newsletter services, or perhaps special on-topic reports.

4.0 Market Analysis Summary

Acme will be focusing on high-technology manufacturers of computer hardware and software, services, and networking, who want to sell into markets in the United States, Europe, and Latin America. These are mostly larger companies, and occasionally medium-sized companies.

Our most important group of potential customers are executives in larger corporations. These are marketing managers, general managers, sales managers, sometimes charged with international focus and sometimes charged with market or even specific channel focus. They do not want to waste their time or risk their money looking for bargain information or questionable expertise. As they go into markets looking at new opportunities, they are very sensitive to risking their company's name and reputation.

4.1 Market Segmentation

Large manufacturer corporations: Our most important market segment is the large manufacturer of high-technology products, such as Apple, Hewlett-Packard, IBM, Microsoft, Siemens, or Olivetti. These companies will be calling on Acme for development functions that are better spun off than managed in-house, for market research, and for market forums.

Medium-sized growth companies: particularly in software, multimedia, and some related high-growth fields, Acme will offer an attractive development alternative to the company that is management constrained and unable to address opportunities in new markets and new market segments.

Potential Market

- U.S. High Tech
- European High Tech
- Latin America
- Other

Table 4.1: Market Analysis

Potential Customers	Growth	1996	1997	1998	1999	2000	CAGR
U.S. High Tech	10%	5,000	5,500	6,050	6,655	7,321	10.00%
European High Tech	15%	1,000	1,150	1,323	1,521	1,749	15.00%
Latin America	35%	250	338	456	616	832	35.07%
Other	2%	10,000	10,200	10,404	10,612	10,824	2.00%
Total	6.27%	16,250	17,188	18,233	19,404	20,726	6.27%

4.2 Target Market Segment Strategy

As indicated by the previous table and Illustration, we must focus on a few thousand well-chosen potential customers in the United States, Europe, and Latin America. These few thousand high-tech manufacturing companies are the key customers for Acme.

4.3 Service Business Analysis

The consulting "industry" is pulverized and disorganized, with thousands of smaller consulting organizations and individual consultants for every one of the few dozen well-known companies.

Consulting participants range from major international name-brand consultants to tens of thousands of individuals. One of Acme's challenges will be establishing itself as a *real* consulting company, positioned as a relatively risk-free corporate purchase.

4.3.1 Business Participants

At the highest level are the few well-established major names in management consulting. Most of these are organized as partnerships established in major markets around the world, linked together by interconnecting directors and sharing the name and corporate wisdom. Some evolved from accounting companies (e.g. Arthur Andersen, Touche Ross) and some from management consulting (McKinsey, Bain). These companies charge very high rates for consulting, and maintain relatively high overhead structures and fulfillment structures based on partners selling and junior associates fulfilling.

At the intermediate level are some function-specific or market-specific consultants, such as the market research firms (IDC, Dataquest) or channel development firms (ChannelCorp, Channel Strategies, ChannelMark).

Some kinds of consulting are little more than contract expertise provided by somebody who, while temporarily out of work, offers consulting services.

4.3.2 Distributing a Service

Consulting is sold and purchased mainly on a word-of-mouth basis, with relationships and previous experience being, by far, the most important factor.

The major name-brand houses have locations in major cities and major markets, and executive-level managers or partners develop new business through industry associations, business associations, chambers of commerce and industry, etc., and in some cases social associations such as country clubs.

The medium-level houses are generally area specific or function specific, and are not easily able to leverage their business through distribution.

4.3.3 Competition and Buying Patterns

The key element in purchase decisions made at the Acme client level is trust in the professional reputation and reliability of the consulting firm.

4.3.4 Main Competitors

1. The high-level prestige management consulting:

   Strengths: International locations managed by owner-partners with a high level of presentation and understanding of general business. Enviable reputations which make purchase of consulting an easy decision for a manager, despite the very high prices.

   Weaknesses: General business knowledge doesn't substitute for the specific market, channel, and distribution expertise of Acme, focusing on high-technology markets and products only. Also, fees are extremely expensive, and work is generally done by very junior-level consultants, even though sold by high-level partners.

2. The international market research company:

   Strengths: International offices, specific market knowledge, permanent staff developing market research information on permanent basis, good relationships with potential client companies.

   Weaknesses: Market numbers are not marketing, not channel development nor market development. Although these companies compete for some of the business Acme is after, they cannot really offer the same level of business understanding at a high level.

3. Market specific or function specific experts:

   Strengths: Expertise in market or functional areas. Acme should not try to compete with Normura or Select in their markets with market research, or with ChannelCorp in channel management.

   Weaknesses: The inability to spread beyond a specific focus, or to rise above a specific focus, to provide actual management expertise, experience, and wisdom beyond the specifics.

4. The most significant competition is no consulting at all, companies choosing to do business development, channel development, and market research in-house.

   Strengths: No incremental cost except travel; the general work is done by the people who are responsible, the planning by those who will implement it.

   Weaknesses: Most managers are terribly overburdened already, unable to find incremental resources in time and people to apply to incremental opportunities. Also, there is a lot of additional risk in market and channel development done in-house from the ground up. Finally, retainer-based antenna consultants can greatly enhance a company's reach and extend its position into conversations that might otherwise never have taken place.

5.0 Strategy and Implementation Summary

Acme will focus on three geographical markets, the United States, Europe, and Latin America, and in limited product segments: personal computers, software, networks, telecommunications, personal organizers, and technology integration products.

The target customer is usually a manager in a larger corporation, and occasionally an owner or president of a medium-sized corporation in a high-growth period.

5.1 Pricing Strategy

Acme Consulting will be priced at the upper edge of what the market will bear, competing with the name-brand consultants. The pricing fits with the general positioning of Acme as providing high-level expertise.

Consulting should be based on $5,000 per day for project consulting, $2,000 per day for market research, and $10,000 per month and up for retainer consulting. Market research reports should be priced at $5,000 per report, which will, of course, require that reports be very well planned, focused on very important topics, and very well presented.

5.2 Sales Forecast

The sales forecast monthly summary is included in the appendix. The annual sales projections are included here in Table 5.2.

Total Sales by Month in Year 1

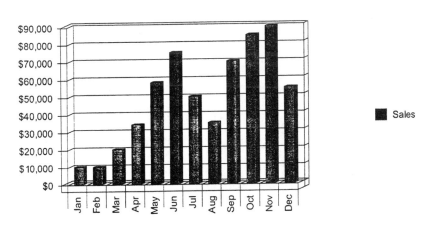

Table 5.2: Sales Forecast

Sales	1996	1997	1998
Retainer Consulting	$200,000	$350,000	$425,000
Project Consulting	$270,000	$325,000	$350,000
Market Research	$122,000	$150,000	$200,000
Strategic Reports	$0	$50,000	$125,000
Other	$0	$0	$0
Total Sales	$592,000	$875,000	$1,100,000

Direct Cost of sales	1996	1997	1998
Retainer Consulting	$30,000	$38,000	$48,000
Project Consulting	$45,000	$56,000	$70,000
Market Research	$84,000	$105,000	$131,000
Strategic Reports	$0	$20,000	$40,000
Other	$0	$0	$0
Subtotal Cost of Sales	$159,000	$219,000	$289,000

5.3 Strategic Alliances

At this writing, strategic alliances with Smith and Jones are possibilities, given the content of existing discussions. Given the background of prospective partners, we might also be talking to European companies including Siemens, Olivetti, and others, and to United States companies related to Apple Computer. In Latin America we would be looking at the key local high-technology vendors, beginning with Printaform.

6.0 Management Summary

The initial management team depends on the founders themselves, with little back-up. As we grow, we will take on additional consulting help, plus graphic/editorial, sales, and marketing.

6.1 Organizational Structure

Acme should be managed by working partners, in a structure taken mainly from Smith Partners. In the beginning we assume 3-5 partners:

- Ralph Sampson

- At least one, probably two, partners from Smith and Jones

- One strong European partner, based in Paris.

  The organization has to be very flat in the beginning, with each of the founders reponsible for his or her own work and management.

- One other strong partner

6.2 Management Team

The Acme business requires a very high level of international experience and expertise, which means that it will not be easily leveragable in the common consulting company mode in which partners run the business and make sales, while associates fulfill. Partners will necessarily be involved in the fulfillment of the core business proposition, providing the expertise to the clients. The initial personnel plan is still tentative. It should involve 3-5 partners, 1-3 consultants, one strong editorial/graphic person with good staff support, one strong marketing person, an office manager, and a secretary. Later, we add more partners, consultants, and sales staff. Founders' resumes are included as an attachment to this plan.

6.3 Personnel Plan

The detailed monthly personnel plan for the first year is included in the appendix. The annual personnel estimates are included here.

Table 6.3: Personnel Plan

Personnel		1996	1997	1998
Partners	1.4	$144,000	$175,000	$200,000
Consultants	1.25	$0	$50,000	$63,000
Editorial/graphic	1.2	$18,000	$22,000	$26,000
VP Marketing	1.1	$20,000	$50,000	$55,000
Sales people	1.1	$0	$30,000	$33,000
Office Manager	1.1	$7,500	$30,000	$33,000
Secretarial	1.1	$5,250	$20,000	$22,000
Other	1.1	$0	$0	$0
Other		$0	$0	$0
Total Payroll		$194,750	$377,000	$432,000
Total Headcount		0	0	0
Payroll Burden		$27,265	$52,780	$60,480
Total Payroll Expenditures		$222,015	$429,780	$492,480

7.0 Financial Plan

7.1 Important Assumptions

Table 7.1 summarizes key financial assumptions, including 45-day average collection days, sales entirely on invoice basis, expenses mainly on net 30 basis, 35 days on average for payment of invoices, and present-day interest rates.

Table 7.1: General Assumptions

	1996	1997	1998
Short-term Interest Rate %	8.00%	8.00%	8.00%
Long-term Interest Rate %	10.00%	10.00%	10.00%
Payment Days Estimator	35	35	35
Collection Days Estimator	45	45	45
Tax Rate %	25.00%	25.00%	25.00%
Expenses in Cash %	25.00%	25.00%	25.00%
Sales on Credit %	100.00%	100.00%	100.00%
Personnel Burden %	14.00%	14.00%	14.00%

7.2 Key Financial Indicators

The following benchmark chart indicates our key financial indicators for the first three years. We foresee major growth in sales and operating expenses, and a bump in our collection days as we spread the business during expansion.

Benchmark Comparison

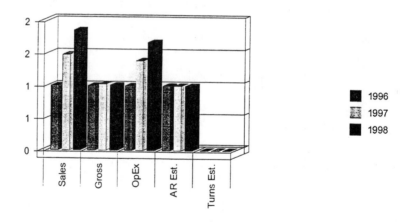

7.3 Break-even Analysis

Table 7.3 summarizes the break-even analysis, including monthly units and sales break-even points.

Breakeven Analysis

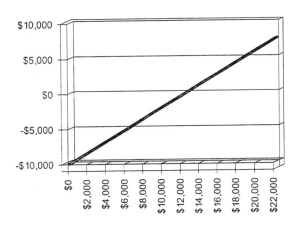

Table 7.3: Break-even Analysis

Monthly Units Break-even	12,500
Monthly Sales Break-even	$12,500
Assumptions:	
Average Per-Unit Revenue	$1.00
Average Per-Unit Variable Cost	$0.20
Estimated Monthly Fixed Cost	$10,000

7.4 Projected Profit and Loss

The detailed monthly pro-forma income statement for the first year is included in the appendix. The annual estimates are included here.

Table 7.4: Projected Profit and Loss

	1996	1997	1998
Sales	$592.000	$875.000	$1.100.000
Direct Cost of Sales	$159.000	$219.000	$289.000
Other	$0	$0	$0
	------------	------------	------------
Total Cost of Sales	$159.000	$219.000	$289.000
Gross Margin	$433.000	$656.000	$811.000
Gross Margin %	73.14%	74.97%	73.73%
Operating expenses:			
Advertising/Promotion	$36.000	$40.000	$44.000
Public Relations	$30.000	$30.000	$33.000
Travel	$90.000	$60.000	$110.000
Miscellaneous	$6.000	$7.000	$8.000
Travel	$0	$0	$0
Miscellaneous	$0	$0	$0
General and Administrative Payroll	$0	$0	$0
Payroll Expense	$194.750	$377.000	$432.000
Payroll Burden	$27.265	$52.780	$60.480
Depreciation	$0	$0	$0
Leased Equipment	$6.000	$7.000	$7.000
Utilities	$12.000	$12.000	$12.000
Insurance	$3.600	$2.000	$2.000
Rent	$18.000	$0	$0
Other	$0	$0	$0
Contract/Consultants	$0	$0	$0
	------------	------------	------------
Total Operating Expenses	$423.615	$587.780	$708.480
Profit Before Interest and Taxes	$9.385	$68.220	$102.520
Interest Expense Short-term	$3.600	$8.800	$12.800
Interest Expense Long-term	$5.000	$5.000	$5.000
Taxes Incurred	$196	$13.605	$21.180
Net Profit	$589	$40.815	$63.540
Net Profit/Sales	0.10%	4.66%	5.78%

7.5 Projected Cash Flow

Cash flow projections are critical to our success. The monthly cash flow is shown in the illustration, with one bar representing the cash flow per month and the other representing the monthly balance. The annual cash flow figures are included here as Table 7.5. Detailed monthly numbers are included in the appendix.

Cash Analysis

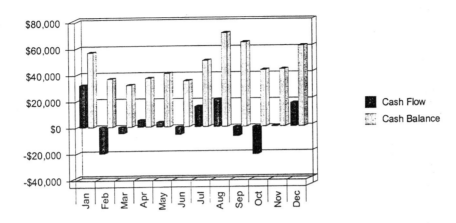

Table 7.5: Projected Cash Flow

	1996	1997	1998
Net Profit	$589	$40,815	$63,540
Plus:			
Depreciation	$0	$0	$0
Change in Accounts Payable	$25,896	$1,405	$10,967
Current Borrowing (repayment)	$60,000	$100,000	$0
Increase (decrease) Other Liabilities	$0	$0	$0
Long-term Borrowing (repayment)	$50,000	$0	$0
Capital Input	$0	$0	$0
Subtotal	$136,485	$142,220	$74,507
Less:	1996	1997	1998
Change in Accounts Receivable	$100,000	$47,804	$38,007
Change in Other ST Assets	$0	$0	$0
Capital Expenditure	$0	$0	$0
Dividends	$0	$0	$0
Subtotal	$100,000	$47,804	$38,007
Net Cash Flow	$36,485	$94,416	$36,500
Cash Balance	$61,485	$155,901	$192,401

7.6 Projected Balance Sheet

The balance sheet shows healthy growth of net worth, and strong financial position. The monthly estimates are included in the appendix.

Table 7.6: Projected Balance Sheet

Assets

	Starting Balances	1996	1997	1998
Short-term Assets				
Cash	$25,000	$61,485	S155,901	S192,401
Accounts Receivable	$0	$100,000	S147,804	S185,811
Other Short-term Assets	S7,000	S7,000	S7,000	S7,000
Total Short-term Assets	$32,000	$168,485	S310,705	$385,212
Long-term Assets				
Capital Assets	$0	$0	S0	S0
Accumulated Depreciation	$0	$0	S0	S0
Total Long-term Assets	S0	$0	S0	S0
Total Assets	$32,000	$168,485	$310,705	$385,212

Liabilities and Capital

		1996	1997	1998
Accounts Payable	$5,000	$30,896	S32,301	$43,268
Short-term Notes	$0	$60,000	$160,000	$160,000
Other Short-term Liabilities	$0	$0	S0	$0
Subtotal Short-term Liabilities	$5,000	$90,896	$192,301	$203,268
Long-term Liabilities	S0	$50,000	$50,000	$50,000
Total Liabilities	S5,000	S140,896	$242,301	$253,268
Paid in Capital	S50,000	S50,000	$50,000	$50,000
Retained Earnings	($23,000)	($23,000)	($22,411)	$18,404
Earnings	$0	$589	$40,815	$63,540
Total Capital	$27,000	$27,589	S68,404	$131,944
Total Liabilities and Capital	$32,000	$168,485	S310,705	S385,212
Net Worth	$27,000	$27,589	$68,404	S131,944

7.7 Business Ratios

The following table shows the projected business ratios. We expect to maintain healthy ratios for profitability, risk, and return.

Table 7.7: Projected Business Ratios

Profitability Ratios:	1996	1997	1998	RMA
Gross Margin	73.14%	74.97%	73.73%	0
Net Profit Margin	0.10%	4.66%	5.78%	0
Return on Assets	0.35%	13.14%	16.49%	0
Return on Equity	2.13%	59.67%	48.16%	0
Activity Ratios	1996	1997	1998	RMA
AR Turnover	5.92	5.92	5.92	0
Collection Days	31	52	55	0
Inventory Turnover	0.00	0.00	0.00	0
Accts Payable Turnover	8.75	8.75	8.75	0
Total Asset Turnover	3.51	2.82	2.86	0
Debt Ratios	1996	1997	1998	RMA
Debt to Net Worth	5.11	3.54	1.92	0
Short-term Liab. to Liab.	0.65	0.79	0.80	0
Liquidity Ratios	1996	1997	1998	RMA
Current Ratio	1.85	1.62	1.90	0
Quick Ratio	1.85	1.62	1.90	0
Net Working Capital	$77,589	$118,404	$181,944	0
Interest Coverage	1.09	4.94	5.76	0
Additional Ratios	1996	1997	1998	RMA
Assets to Sales	0.28	0.36	0.35	0
Debt/Assets	84%	78%	66%	0
Current Debt/Total Assets	54%	62%	53%	0
Acid Test	0.75	0.85	0.98	0
Asset Turnover	3.51	2.82	2.86	0
Sales/Net Worth	21.46	12.79	8.34	0

Table 7.6: Projected Balance Sheet

Assets

	Starting Balances	Jan	Feb	Mar	Apr	May	Jun	Jul	Aug	Sep	Oct	Nov	Dec
Short-term Assets													
Cash	$25,000	$56,928	$36,767	$31,994	$37,163	$40,812	$35,086	$50,572	$71,398	$64,176	$43,072	$43,674	$61,485
Accounts Receivable	$0	$10,000	$14,795	$29,589	$44,000	$75,000	$104,000	$87,500	$60,000	$87,500	$120,000	$132,500	$100,000
Other Short-term Assets	$7,000	$7,000	$7,000	$7,000	$7,000	$7,000	$7,000	$7,000	$7,000	$7,000	$7,000	$7,000	$7,000
Total Short-term Assets	$32,000	$73,928	$58,561	$68,583	$88,163	$122,812	$146,086	$145,072	$138,398	$158,676	$170,072	$183,174	$168,485
Long-term Assets													
Capital Assets	$0	$0	$0	$0	$0	$0	$0	$0	$0	$0	$0	$0	$0
Accumulated Depreciation	$0	$0	$0	$0	$0	$0	$0	$0	$0	$0	$0	$0	$0
Total Long-term Assets	$0	$0	$0	$0	$0	$0	$0	$0	$0	$0	$0	$0	$0
Total Assets	$32,000	$73,928	$58,561	$68,583	$88,163	$122,812	$146,086	$145,072	$138,398	$158,676	$170,072	$183,174	$168,485

Liabilities and Capital

	Starting Balances	Jan	Feb	Mar	Apr	May	Jun	Jul	Aug	Sep	Oct	Nov	Dec
Accounts Payable	$5,000	$14,475	$16,656	$17,951	$21,403	$26,149	$30,896	$24,855	$21,403	$33,053	$35,211	$36,074	$30,896
Short-term Notes	$0	$0	$0	$20,000	$40,000	$60,000	$60,000	$60,000	$60,000	$60,000	$60,000	$60,000	$60,000
Other Short-term Liabilities	$0	$0	$0	$0	$0	$0	$0	$0	$0	$0	$0	$0	$0
Subtotal Short-term Liabilities	$5,000	$14,475	$16,656	$37,951	$61,403	$86,149	$90,896	$84,855	$81,403	$93,053	$95,211	$96,074	$90,896
Long-term Liabilities	$0	$50,000	$50,000	$50,000	$50,000	$50,000	$50,000	$50,000	$50,000	$50,000	$50,000	$50,000	$50,000
Total Liabilities	$5,000	$64,475	$66,656	$87,951	$111,403	$136,149	$140,896	$134,855	$131,403	$143,053	$145,211	$146,074	$140,896
Paid in Capital	$50,000	$50,000	$50,000	$50,000	$50,000	$50,000	$50,000	$50,000	$50,000	$50,000	$50,000	$50,000	$50,000
Retained Earnings	($23,000)	($23,000)	($23,000)	($23,000)	($23,000)	($23,000)	($23,000)	($23,000)	($23,000)	($23,000)	($23,000)	($23,000)	($23,000)
Earnings	$0	($17,548)	($35,095)	($46,368)	($50,240)	($40,338)	($21,810)	($16,783)	($20,005)	($11,378)	($2,139)	$10,100	$589
Total Capital	$27,000	$9,453	($8,095)	($19,368)	($23,240)	($13,338)	$5,190	$10,218	$6,995	$15,623	$24,861	$37,100	$27,589
Total Liabilities and Capital	$32,000	$73,928	$58,561	$68,583	$88,163	$122,812	$146,086	$145,072	$138,398	$158,676	$170,072	$183,174	$168,485
Net Worth	$27,000	$9,453	($8,095)	($19,368)	($23,240)	($13,338)	$5,190	$10,218	$6,995	$15,623	$24,861	$37,100	$27,589

Table 7.5: Projected Cash Flow

	Jan	Feb	Mar	Apr	May	Jun	Jul	Aug	Sep	Oct	Nov	Dec
Net Profit	($17,548)	($17,548)	($11,273)	($3,873)	$9,903	$18,528	$5,028	($3,223)	$8,628	$9,239	$12,239	($9,511)
Plus:												
Depreciation	$0	$0	$0	$0	$0	$0	$0	$0	$0	$0	$0	$0
Change in Accounts Payable	$9,475	$2,181	$1,295	$3,452	$4,747	$4,747	($6,041)	($3,452)	$11,651	$2,158	$863	($5,178)
Current Borrowing (repayment)	$0	$0	$20,000	$20,000	$20,000	$0	$0	$0	$0	$0	$0	$0
Increase (decrease) Other Liabilities	$0	$0	$0	$0	$0	$0	$0	$0	$0	$0	$0	$0
Long-term Borrowing (repayment)	$50,000	$0	$0	$0	$0	$0	$0	$0	$0	$0	$0	$0
Capital Input	$0	$0	$0	$0	$0	$0	$0	$0	$0	$0	$0	$0
Subtotal	$41,928	($15,366)	$10,022	$19,580	$34,649	$23,274	($1,014)	($6,675)	$20,278	$11,396	$13,102	($14,689)
Less:	Jan	Feb	Mar	Apr	May	Jun	Jul	Aug	Sep	Oct	Nov	Dec
Change in Accounts Receivable	$10,000	$4,795	$14,795	$14,411	$31,000	$29,000	($16,500)	($27,500)	$27,500	$32,500	$12,500	($32,500)
Change in Other ST Assets	$0	$0	$0	$0	$0	$0	$0	$0	$0	$0	$0	$0
Capital Expenditure	$0	$0	$0	$0	$0	$0	$0	$0	$0	$0	$0	$0
Dividends	$0	$0	$0	$0	$0	$0	$0	$0	$0	$0	$0	$0
Subtotal	$10,000	$4,795	$14,795	$14,411	$31,000	$29,000	($16,500)	($27,500)	$27,500	$32,500	$12,500	($32,500)
Net Cash Flow	$31,928	($20,161)	($4,773)	$5,169	$3,649	($5,726)	$15,486	$20,825	($7,222)	($21,104)	$602	$17,811
Cash Balance	$56,928	$36,767	$31,994	$37,163	$40,812	$35,086	$50,572	$71,398	$64,176	$43,072	$43,674	$61,485

Table 7.1: General Assumptions

	Jan	Feb	Mar	Apr	May	Jun	Jul	Aug	Sep	Oct	Nov	Dec
Short-term Interest Rate %	8.00%	8.00%	8.00%	8.00%	8.00%	8.00%	8.00%	8.00%	8.00%	8.00%	8.00%	8.00%
Long-term Interest Rate %	10.00%	10.00%	10.00%	10.00%	10.00%	10.00%	10.00%	10.00%	10.00%	10.00%	10.00%	10.00%
Payment Days Estimator	35	35	35	35	35	35	35	35	35	35	35	35
Collection Days Estimator	45	45	45	45	45	45	45	45	45	45	45	45
Tax Rate %	25.00%	25.00%	25.00%	25.00%	25.00%	25.00%	25.00%	25.00%	25.00%	25.00%	25.00%	25.00%
Expenses in Cash %	25.00%	25.00%	25.00%	25.00%	25.00%	25.00%	25.00%	25.00%	25.00%	25.00%	25.00%	25.00%
Sales on Credit %	100.00%	100.00%	100.00%	100.00%	100.00%	100.00%	100.00%	100.00%	100.00%	100.00%	100.00%	100.00%
Personnel Burden %	14.00%	14.00%	14.00%	14.00%	14.00%	14.00%	14.00%	14.00%	14.00%	14.00%	14.00%	14.00%

Table 6.3: Personnel Plan

Personnel		Jan	Feb	Mar	Apr	May	Jun	Jul	Aug	Sep	Oct	Nov	Dec
Partners	1.4	$12,000	$12,000	$12,000	$12,000	$12,000	$12,000	$12,000	$12,000	$12,000	$12,000	$12,000	$12,000
Consultants	1.25	$0	$0	$0	$0	$0	$0	$0	$0	$0	$0	$0	$0
Editorial/graphic	1.2	$0	$0	$0	$0	$0	$0	$0	$0	$0	$6,000	$6,000	$6,000
VP Marketing	1.1	$0	$0	$0	$0	$0	$0	$0	$0	$5,000	$5,000	$5,000	$5,000
Sales people	1.1	$0	$0	$0	$0	$0	$0	$0	$0	$0	$0	$0	$0
Office Manager	1.1	$0	$0	$0	$0	$0	$0	$0	$0	$0	$2,500	$2,500	$2,500
Secretarial	1.1	$0	$0	$0	$0	$0	$0	$0	$0	$0	$1,750	$1,750	$1,750
Other	1.1	$0	$0	$0	$0	$0	$0	$0	$0	$0	$0	$0	$0
Other		$0	$0	$0	$0	$0	$0	$0	$0	$0	$0	$0	$0
Total Payroll		$12,000	$12,000	$12,000	$12,000	$12,000	$12,000	$12,000	$12,000	$17,000	$27,250	$27,250	$27,250
Total Headcount		0	0	0	0	0	0	0	0	0	0	0	0
Payroll Burden		$1,680	$1,680	$1,680	$1,680	$1,680	$1,680	$1,680	$1,680	$2,380	$3,815	$3,815	$3,815
Total Payroll Expenditures		$13,680	$13,680	$13,680	$13,680	$13,680	$13,680	$13,680	$13,680	$19,380	$31,065	$31,065	$31,065

Table 7.4: Projected Profit and Loss

	Jan	Feb	Mar	Apr	May	Jun	Jul	Aug	Sep	Oct	Nov	Dec
Sales	$10,000	$10,000	$20,000	$34,000	$58,000	$75,000	$50,000	$35,000	$70,000	$85,000	$90,000	$55,000
Direct Cost of Sales	$2,500	$2,500	$4,000	$8,000	$13,500	$19,000	$12,000	$8,000	$21,500	$24,000	$25,000	$19,000
Other	$0	$0	$0	$0	$0	$0	$0	$0	$0	$0	$0	$0
Total Cost of Sales	$2,500	$2,500	$4,000	$8,000	$13,500	$19,000	$12,000	$8,000	$21,500	$24,000	$25,000	$19,000
Gross Margin	$7,500	$7,500	$16,000	$26,000	$44,500	$56,000	$38,000	$27,000	$48,500	$61,000	$65,000	$36,000
Gross Margin %	75.00%	75.00%	80.00%	76.47%	76.72%	74.67%	76.00%	77.14%	69.29%	71.76%	72.22%	65.45%
Operating expenses:												
Advertising/Promotion	$3,000	$3,000	$3,000	$3,000	$3,000	$3,000	$3,000	$3,000	$3,000	$3,000	$3,000	$3,000
Public Relations	$2,500	$2,500	$2,500	$2,500	$2,500	$2,500	$2,500	$2,500	$2,500	$2,500	$2,500	$2,500
Travel	$7,500	$7,500	$7,500	$7,500	$7,500	$7,500	$7,500	$7,500	$7,500	$7,500	$7,500	$7,500
Miscellaneous	$500	$500	$500	$500	$500	$500	$500	$500	$500	$500	$500	$500
Travel	$0	$0	$0	$0	$0	$0	$0	$0	$0	$0	$0	$0
Miscellaneous	$0	$0	$0	$0	$0	$0	$0	$0	$0	$0	$0	$0
General and Administrative Payroll	$0	$0	$0	$0	$0	$0	$0	$0	$0	$0	$0	$0
Payroll Expense	$12,000	$12,000	$12,000	$12,000	$12,000	$12,000	$12,000	$12,000	$17,000	$27,250	$27,250	$27,250
Payroll Burden	$1,680	$1,680	$1,680	$1,680	$1,680	$1,680	$1,680	$1,680	$2,380	$3,815	$3,815	$3,815
Depreciation	$0	$0	$0	$0	$0	$0	$0	$0	$0	$0	$0	$0
Leased Equipment	$500	$500	$500	$500	$500	$500	$500	$500	$500	$500	$500	$500
Utilities	$1,000	$1,000	$1,000	$1,000	$1,000	$1,000	$1,000	$1,000	$1,000	$1,000	$1,000	$1,000
Insurance	$300	$300	$300	$300	$300	$300	$300	$300	$300	$300	$300	$300
Rent	$1,500	$1,500	$1,500	$1,500	$1,500	$1,500	$1,500	$1,500	$1,500	$1,500	$1,500	$1,500
Other	$0	$0	$0	$0	$0	$0	$0	$0	$0	$0	$0	$0
Contract/Consultants	$0	$0	$0	$0	$0	$0	$0	$0	$0	$0	$0	$0
Total Operating Expenses	$30,480	$30,480	$30,480	$30,480	$30,480	$30,480	$30,480	$30,480	$36,180	$47,865	$47,865	$47,865
Profit Before Interest and Taxes	($22,980)	($22,980)	($14,480)	($4,480)	$14,020	$25,520	$7,520	($3,480)	$12,320	$13,135	$17,135	($11,865)
Interest Expense Short-term	$0	$0	$133	$267	$400	$400	$400	$400	$400	$400	$400	$400
Interest Expense Long-term	$417	$417	$417	$417	$417	$417	$417	$417	$417	$417	$417	$417
Taxes Incurred	($5,849)	($5,849)	($3,758)	($1,291)	$3,301	$6,176	$1,676	($1,074)	$2,876	$3,080	$4,080	($3,170)
Net Profit	($17,548)	($17,548)	($11,273)	($3,873)	$9,903	$18,528	$5,028	($3,223)	$8,628	$9,239	$12,239	($9,511)

Table 5.2: Sales Forecast

Sales	Jan	Feb	Mar	Apr	May	Jun	Jul	Aug	Sep	Oct	Nov	Dec
Retainer Consulting	$10,000	$10,000	$10,000	$10,000	$20,000	$20,000	$20,000	$20,000	$20,000	$20,000	$20,000	$20,000
Project Consulting	$0	$0	$10,000	$20,000	$30,000	$40,000	$20,000	$10,000	$30,000	$45,000	$50,000	$15,000
Market Research	$0	$0	$0	$4,000	$8,000	$15,000	$10,000	$5,000	$20,000	$20,000	$20,000	$20,000
Strategic Reports	$0	$0	$0	$0	$0	$0	$0	$0	$0	$0	$0	$0
Other	$0	$0	$0	$0	$0	$0	$0	$0	$0	$0	$0	$0
Total Sales	$10,000	$10,000	$20,000	$34,000	$58,000	$75,000	$50,000	$35,000	$70,000	$85,000	$90,000	$55,000

Direct Cost of sales	Jan	Feb	Mar	Apr	May	Jun	Jul	Aug	Sep	Oct	Nov	Dec
Retainer Consulting	$2,500	$2,500	$2,500	$2,500	$2,500	$2,500	$2,500	$2,500	$2,500	$2,500	$2,500	$2,500
Project Consulting	$0	$0	$1,500	$3,500	$5,000	$6,500	$3,500	$1,500	$5,000	$7,500	$8,500	$2,500
Market Research	$0	$0	$0	$2,000	$6,000	$10,000	$6,000	$4,000	$14,000	$14,000	$14,000	$14,000
Strategic Reports	$0	$0	$0	$0	$0	$0	$0	$0	$0	$0	$0	$0
Other	$0	$0	$0	$0	$0	$0	$0	$0	$0	$0	$0	$0
Subtotal Cost of Sales	$2,500	$2,500	$4,000	$8,000	$13,500	$19,000	$12,000	$8,000	$21,500	$24,000	$25,000	$19,000

This page intentionally blank.

Sample Plan: **AMT, Inc.**

American Management Technologies, Inc.

This sample business plan has been made available to users of Business Plan Pro™, business plan software published by Palo Alto Software. It is based on a real business plan of an existing company. Names and numbers have been changed, and substantial portions of text may have been omitted to preserve confidential information.

You are welcome to use this plan as a starting point to create your own, but you do not have permission to reproduce, publish, distribute, or even copy this plan as it exists here.

Requests for reprints, academic use, and other dissemination of this sample plan should be addressed to the marketing department of Palo Alto Software.

Table Of Contents

Confidentiality Agreement

The undersigned reader acknowledges that the information provided by _____ in this business plan is confidential; therefore, reader agrees not to disclose it without the express written permission of _____.

It is acknowledged by reader that information to be furnished in this business plan is in all respects confidential in nature, other than information which is in the public domain through other means and that any disclosure or use of same by reader, may cause serious harm or damage to _____.

Upon request, this document is to be immediately returned to _____.

_____
Signature

_____
Date

_____
Name (typed or printed)

This is a business plan. It does not imply an offering of securities.

1.0 Executive Summary

By focusing on its strengths, its key customers, and the underlying values they need, American Management Technology will increase sales to more than $10 million in three years, while also improving the gross margin on sales and cash management and working capital.

This business plan leads the way. It renews our vision and strategic focus: adding value to our target market segments, the small business and high-end home office users, in our local market. It also provides the step-by-step plan for improving our sales, gross margin, and profitability.

This plan includes this summary, and chapters on the company, products and services, market focus, action plans and forecasts, management team, and financial plan.

Business Plan Highlights

1.1 Objectives

1. Sales increasing to more than $8 million by the third year.

2. Bring gross margin back up to above 30%, and maintain that level.

3. Sell $2 million of service, support, and training by 1998.

4. Improve inventory turnover to 6 turns next year, 7 in 1996, and 8 in 1997.

1.2 Mission

AMT is built on the assumption that the management of information technology for business is like legal advice, accounting, graphic arts, and other bodies of knowledge, in that it is not inherently a do-it-yourself prospect. Smart business people who aren't computer hobbyists need to find quality vendors of reliable hardware, software, service, and support. They need to use these quality vendors as they use their other professional service suppliers, as trusted allies.

AMT is such a vendor. It serves its clients as a trusted ally, providing them with the loyalty of a business partner and the economics of an outside vendor. We make sure that our clients have what they need to run their businesses as well as possible, with maximum efficiency and reliability. Many of our information applications are mission critical, so we give our clients the assurance that we will be there when they need us.

1.3 Keys to Success

1. Differentiate from box-pushing, price-oriented businesses by offering and delivering service and support -- and charging for it.

2. Increase gross margin to more than 25%.

3. Increase our non-hardware sales to 20% of the total sales by the third year.

2.0 Company Summary

AMT is a computer reseller based in the Uptown area. It was founded as a consulting-oriented VAR, became a reseller to fill the market need for personal computers, and is emphasizing service and support to differentiate itself from more price oriented national chains.

2.1 Company Ownership

AMT is a privately-held C corporation owned in majority by its founder and president, Ralph Jones. There are six part owners, including four investors and two past employees. The largest of these (in percent of ownership) are Frank Dudley, our attorney, and Paul Karots, our public relations consultant. Neither owns more than 15%, but both are active participants in management decisions.

2.2 Company History

AMT has been caught in the vise grip of margin squeezes that have affected computer resellers worldwide. Although the chart titled Past Financial Performance shows that we have had healthy growth in sales, it also shows declining gross margin and declining profits.

The more detailed numbers in Table 2.2 include other indicators of some concern:

The gross margin % has been declining steadily, as we see in the chart.

Inventory turnover is getting steadily worse.

All of these concerns are part of the general trend affecting computer resellers. The margin squeeze is happening throughout the computer industry worldwide.

Past Financial Performance

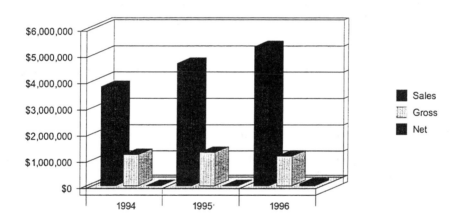

Table 2.2: Past Performance

	1994	1995	1996
Sales	$3,773,889	$4,661,902	$5,301,059
Gross Margin	$1,189,495	$1,269,261	$1,127,568
Gross % (calculated)	31.52%	27.23%	21.27%
Operating Expenses	$752,083	$902,500	$1,052,917
Collection period (days)	48	52	65
Inventory turnover	7	6	5

Balance Sheet			
Short-term Assets	1994	1995	1996
Cash	$0	$0	$55,432
Accounts receivable	$0	$0	$395,107
Inventory	$0	$0	$251,012
Other Short-term Assets	$0	$0	$25,000
Total Short-term Assets	$0	$0	$726,551
Long-term Assets			
Capital Assets	$0	$0	$350,000
Accumulated Depreciation	$0	$0	$50,000
Total Long-term Assets	$0	$0	$300,000
Total Assets	$0	$0	$1,026,551

Capital and Liabilities			
	1994	1995	1996
Accounts Payable	$0	$0	$223,897
Short-term Notes	$0	$0	$90,000
Other ST Liabilities	$0	$0	$15,000
Subtotal Short-term Liabilities	$0	$0	$328,897
Long-term Liabilities	$0	$0	$284,862
Total Liabilities	$0	$0	$613,759
Paid in Capital	$0	$0	$500,000
Retained Earnings	$0	$0	($161,860)
Earnings	$0	$0	$74,652
Total Capital	$0	$0	$412,792
Total Capital and Liabilities	$0	$0	$1,026,551

Other Inputs	1994	1995	1996
Payment days	0	0	30
Sales on credit	$0	$0	$3,445,688
Receivables turnover	0.00	0.00	8.72

2.3 Company Locations and Facilities

We have one location--a 7,000 square foot store in a suburban shopping center located conveniently close to the downtown area. It includes a training area, service department, offices, and showroom area.

3.0 Products and Services

AMT provides both computer products and services to make them useful to small business. We are especially focused on providing network systems and services to small and medium business. The systems include both PC-based LAN systems and minicomputer server-based systems. Our services include design and installation of network systems, training, and support.

3.1 Product and Service Description

In personal computers, we support three main lines:

The Super Home is our smallest and least expensive line, initially positioned by its manufacturer as a home computer. We use it mainly as a cheap workstation for small business installations. Its specifications include ...[additional specifics omitted]

The Power User is our main up-scale line. It is our most important system for high-end home and small business main workstations, because of .... Its key strengths are .... Its specifications include ....[additional specifics omitted]

The Business Special is an intermediate system, used to fill the gap in the positioning. Its specifications include ... [additional specifics omitted]

In peripherals, accessories and other hardware, we carry a complete line of necessary items from cables to forms to mousepads ... [additional specifics omitted]

In service and support, we offer a range of walk-in or depot service, maintenance contracts and on-site guarantees. We have not had much success selling service contracts. Our networking capabilities ...[additional specifics omitted]

In software, we sell a complete line of ... [additional specifics omitted]

In training, we offer ... [additional specifics omitted]

3.2 Competitive Comparison

The only way we can hope to differentiate well is to define the vision of the company to be an information technology ally to our clients. We will not be able to compete in any effective way with the chains using boxes or products as appliances. We need to offer a real alliance.

The benefits we sell include many intangibles: confidence, reliability, knowing that somebody will be there to answer questions and help at the important times.

These are complex products, products that require serious knowledge and experience to use, and our competitors sell only the products themselves.

Unfortunately, we cannot sell the products at a higher price just because we offer services; the market has shown that it will not support that concept. We have to also sell the service and charge for it separately.

3.3 Sales Literature

Copies of our brochure and advertisements are attached as appendices. Of course, one of our first tasks will be to change the message of our literature to make sure we are selling the company, rather than the product.

3.4 Sourcing

Our costs are part of the margin squeeze. As competition on price increases, the squeeze between manufacturers' price into channels and end-users' ultimate buying price continues.

With the hardware lines, our margins are declining steadily. We generally buy at ... Our margins are thus being squeezed from the 25% of five years ago to more like 13-15% at present. In the main-line peripherals a similar trend shows, with prices for printers and monitors declining steadily. We are also starting to see that same trend with software ....

In order to hold costs down as much as possible, we concentrate our purchasing with Hauser, which offers 30-day net terms and overnight shipping from the warehouse in Dayton. We need to concentrate on making sure our volume gives us negotiating strength.

In accessories and add-ons we can still get decent margins, 25% to 40%.

For software, margins are ...

3.5 Technology

We have for years supported both Windows and Macintosh technology for CPUs, although we've switched vendors many times for the Windows (and previously DOS) lines. We are also supporting Novell, Banyon, and Microsoft networking, Xbase database software, and Claris application products.

3.6 Service and Support

Our strategy hinges on providing excellent service and support. This is critical. We need to differentiate on service and support, and to therefore deliver as well.

1. Training: details are essential in a real business plan, but not this sample plan.

2. Upgrade offers: details are essential in a real business plan, but not in this sample plan.

3. Our own internal training: details are essential in a real business plan, but not in this sample plan.

4. Installation services: details are essential in a real business plan, but not in this sample plan.

5. Custom software services: details are essential in a real business plan, but not in this sample plan.

6. Network configuration services: details are essential in a real business plan, but not in this sample plan.

3.7 Future Products and Services

We must remain on top of the new technologies, because this is our bread and butter. For networking, we need to provide better knowledge of cross platform technologies. Also, we are under pressure to improve our understanding of direct-connect internet and related communications. Finally, although we have a good command of desktop publishing, we are concerned about getting better at the integration of technologies that creates fax, copier, printer, and voice mail as part of the computer system.

4.0 Market Analysis Summary

AMT focuses on local markets, small business and home office, with special focus on the high-end home office and the 5-20 unit small business office.

4.1 Market Segmentation

The segmentation allows some room for estimates and nonspecific definitions. We focus on a small-medium level of small business, and it is hard to find information to make an exact classification. Our target companies are large enough to need the high-quality information technology management we offer, but too small to have a separate computer management staff such as an MIS department. We say that our target market has 10-50 employees, and needs 5-20 workstations tied together in a local area network; the definition is flexible.

Defining the high-end home office is even more difficult. We generally know the characteristics of our target market, but we can't find easy classifications that fit into available demographics. The high-end home office business is a business, not a hobby. It generates enough money to merit the owner's paying real attention to the quality of information technology management, meaning that there is both budget and concerns that warrant working with our level of quality service and support. We can assume that we aren't talking about home offices used only part-time by people who work elsewhere during the day, and that our target market home office wants to have powerful technology and a lot of links between computing, telecommunications, and video.

Potential Market

Table 4.1: Market Analysis

Potential Customers	Growth	1997	1998	1999	2000	2001	CAGR
Consumer	2%	12,000	12,240	12,485	12,735	12,990	2.00%
Small Business	5%	15,000	15,750	16,538	17,365	18,233	5.00%
Large Business	8%	33,000	35,640	38,491	41,570	44,896	8.00%
Government	-2%	36,000	35,280	34,574	33,883	33,205	-2.00%
Other	0%	19,000	19,000	19,000	19,000	19,000	0.00%
Total	2.78%	115,000	117,910	121,088	124,553	128,324	2.78%

4.2 Target Market Segment Strategy

We are part of the computer reselling business, which includes several kinds of businesses:

1. Computer dealers: storefront computer resellers, usually less than 5,000 square feet, often focused on a few main brands of hardware, usually offering only a minimum of software, and variable amounts of service and support. These are usually old-fashioned (1980s-style) computer stores and they usually offer relatively few reasons for buyers to shop with them. Their service and support is not usually very good and their prices are usually higher than the larger stores.

2. Chain stores and computer superstores: these include major chains such as CompUSA, Computer City, Future Shop, etc. They are almost always more than 10,000 square feet of space, usually offer decent walk-in service, and are often warehouse-like locations where people go to find products in boxes with very aggressive pricing, and little support.

3. Mail order: the market is served increasingly by mail order businesses that offer aggressive pricing of boxed product. For the purely price-driven buyer, who buys boxes and expects no service, these are very good options.

4. Others: there are many other channels through which people buy their computers, usually variations of the main three types above.

4.2.1 Market Needs

Since our target market is the service seeker, the most important market needs are support, service, training, and installation, in that order. One of the key points of our strategy is the focus on target segments that know and understand these needs and are willing to pay to have them filled.

All personal computer users need support and service. The self reliant ones, however, supply those needs themselves. In home offices, these are the knowledgeable computer users who like to do it themselves. Among the businesses, these are businesses that have people on staff.

4.2.2 Market Trends

The most obvious and important trend in the market is declining prices. This has been true for years, but the trend seems to be accelerating. We see the major brand-name manufacturers putting systems together with amazing specs--more power, more speed, more memory, more disk storage--at amazing prices. The major chain shops are selling brand-name powerful computers for less than $1,000.

This may be related to a second trend, which is the computer as throw-away appliance. By the time a system needs upgrading, it is cheaper to buy completely new. The increasing power and storage of a sub-$1000 system means buyers are asking for less service.

A third trend is ever greater connectivity. Everybody wants onto the internet, and every small office wants a LAN. A lot of small offices want their LAN connected to the internet.

4.2.3 Market Growth

As prices fall, unit sales increase. The published market research on sales of personal computers is astounding, as the United States market alone is absorbing more than 30 million units per year, and sales are growing at more than 20 percent per year. We could quote Dataquest, Infocorp, IDC, or others; it doesn't matter, they all agree on high growth of CPU sales.

Where growth is not as obvious is the retail market. A report in CRW says Dell is now selling $5 million monthly over the web, and we assume Gateway and Micron are both close to that. Direct mail has given way to the web, but catalogs are still powerful, and the non-retail sale is more accepted every day. The last study we saw published has retail sales growing at 5% per year, while web sales and direct sales are growing at 25% or 30%.

4.3 Industry Analysis

We are part of the computer reselling business, which includes several kinds of businesses:

1. Computer dealers: storefront computer resellers, usually less than 5,000 square feet, often focused on a few main brands of hardware, usually offering only a minimum of software, and variable amounts of service and support. These are usually old-fashioned (1980s-style) computer stores and they usually offer relatively few reasons for buyers to shop with them. Their service and support is not usually very good and their prices are usually higher than the larger stores.

2. Chain stores and computer superstores: these include major chains such as CompUSA, Computer City, Future Shop, etc. They are almost always more than 10,000 square feet of space, usually offer decent walk-in service, and are often warehouse-like locations where people go to find products in boxes with very aggressive pricing, and little support.

3. Mail order: the market is served increasingly by mail order businesses that offer aggressive pricing of boxed product. For the purely price-driven buyer, who buys boxes and expects no service, these are very good options.

4. Others: there are many other channels through which people buy their computers, usually variations of the main three types above.

4.3.1 Industry Participants

1. The national chains are a growing presence. CompUSA, Computer City, Incredible Universe, Babbages, Egghead, and others. They benefit from national advertising, economies of scale, volume buying, and a general trend toward name-brand loyalty for buying in the channels as well as for products.

2. Local computer stores are threatened. These tend to be small businesses, owned by people who started them because they liked computers. They are under-capitalized and under-managed. Margins are squeezed as they compete against the chains, in a competition based on price more than on service and support.

4.3.2 Distribution Patterns

Small Business buyers are accustomed to buying from vendors who visit their offices. They expect the copy machine vendors, office products vendors, and office furniture vendors, as well as the local graphic artists, freelance writers, or whomever, to visit their office to make their sales.

There is usually a lot of leakage in ad-hoc purchasing through local chain stores and mail order. Often the administrators try to discourage this, but are only partially successful. Unfortunately our Home Office target buyers may not expect to buy from us. Many of them turn immediately to the superstores (office equipment, office supplies, and electronics) and mail order to look for the best price, without realizing that there is a better option for them at only a little bit more.

4.3.3 Competition and Buying Patterns

The small business buyers understand the concept of service and support, and are much more likely to pay for it when the offering is clearly stated.

There is no doubt that we compete much more against all the box pushers than against other service providers. We need to effectively compete against the idea that businesses should buy computers as plug-in appliances that don't need ongoing service, support, and training.

Our focus group sessions indicated that our target Home Offices think about price but would buy based on quality service if the offering were properly presented. They think about price because that's all they ever see. We have very good indications that many would rather pay 10-20% more for a relationship with a long-term vendor providing back-up and quality service and support; they end up in the box-pusher channels because they aren't aware of the alternatives.

Availability is also very important. The Home Office buyers tend to want immediate, local solutions to problems.

4.3.4 Main Competitors

Chain stores:

We have Store 1 and Store 2 already within the valley, and Store 3 is expected by the end of next year. If our strategy works, we will have differentiated ourselves sufficiently to not have to compete against these stores.

Strengths: national image, high volume, aggressive pricing, economies of scale.

Weaknesses: lack of product, service and support knowledge, lack of personal attention.

Other local computer stores:

Store 4 and Store 5 are both in the downtown area. They are both competing against the chains in an attempt to match prices. When asked, the owners will complain that margins are squeezed by the chains and customers buy on price only. They say they tried offering services and that buyers didn't care, instead preferring lower prices. We think the problem is also that they didn't really offer good service, and also that they didn't differentiate from the chains.

5.0 Strategy and Implementation Summary

The home offices in Tintown are an important growing market segment. Nationally, there are approximately 30 million home offices, and the number is growing at 10% per year. Our estimate in this plan for the home offices in our market service area is based on an analysis published four months ago in the local newspaper.

Home offices include several types. The most important, for our plan's focus, are the home offices that are the only offices of real businesses, from which people make their primary living. These are likely to be professional services such as graphic artists, writers, and consultants, some accountants and the occasional lawyer, doctor, or dentist. There are also part-time home offices with people who are employed during the day but work at home at night, people who work at home to provide themselves with a part-time income, or people who maintain home offices relating to their hobbies; we will not be focusing on this segment.

Small business within our market includes virtually any business with a retail, office, professional, or industrial location outside of someone's home, and fewer than 30 employees. We estimate 45,000 such businesses in our market area.

The 30-employee cutoff is arbitrary. We find that the larger companies turn to other vendors, but we can sell to departments of larger companies, and we shouldn't be giving up leads when we get them.

5.1 Strategy Pyramids

For placing emphasis on service and support, our main tactics are networking expertise, excellent training, and developing our own proprietary software/network administrative system. Our specific programs for networking include mailers and internal training. Specific programs for training include direct mail promotion, and train-the-trainers programs. For developing our own proprietary systems, our programs are company direct mail marketing, and working with VARs.

Our second strategy is emphasizing relationships. The tactics are marketing the company (instead of the products), more regular contacts with the customer, and increasing sales per customer. Programs for marketing the company include new sales literature, revised ad strategy, and direct mail. Programs for more regular contacts include call-backs after installation, direct mail, and sales management. Programs for increasing sales per customer include upgrade mailings and sales training.

5.2 Value Proposition

Our value proposition has to be different from the standard box-oriented retail chain. We offer our target customer, who is service seeking and not self reliant, a vendor who acts as a strategic ally, at a premium price that reflects the value of reassurance that systems will work.

5.3 Competitive Edge

Our competitive edge is our positioning as strategic ally with our clients, who are clients more than customers. By building a business based on long-standing relationships with satisfied clients, we simultaneously build defenses against competition. The longer the relationship stands, the more we help our clients understand what we offer them and why they need it.

5.4 Marketing Strategy

The marketing strategy is the core of the main strategy:

1. Emphasize service and support.

2. Build a relationship business.

3. Focus on small business and high-end home office as key target markets.

5.4.1 Positioning Statements

For businesspeople who want to be sure their computer systems are always working reliably, AMT is a vendor and trusted strategic ally who makes sure their systems work, their people are trained, and their down time is minimal. Unlike the chain retail stores, it knows the customer and goes to his or her site when needed, and offers proactive support, service, training, and installation.

5.4.2 Pricing Strategy

We must charge appropriately for the high-end, high-quality service and support we offer. Our revenue structure has to match our cost structure, so the salaries we pay to assure good service and support must be balanced by the revenue we charge.

We cannot build the service and support revenue into the price of products. The market can't bear the higher prices and the buyer feels ill-used when they see the same product priced lower at the chains. Despite the logic behind this, the market doesn't support this concept.

Therefore, we must make sure that we deliver and charge for service and support. Training, service, installation, networking support--all of this must be readily available and priced to sell and deliver revenue.

5.4.3 Promotion Strategy

We depend on newspaper advertising as our main way to reach new buyers. As we change strategies, however, we need to change the way we promote ourselves:

1. Advertising

We'll be developing our core positioning message: "24 Hour On-Site Service - 365 Days a Year
With No Extra Charges" to differentiate our service from the competition. We will be using local newspaper advertising, radio, and cable TV to launch the initial campaign.

2. Sales Brochure

Our collaterals have to sell the store, and visiting the store, not the specific book or discount pricing.

3. Direct Mail

We must radically improve our direct mail efforts, reaching our established customers with training, support services, upgrades, and seminars.

4. Local Media

It's time to work more closely with the local media. We could offer the local radio a regular talk show on technology for small business, as one example.

5.4.4 Distribution Strategy

Our most important marketing program is [specifics omitted]. Leslie Doe will be responsible, with budget of $XX,XXX and milestone date of the 15th of May. This program is intended to [objectives omitted]. Achievement should be measured by [specific concrete measurement].

Another key marketing program is [specifics omitted]. [Name] will be responsible, with budget of $XX,XXX and milestone date of [date]. This program is intended to [objectives omitted]. Achievement should be measured by [specific concrete measurement].

5.5 Sales Strategy

1. We need to sell the company, not the product. We sell AMT, not Apple, IBM, Hewlett-Packard, or Compaq, or any of our software brand names.

2. We have to sell our service and support. The hardware is like the razor, and the support, service, software services, training, and seminars are the razor blades. We need to serve our customers with what they really need.

3. The Yearly Total Sales chart summarizes our ambitious sales forecast. We expect sales to increase from $5.3 million last year to more than $7 million next year and to more than $10 million in the last year of this plan.

Yearly Total Sales

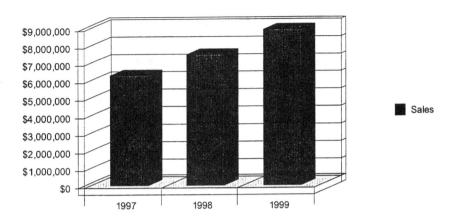

5.5.1 Sales Forecast

The important elements of the sales forecast are shown in the Total Sales by Month in Year 1 table. The non-hardware sales increase to about $2 million total in the third year.

Total Sales by Month in Year 1

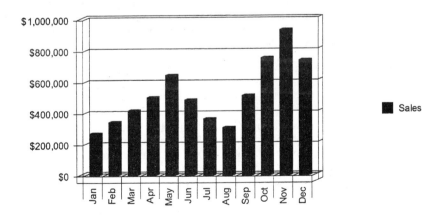

Table 5.5.1: Sales Forecast

Unit Sales		1997	1998	1999
Systems		2,255	2,500	2,800
Service		3,128	6,000	7,500
Software		3,980	5,000	6,500
Training		2,230	4,000	8,000
Other		2,122	2,500	3,000
Total Unit Sales		13,715	20,000	27,800
Unit Prices		1997	1998	1999
Systems		$1,980.80	$1,984.50	$1,980.80
Service		$68.47	$84	$87
Software		$212.86	$195	$180
Training		$46.58	$72	$79
Other		$300.00	$300	$300
Sales				
Systems		$4,466,708	$4,961,240	$5,546,245
Service		$214,159	$504,000	$652,500
Software		$847,183	$975,000	$1,170,000
Training		$103,865	$288,000	$632,000
Other		$636,600	$750,000	$900,000
Total Sales		$6,268,514	$7,478,240	$8,900,745
Direct Unit Costs		1997	1998	1999
Systems	85.00%	$1,700.00	$1,686.82	$1,683.68
Service	40.00%	$58.08	$33.60	$34.80
Software	60.00%	$120.00	$117.00	$108.00
Training	30.00%	$11.10	$21.60	$23.70
Other	30.00%	$90.00	$90.00	$118.26
Direct Cost of Sales		1997	1998	1999
Systems		$3,833,500	$4,217,054	$4,714,308
Service		$181,680	$201,600	$261,000
Software		$477,600	$585,000	$702,000
Training		$24,753	$86,400	$189,600
Other		$190,980	$225,000	$354,792
Subtotal Direct Cost of Sales		$4,708,513	$5,315,054	$6,221,700

5.5.2 Sales Programs

1. Direct mail: Use great detail to describe your company's programs here.

2. Seminars: Use great detail to describe your company's programs here.

5.6 Strategic Alliances

Our important milestones are shown on the following table. Row by row, they track the need to follow up on strategy with specific activities. Most of the activities on the list can be easily tied to our strategic goals of selling more service and enhancing the relationship with the customer.

Table 5.6: Milestones

Milestone	Manager	Planned Date	Department	Budget
Corporate Identity	TJ	12/17/95	Marketing	$10,000
Seminar implementation	IR	1/10/96	Sales	$1,000
Business Plan Review	RJ	1/10/96	GM	$0
Upgrade mailer	IR	1/16/96	Sales	$5,000
New corporate brochure	TJ	1/16/96	Marketing	$5,000
Delivery vans	SD	1/25/96	Service	$12,500
Direct mail	IR	2/16/96	Marketing	$3,500
Advertising	RJ	2/16/96	GM	S115,000
X4 Prototype	SG	2/25/96	Product	$2,500
Service revamp	SD	2/25/96	Product	$2,500
6 Presentations	IR	2/25/96	Sales	$0
X4 Testing	SG	3/6/96	Product	$1,000
3 Accounts	SD	3/17/96	Sales	$0
L30 Prototype	PR	3/26/96	Product	$2,500
Tech95 Expo	TB	4/12/96	Marketing	$15,000
VP S&M hired	JK	6/11/96	Sales	$1,000
Mailing system	SD	7/25/96	Service	$5,000
Totals				$181,500

6.0 Management Summary

Our management philosophy is based on responsibility and mutual respect. People who work at AMT want to work at AMT because we have an environment that encourages creativity and achievement.

6.1 Organizational Structure

1. The team includes 22 employees, under a president and four managers.

2. Our main management divisions are sales, marketing, service, and administration. Service handles service, support, training, and development.

6.2 Management Team

Ralph Jones, President: 46 years old, founded AMT in 1984 to focus on reselling high-powered personal computers to small business. Degree in computer science, 15 years with Large Computer Company, Inc. in positions ending with project manager. Ralph has been attending courses at the local Small Business Development Center for more than six years now, steadily adding business skills and business training to his technical background.

Sabrina Benson, VP Marketing: 36 years old, joined us last year following a very successful career with Continental Computers. Her hiring was the culmination of a long recruiting search. With Continental she managed the VAR marketing division. She is committed to re-engineering AMT to be a service and support business that sells computers, not vice-versa. MBA, undergraduate degree in history.

Gary Andrews, VP Service and Support: 48 years old, 18 years with Large Computers, Inc. in programming and service-related positions, 7 years with AMT. MS in computer science and BS in electrical engineering.

Laura Dannis, VP Sales: 32, former teacher, joined AMT part-time in 1991 and went full-time in 1992. Very high people skills, BA in elementary education. She has taken several sales management courses at the local SBDC.

John Peters, Director of Administration: 43, started with AMT as a part-time bookkeeper in 1987, and has become full-time administrative and financial backbone of the company.

6.3 Management Team Gaps

At present we believe we have a good team for covering the main points of the business plan. The addition of Sabrina Benson was important as a way to cement our fundamental re-positioning and re-engineering.

At present, we are weakest in the area of technical capabilities to manage the database marketing programs and upgraded service and support, particularly with cross-platform networks. We also need to find a training manager.

6.4 Personnel Plan

The Personnel Plan reflects the need to bolster our capabilities to match our positioning. Our total headcount should increase to 22 this first year, and to 30 by the third year. Detailed monthly projections are included in the appendices.

Table 6.4: Personnel Plan

	1997	1998	1999
Production			
Manager	$12,000	$13,000	$14,000
Assistant	$36,000	$40,000	$40,000
Technical	$12,500	$35,000	$35,000
Technical	$12,500	$35,000	$35,000
Technical	$24,000	$27,500	$27,500
Fulfillment	$24,000	$30,000	$60,000
Fulfillment	$18,000	$22,000	$50,000
Other	$0	$0	$0
Subtotal	$139,000	$202,500	$261,500
Sales and Marketing Personnel			
Manager	$72,000	$76,000	$80,000
Technical sales	$60,000	$63,000	$85,000
Technical sales	$45,500	$46,000	$46,000
Salesperson	$40,500	$55,000	$64,000
Salesperson	$40,500	$50,000	$55,000
Salesperson	$33,500	$34,000	$45,000
Salesperson	$31,000	$38,000	$45,000
Salesperson	$21,000	$30,000	$33,000
Salesperson	$0	$30,000	$33,000
Other	$0	$0	$0
Subtotal	$344,000	$422,000	$486,000
General and Administrative Personnel			
President	$66,000	$69,000	$95,000
Finance	$28,000	$29,000	$30,000
Admin Assistant	$24,000	$26,000	$28,000
Bookkeeping	$18,000	$25,000	$30,000
Clerical	$12,000	$15,000	$18,000
Clerical	$7,000	$15,000	$18,000
Clerical	$0	$0	$15,000
Other	$0	$0	$0
Subtotal	$155,000	$179,000	$234,000
Other Personnel			
Programming	$36,000	$40,000	$44,000
Other technical	$0	$30,000	$33,000
Other	$0	$0	$0
Subtotal	$36,000	$70,000	$77,000
Total Headcount	0	0	0
Total Payroll	$674,000	$873,500	$1,058,500
Payroll Burden	$107,840	$139,760	$169,360
Total Payroll Expenditures	$781,840	$1,013,260	$1,227,860

6.5 Other Management Considerations

Our attorney, Frank Dudley, is also a co-founder. He invested significantly in the company over a period of time during the 1980's. He remains a good friend of Ralph and has been a steady source of excellent legal and business advice.

Paul Karots, public relations consultant, is also a co-founder and co-owner. Like Dudley, he invested in the early stages and remains a trusted confidant and vendor of public relations and advertising services.

7.0 Financial Plan

The most important element in the financial plan is the critical need for improving several of the key factors that impact cash flow:

1. We must at any cost stop the slide in inventory turnover and develop better inventory management to bring the turnover back up to 8 turns by the third year. This should also be a function of the shift in focus towards service revenues to add to the hardware revenues.

2. We must also bring the gross margin back up to 25%. This too is related to improving the mix between hardware and service revenues, because the service revenues offer much better margins.

3. We plan to borrow another $150,000 long-term this year. The amount seems in line with the balance sheet capabilities.

7.1 Important Assumptions

The financial plan depends on important assumptions, most of which are shown in Table 7.1. The key underlying assumptions are:

1. We assume a slow-growth economy, without major recession.

2. We assume of course that there are no unforeseen changes in technology to make products immediately obsolete.

On our General Assumptions table, the most ambitious and also the most questionable assumption is our projected improvement in inventory turnover. This is critical to healthy cash flow, but will also be difficult.

Table 7.1: General Assumptions

	1997	1998	1999
Short-term Interest Rate %	8.00%	8.00%	8.00%
Long-term Interest Rate %	8.50%	8.50%	8.50%
Payment Days Estimator	45	45	45
Collection Days Estimator	45	45	45
Inventory Turnover Estimator	7.00	7.00	7.00
Tax Rate %	20.00%	20.00%	20.00%
Expenses in Cash %	14.00%	14.00%	14.00%
Sales on Credit %	70.00%	70.00%	70.00%
Personnel Burden %	16.00%	16.00%	16.00%

7.2 Key Financial Indicators

The Benchmark Comparison chart highlights our ambitious plans to correct declining gross margin and inventory turnover. The chart illustrates why we think the ambitious sales increases we plan are reasonable. We have had similar increases in the recent past.

Benchmark Comparison

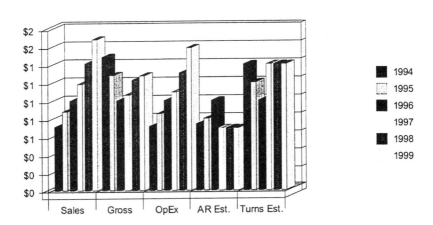

7.3 Break-even Analysis

For our break-even analysis, we assume running costs of approximately $96,000 per month, which includes our full payroll, rent, and utilities, and an estimation of other running costs. Payroll alone, at our present run rate, is only about $55,000.

Margins are harder to assume. Our overall average of $343/248 is based on past sales. We hope to attain a margin that high in the future.

The chart shows that we need to sell about $350,000 per month to break even, according to these assumptions. This is about half of our planned 1997 sales level, and significantly below our last year's sales level, so we believe we can maintain it.

Breakeven Analysis

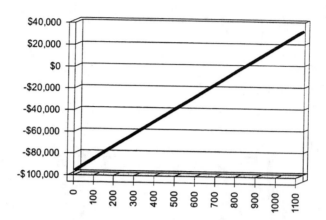

Table 7.3: **Break-even Analysis**

Monthly Units Break-even	824
Monthly Sales Break-even	$352,336
Assumptions:	
Average Per-Unit Revenue	$427.69
Average Per-Unit Variable Cost	$311.41
Estimated Monthly Fixed Cost	$95,792

7.4 Projected Profit and Loss

The most important assumption in the Projected Profit and Loss statement is the gross margin, which is supposed to increase. This is up from barely 21% in the last year. The increase in gross margin is based on changing our sales mix, and it is critical.

Month-by-month assumptions for profit and loss are included in the appendices.

AMT, Inc.

Table 7.4: Projected Profit and Loss

	1997	1998	1999
Sales	$6,268,514	$7,478,240	$8,900,745
Direct Cost of Sales	$4,708,513	$5,315,054	$6,221,700
Production payroll	$139,000	$202,500	$261,500
Other	$6,000	$6,600	$7,260
Total Cost of Sales	$4,853,513	$5,524,154	$6,490,460
Gross Margin	$1,415,001	$1,954,086	$2,410,285
Gross Margin %	22.57%	26.13%	27.08%
Operating expenses:			
Sales and Marketing Expenses			
Sales and Marketing Payroll	$344,000	$422,000	$486,000
Ads	$125,000	$140,000	$175,000
Catalog	$25,000	$19,039	$19,991
Mailing	$113,300	$120,000	$150,000
Promo	$16,000	$20,000	$25,000
Shows	$20,200	$25,000	$30,000
Literature	$7,000	$10,000	$12,500
PR	$1,000	$1,250	$1,500
Seminar	$31,000	$45,000	$60,000
Service	$10,250	$12,000	$15,000
Training	$5,400	$7,000	$15,000
Total Sales and Marketing Expenses	$698,150	$821,289	$989,991
Sales and Marketing %	11.14%	10.98%	11.12%
General and Administrative Expenses			
General and Administrative Payroll	$155,000	$179,000	$234,000
Payroll Burden	$107,840	$139,760	$169,360
Depreciation	$12,681	$13,315	$13,981
Leased Equipment	$30,000	$31,500	$33,075
Utilities	$9,000	$9,450	$9,923
Insurance	$6,000	$6,300	$6,615
Rent	$84,000	$88,200	$92,610
Other	$0	$0	$0
Other	$6,331	$6,648	$6,980
Total General and Administrative Expenses	$410,852	$474,173	$566,544
General and Administrative %	6.55%	6.34%	6.37%
Other Expenses			
Other Payroll	$36,000	$70,000	$77,000
Contract/Consultants	$1,500	$5,000	$30,000
Other	------------	8/15/08	1/20/09
Total Other Expenses	$37,500	$78,150	$110,308
Other %	0.60%	1.05%	1.24%
Total Operating Expenses	$1,149,502	$1,373,612	$1,666,843
Profit Before Interest and Taxes	$265,499	$580,474	$743,442
Interest Expense Short-term	$15,133	$19,400	$26,400
Interest Expense Long-term	$29,628	$26,833	$21,162
Taxes Incurred	$44,148	$106,848	$139,176
Net Profit	$176,590	$427,393	$556,704
Net Profit/Sales	2.82%	5.72%	6.25%

AMT, Inc.

7.5 Projected Cash Flow

The cash flow depends on assumptions for inventory turnover, payment days, and accounts receivable management. Our projected 45-day collection days is critical, and it is also reasonable. We need $150,000 in new financing in March to get through a cash flow dip as we build up for mid-year sales.

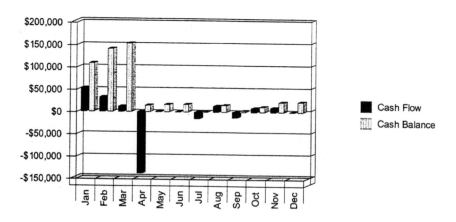

Table 7.5: Projected Cash Flow

	1997	1998	1999
Net Profit	$176,590	$427,393	$556,704
Plus:			
Depreciation	$12,681	$13,315	$13,981
Change in Accounts Payable	$537,079	$96,679	$152,297
Current Borrowing (repayment)	$140,000	$25,000	$150,000
Increase (decrease) Other Liabilities	$0	$0	$0
Long-term Borrowing (repayment)	$63,292	($64,953)	($68,484)
Capital Input	$325,000	$0	$0
Subtotal	$1,254,642	$497,435	$804,499
Less:	1997	1998	1999
Change in Accounts Receivable	$449,771	$163,048	$191,727
Change in Inventory	$746,874	$137,884	$198,673
Change in Other ST Assets	$0	$0	$0
Capital Expenditure	$90,000	$200,000	$400,000
Dividends	$0	$0	$0
Subtotal	$1,286,645	$500,933	$790,400
Net Cash Flow	($32,003)	($3,498)	$14,099
Cash Balance	$23,429	$19,931	$34,030

7.6 Projected Balance Sheet

The Projected Balance Sheet is quite solid. We do not project any real trouble meeting our debt obligations--as long as we can achieve our specific objectives.

Table 7.6: Projected Balance Sheet

Assets

	Starting Balances	1997	1998	1999
Short-term Assets				
Cash	$55,432	$23,429	$19,931	$34,030
Accounts Receivable	$395,107	$844,878	$1,007,927	$1,199,654
Inventory	$251,012	$997,886	$1,135,770	$1,334,443
Other Short-term Assets	$25,000	$25,000	$25,000	$25,000
Total Short-term Assets	$726,551	$1,891,193	$2,188,628	$2,593,126
Long-term Assets				
Capital Assets	$350,000	$440,000	$640,000	$1,040,000
Accumulated Depreciation	$50,000	$62,681	$75,996	$89,977
Total Long-term Assets	$300,000	$377,319	$564,004	$950,023
Total Assets	$1,026,551	$2,268,512	$2,752,632	$3,543,149

Liabilities and Capital

		1997	1998	1999
Accounts Payable	$223,897	$760,976	$857,655	$1,009,953
Short-term Notes	$90,000	$230,000	$255,000	$405,000
Other Short-term Liabilities	$15,000	$15,000	$15,000	$15,000
Subtotal Short-term Liabilities	$328,897	$1,005,976	$1,127,655	$1,429,953
Long-term Liabilities	$284,862	$348,154	$283,201	$214,717
Total Liabilities	$613,759	$1,354,130	$1,410,857	$1,644,670
Paid in Capital	$500,000	$825,000	$825,000	$825,000
Retained Earnings	($161,860)	($87,208)	$89,382	$516,775
Earnings	$74,652	$176,590	$427,393	$556,704
Total Capital	$412,792	$914,382	$1,341,775	$1,898,480
Total Liabilities and Capital	$1,026,551	$2,268,512	$2,752,632	$3,543,149
Net Worth	$412,792	$914,382	$1,341,775	$1,898,480

7.7 Business Ratios

The table follows with our main business ratios. We do intend to improve gross margin, collection days, and inventory turnover.

Table 7.7: Projected Business Ratios

Profitability Ratios:	1997	1998	1999	RMA
Gross Margin	22.57%	26.13%	27.08%	0
Net Profit Margin	2.82%	5.72%	6.25%	0
Return on Assets	7.78%	15.53%	15.71%	0
Return on Equity	19.31%	31.85%	29.32%	0
Activity Ratios	1997	1998	1999	RMA
AR Turnover	5.19	5.19	5.19	0
Collection Days	52	65	65	0
Inventory Turnover	7.77	5.18	5.25	0
Accts Payable Turnover	5.90	5.90	5.90	0
Total Asset Turnover	2.76	2.72	2.51	0
Debt Ratios	1997	1998	1999	RMA
Debt to Net Worth	1.48	1.05	0.87	0
Short-term Liab. to Liab.	0.74	0.80	0.87	0
Liquidity Ratios	1997	1998	1999	RMA
Current Ratio	1.88	1.94	1.81	0
Quick Ratio	0.89	0.93	0.88	0
Net Working Capital	$885,217	$1,060,972	$1,163,174	0
Interest Coverage	5.93	12.56	15.63	0
Additional Ratios	1997	1998	1999	RMA
Assets to Sales	0.36	0.37	0.40	0
Debt/Assets	60%	51%	46%	0
Current Debt/Total Assets	44%	41%	40%	0
Acid Test	0.05	0.04	0.04	0
Asset Turnover	2.76	2.72	2.51	0
Sales/Net Worth	6.86	5.57	4.69	0

Appendix: AMT, Inc.

Table 7.6: Projected Balance Sheet

Assets

	Starting Balances	Jan	Feb	Mar	Apr	May	Jun	Jul	Aug	Sep	Oct	Nov	Dec
Short-term Assets													
Cash	$55,432	$108,508	$141,078	$153,148	$14,875	$16,684	$17,118	$2,010	$15,593	$3,209	$12,422	$22,817	$23,429
Accounts Receivable	$395,107	$277,923	$354,332	$430,575	$496,730	$626,284	$565,392	$423,890	$341,268	$466,541	$707,840	$918,115	$844,878
Inventory	$251,012	$333,445	$444,104	$544,477	$699,578	$879,836	$648,051	$459,866	$401,460	$666,411	$994,975	$1,250,220	$997,886
Other Short-term Assets	$25,000	$25,000	$25,000	$25,000	$25,000	$175,000	$175,000	$475,000	$475,000	$325,000	$25,000	$25,000	$25,000
Total Short-term Assets	$726,551	$744,876	$964,514	$1,153,200	$1,236,182	$1,697,804	$1,405,562	$1,360,765	$1,233,320	$1,461,161	$1,740,236	$2,216,152	$1,891,193
Long-term Assets													
Capital Assets	$350,000	$375,000	$375,000	$390,000	$390,000	$440,000	$440,000	$440,000	$440,000	$440,000	$440,000	$440,000	$440,000
Accumulated Depreciation	$50,000	$51,000	$52,010	$53,030	$54,060	$55,100	$56,150	$57,211	$58,283	$59,366	$60,460	$61,565	$62,681
Total Long-term Assets	$300,000	$324,000	$322,990	$336,970	$335,940	$384,900	$383,850	$382,789	$381,717	$380,634	$379,540	$378,435	$377,319
Total Assets	$1,026,551	$1,068,876	$1,287,504	$1,490,170	$1,572,122	$2,082,704	$1,789,412	$1,743,554	$1,615,037	$1,841,795	$2,119,776	$2,594,587	$2,268,512

Liabilities and Capital

	Starting Balances	Jan	Feb	Mar	Apr	May	Jun	Jul	Aug	Sep	Oct	Nov	Dec
Accounts Payable	$223,897	$268,569	$369,549	$428,414	$560,724	$702,163	$514,886	$378,036	$324,275	$555,293	$795,989	$984,178	$760,976
Short-term Notes	$90,000	$90,000	$190,000	$220,000	$170,000	$215,000	$105,000	$205,000	$155,000	$155,000	$155,000	$380,000	$230,000
Other Short-term Liabilities	$15,000	$15,000	$15,000	$15,000	$15,000	$15,000	$15,000	$15,000	$15,000	$15,000	$15,000	$15,000	$15,000
Subtotal Short-term Liabilities	$328,897	$373,569	$574,549	$663,414	$745,724	$932,163	$634,886	$598,036	$494,275	$725,293	$965,989	$1,379,178	$1,005,976
Long-term Liabilities	$284,862	$281,920	$278,958	$375,974	$372,970	$369,944	$366,897	$363,828	$360,737	$357,624	$354,490	$351,333	$348,154
Total Liabilities	$613,759	$655,489	$853,506	$1,039,388	$1,118,694	$1,302,107	$1,001,783	$961,863	$855,012	$1,082,917	$1,320,479	$1,730,511	$1,354,130
Paid in Capital	$500,000	$500,000	$525,000	$525,000	$525,000	$825,000	$825,000	$825,000	$825,000	$825,000	$825,000	$825,000	$825,000
Retained Earnings	($161,860)	($87,208)	($87,208)	($87,208)	($87,208)	($87,208)	($87,208)	($87,208)	($87,208)	($87,208)	($87,208)	($87,208)	($87,208)
Earnings	$74,652	$595	($3,795)	$12,990	$15,636	$42,804	$49,837	$43,899	$22,234	$21,086	$61,505	$126,284	$176,590
Total Capital	$412,792	$413,387	$433,997	$450,782	$453,428	$780,596	$787,629	$781,691	$760,026	$758,878	$799,297	$864,076	$914,382
Total Liabilities and Capital	$1,026,551	$1,068,876	$1,287,504	$1,490,170	$1,572,122	$2,082,704	$1,789,412	$1,743,554	$1,615,037	$1,841,795	$2,119,776	$2,594,587	$2,268,512
Net Worth	$412,792	$413,387	$433,997	$450,782	$453,428	$780,596	$787,629	$781,691	$760,026	$758,878	$799,297	$864,076	$914,382

Appendix: AMT, Inc.

Table 7.5: Projected Cash Flow

	Jan	Feb	Mar	Apr	May	Jun	Jul	Aug	Sep	Oct	Nov	Dec
Net Profit	$595	($4,390)	$16,784	$2,647	$27,168	$7,033	($5,938)	($21,665)	($1,148)	$40,419	$64,779	$50,306
Plus:												
Depreciation	$1,000	$1,010	$1,020	$1,030	$1,040	$1,050	$1,061	$1,072	$1,083	$1,094	$1,105	$1,116
Change in Accounts Payable	$44,672	$100,980	$58,866	$132,310	$141,439	($187,277)	($136,850)	($53,761)	$231,018	$240,697	$188,189	($223,202)
Current Borrowing (repayment)	$0	$100,000	$30,000	($50,000)	$45,000	($110,000)	$100,000	($50,000)	$0	$0	$225,000	($150,000)
Increase (decrease) Other Liabilities	$0	$0	$0	$0	$0	$0	$0	$0	$0	$0	$0	$0
Long-term Borrowing (repayment)	($2,942)	($2,962)	$97,017	($3,005)	($3,026)	($3,047)	($3,069)	($3,091)	($3,113)	($3,135)	($3,157)	($3,179)
Capital Input	$0	$25,000	$0	$0	$300,000	$0	$0	$0	$0	$0	$0	$0
Subtotal	$43,325	$219,638	$203,686	$82,982	$511,621	($292,242)	($44,796)	($127,445)	$227,840	$279,075	$475,916	($324,959)
Less:												
Change in Accounts Receivable	($117,184)	$76,409	$76,243	$66,155	$129,554	($60,892)	($141,502)	($82,622)	$125,273	$241,299	$210,276	($73,237)
Change in Inventory	$82,433	$110,659	$100,373	$155,101	$180,258	($231,784)	($188,186)	($58,406)	$264,951	$328,563	$255,245	($252,334)
Change in Other ST Assets	$0	$0	$0	$0	$150,000	$300,000	$0	$0	($150,000)	($300,000)	$0	$0
Capital Expenditure	$25,000	$0	$15,000	$0	$50,000	$0	$0	$0	$0	$0	$0	$0
Dividends	$0	$0	$0	$0	$0	$0	$0	$0	$0	$0	$0	$0
Subtotal	($9,751)	$187,068	$191,616	$221,256	$509,812	($292,676)	($29,688)	($141,028)	$240,224	$269,862	$465,521	($325,571)
Net Cash Flow	$53,076	$32,570	$12,071	($138,274)	$1,809	$435	($15,109)	$13,583	($12,384)	$9,213	$10,395	$612
Cash Balance	$108,508	$141,078	$153,148	$14,875	$16,684	$17,118	$2,010	$15,593	$3,209	$12,422	$22,817	$23,429

Appendix: AMT, Inc.

Table 7.1: General Assumptions

	Jan	Feb	Mar	Apr	May	Jun	Jul	Aug	Sep	Oct	Nov	Dec
Short-term Interest Rate %	8.00%	8.00%	8.00%	8.00%	8.00%	8.00%	8.00%	8.00%	8.00%	8.00%	8.00%	8.00%
Long-term Interest Rate %	8.50%	8.50%	8.50%	8.50%	8.50%	8.50%	8.50%	8.50%	8.50%	8.50%	8.50%	8.50%
Payment Days Estimator	45	45	45	45	45	45	45	45	45	45	45	45
Collection Days Estimator	45	45	45	45	45	45	45	45	45	45	45	45
Inventory Turnover Estimator	7.00	7.00	7.00	7.00	7.00	7.00	7.00	7.00	7.00	7.00	7.00	7.00
Tax Rate %	20.00%	20.00%	20.00%	20.00%	20.00%	20.00%	20.00%	20.00%	20.00%	20.00%	20.00%	20.00%
Expenses in Cash %	14.00%	14.00%	14.00%	14.00%	14.00%	14.00%	14.00%	14.00%	14.00%	14.00%	14.00%	14.00%
Sales on Credit %	70.00%	70.00%	70.00%	70.00%	70.00%	70.00%	70.00%	70.00%	70.00%	70.00%	70.00%	70.00%
Personnel Burden %	16.00%	16.00%	16.00%	16.00%	16.00%	16.00%	16.00%	16.00%	16.00%	16.00%	16.00%	16.00%

Appendix: AMT, Inc.

Table 6.4: Personnel Plan

Production	Jan	Feb	Mar	Apr	May	Jun	Jul	Aug	Sep	Oct	Nov	Dec
Manager	$1,000	$1,000	$1,000	$1,000	$1,000	$1,000	$1,000	$1,000	$1,000	$1,000	$1,000	$1,000
Assistant	$3,000	$3,000	$3,000	$3,000	$3,000	$3,000	$3,000	$3,000	$3,000	$3,000	$3,000	$3,000
Technical	$0	$0	$0	$0	$0	$0	$0	$2,500	$2,500	$2,500	$2,500	$2,500
Technical	$0	$0	$0	$0	$0	$0	$0	$2,500	$2,500	$2,500	$2,500	$2,500
Technical	$2,000	$2,000	$2,000	$2,000	$2,000	$2,000	$2,000	$2,000	$2,000	$2,000	$2,000	$2,000
Fulfillment	$2,000	$2,000	$2,000	$2,000	$2,000	$2,000	$2,000	$2,000	$2,000	$2,000	$2,000	$2,000
Fulfillment	$1,500	$1,500	$1,500	$1,500	$1,500	$1,500	$1,500	$1,500	$1,500	$1,500	$1,500	$1,500
Other	$0	$0	$0	$0	$0	$0	$0	$0	$0	$0	$0	$0
Subtotal	$9,500	$9,500	$9,500	$9,500	$9,500	$9,500	$9,500	$14,500	$14,500	$14,500	$14,500	$14,500

Sales and Marketing Personnel	Jan	Feb	Mar	Apr	May	Jun	Jul	Aug	Sep	Oct	Nov	Dec
Manager	$6,000	$6,000	$6,000	$6,000	$6,000	$6,000	$6,000	$6,000	$6,000	$6,000	$6,000	$6,000
Technical sales	$5,000	$5,000	$5,000	$5,000	$5,000	$5,000	$5,000	$5,000	$5,000	$5,000	$5,000	$5,000
Technical sales	$3,500	$3,500	$3,500	$3,500	$3,500	$4,000	$4,000	$4,000	$4,000	$4,000	$4,000	$4,000
Salesperson	$2,500	$2,500	$2,500	$2,500	$2,500	$4,000	$4,000	$4,000	$4,000	$4,000	$4,000	$4,000
Salesperson	$2,500	$2,500	$2,500	$2,500	$2,500	$4,000	$4,000	$4,000	$4,000	$4,000	$4,000	$4,000
Salesperson	$2,500	$2,500	$2,500	$2,500	$2,500	$3,000	$3,000	$3,000	$3,000	$3,000	$3,000	$3,000
Salesperson	$2,000	$2,000	$2,000	$2,000	$2,000	$3,000	$3,000	$3,000	$3,000	$3,000	$3,000	$3,000
Salesperson	$0	$0	$0	$0	$0	$3,000	$3,000	$3,000	$3,000	$3,000	$3,000	$3,000
Salesperson	$0	$0	$0	$0	$0	$0	$0	$0	$0	$0	$0	$0
Other	$0	$0	$0	$0	$0	$0	$0	$0	$0	$0	$0	$0
Subtotal	$24,000	$24,000	$24,000	$24,000	$24,000	$32,000	$32,000	$32,000	$32,000	$32,000	$32,000	$32,000

General and Administrative Personnel	Jan	Feb	Mar	Apr	May	Jun	Jul	Aug	Sep	Oct	Nov	Dec
President	$5,500	$5,500	$5,500	$5,500	$5,500	$5,500	$5,500	$5,500	$5,500	$5,500	$5,500	$5,500
Finance	$0	$0	$0	$0	$0	$4,000	$4,000	$4,000	$4,000	$4,000	$4,000	$4,000
Admin Assistant	$2,000	$2,000	$2,000	$2,000	$2,000	$2,000	$2,000	$2,000	$2,000	$2,000	$2,000	$2,000
Bookkeeping	$1,500	$1,500	$1,500	$1,500	$1,500	$1,500	$1,500	$1,500	$1,500	$1,500	$1,500	$1,500
Clerical	$1,000	$1,000	$1,000	$1,000	$1,000	$1,000	$1,000	$1,000	$1,000	$1,000	$1,000	$1,000

Appendix: AMT, Inc.

Clerical	$0	$0	$0	$0	$0	$1,000	$1,000	$1,000	$1,000	$1,000	$1,000	$1,000
Clerical	$0	$0	$0	$0	$0	$0	$0	$0	$0	$0	$0	$0
Other	$0	$0	$0	$0	$0	$0	$0	$0	$0	$0	$0	$0
Subtotal	$10,000	$10,000	$10,000	$10,000	$10,000	$15,000	$15,000	$15,000	$15,000	$15,000	$15,000	$15,000
Other Personnel												
Programming	$3,000	$3,000	$3,000	$3,000	$3,000	$3,000	$3,000	$3,000	$3,000	$3,000	$3,000	$3,000
Other technical	$0	$0	$0	$0	$0	$0	$0	$0	$0	$0	$0	$0
Other	$0	$0	$0	$0	$0	$0	$0	$0	$0	$0	$0	$0
Subtotal	$3,000	$3,000	$3,000	$3,000	$3,000	$3,000	$3,000	$3,000	$3,000	$3,000	$3,000	$3,000
Total Headcount	0	0	0	0	0	0	0	0	0	0	0	0
Total Payroll	$46,500	$46,500	$46,500	$46,500	$46,500	$59,500	$59,500	$64,500	$64,500	$64,500	$64,500	$64,500
Payroll Burden	$7,440	$7,440	$7,440	$7,440	$7,440	$9,520	$9,520	$10,320	$10,320	$10,320	$10,320	$10,320
Total Payroll Expenditures	$53,940	$53,940	$53,940	$53,940	$53,940	$69,020	$69,020	$74,820	$74,820	$74,820	$74,820	$74,820

Appendix: AMT, Inc.

Table 7.4: Projected Profit and Loss

	Jan	Feb	Mar	Apr	May	Jun	Jul	Aug	Sep	Oct	Nov	Dec
Sales	$268,365	$342,146	$415,767	$501,731	$643,826	$485,790	$362,662	$306,194	$513,389	$754,505	$934,341	$739,799
Direct Cost of Sales	$184,510	$249,061	$307,612	$398,087	$503,238	$368,030	$258,255	$219,185	$373,740	$565,402	$714,295	$567,100
Production payroll	$9,500	$9,500	$9,500	$9,500	$9,500	$9,500	$9,500	$14,500	$14,500	$14,500	$14,500	$14,500
Other	$500	$500	$500	$500	$500	$500	$500	$500	$500	$500	$500	$500
Total Cost of Sales	$194,510	$259,061	$317,612	$408,087	$513,238	$378,030	$268,255	$234,185	$388,740	$580,402	$729,295	$582,100
Gross Margin	$73,856	$83,086	$98,155	$93,644	$130,589	$107,760	$94,407	$72,009	$124,649	$174,103	$205,046	$157,699
Gross Margin %	27.52%	24.28%	23.61%	18.66%	20.28%	22.18%	26.03%	23.52%	24.28%	23.08%	21.95%	21.32%
Operating expenses:												
Sales and Marketing Expenses												
Sales and Marketing Payroll	$24,000	$24,000	$24,000	$24,000	$24,000	$32,000	$32,000	$32,000	$32,000	$32,000	$32,000	$32,000
Ads	$5,000	$5,000	$7,000	$10,000	$15,000	$10,000	$4,000	$4,000	$20,000	$15,000	$20,000	$10,000
Catalog	$2,000	$3,000	$2,000	$2,000	$2,000	$2,000	$2,000	$2,000	$2,000	$2,000	$2,000	$2,000
Mailing	$3,000	$11,800	$5,500	$10,500	$10,500	$5,500	$10,500	$10,500	$10,500	$22,000	$8,000	$5,000
Promo	$0	$0	$0	$0	$0	$0	$0	$0	$1,000	$0	$15,000	$0
Shows	$0	$7,000	$0	$0	$0	$0	$3,200	$0	$10,000	$7,000	$0	$0
Literature	$0	$0	$0	$0	$0	$0	$0	$0	$0	$0	$0	$0
PR	$0	$0	$0	$1,000	$0	$0	$0	$0	$0	$0	$0	$0
Seminar	$1,000	$0	$0	$5,000	$5,000	$5,000	$5,000	$5,000	$5,000	$0	$0	$0
Service	$2,000	$1,000	$1,000	$500	$2,500	$500	$500	$500	$500	$500	$500	$250
Training	$450	$450	$450	$450	$450	$450	$450	$450	$450	$450	$450	$450
Total Sales and Marketing Expenses	$37,450	$52,250	$39,950	$53,450	$59,450	$55,450	$57,650	$54,450	$81,450	$78,950	$77,950	$49,700
Sales and Marketing %	13.95%	15.27%	9.61%	10.65%	9.23%	11.41%	15.90%	17.78%	15.87%	10.46%	8.34%	6.72%
General and Administrative Expenses												
General and Administrative Payroll	$10,000	$10,000	$10,000	$10,000	$10,000	$15,000	$15,000	$15,000	$15,000	$15,000	$15,000	$15,000
Payroll Burden	$7,440	$7,440	$7,440	$7,440	$7,440	$9,520	$9,520	$10,320	$10,320	$10,320	$10,320	$10,320
Depreciation	$1,000	$1,010	$1,020	$1,030	$1,040	$1,050	$1,061	$1,072	$1,083	$1,094	$1,105	$1,116
Leased Equipment	$2,500	$2,500	$2,500	$2,500	$2,500	$2,500	$2,500	$2,500	$2,500	$2,500	$2,500	$2,500

Appendix: AMT, Inc.

Utilities	$750	$750	$750	$750	$750	$750	$750	$750	$750	$750	$750	$750
Insurance	$500	$500	$500	$500	$500	$500	$500	$500	$500	$500	$500	$500
Rent	$7,000	$7,000	$7,000	$7,000	$7,000	$7,000	$7,000	$7,000	$7,000	$7,000	$7,000	$7,000
Other	$0	$0	$0	$0	$0	$0	$0	$0	$0	$0	$0	$0
Other	$500	$505	$510	$515	$520	$525	$530	$535	$540	$545	$550	$556
Total General and Administrative Expenses	$29,690	$29,705	$29,720	$29,735	$29,750	$36,845	$36,861	$37,677	$37,693	$37,709	$37,725	$37,742
General and Administrative %	11.06%	8.68%	7.15%	5.93%	4.62%	7.58%	10.16%	12.30%	7.34%	5.00%	4.04%	5.10%
Other Expenses												
Other Payroll	$3,000	$3,000	$3,000	$3,000	$3,000	$3,000	$3,000	$3,000	$3,000	$3,000	$3,000	$3,000
Contract/Consultants	$125	$125	$125	$125	$125	$125	$125	$125	$125	$125	$125	$125
Other	9/6/00	9/6/00	9/6/00	9/6/00	9/6/00	9/6/00	9/6/00	9/6/00	9/6/00	9/6/00	9/6/00	9/6/00
Total Other Expenses	$3,375	$3,375	$3,375	$3,375	$3,375	$3,375	$3,375	$3,375	$3,375	$3,375	$3,375	$3,375
Other %	1.26%	0.99%	0.81%	0.67%	0.52%	0.69%	0.93%	1.10%	0.66%	0.45%	0.36%	0.46%
Total Operating Expenses	$70,515	$85,330	$73,045	$86,560	$92,575	$95,670	$97,886	$95,502	$122,518	$120,034	$119,050	$90,817
Profit Before Interest and Taxes	$3,341	($2,244)	$25,110	$7,084	$38,014	$12,090	($3,479)	($23,493)	$2,131	$54,069	$85,996	$66,882
Interest Expense Short-term	$600	$1,267	$1,467	$1,133	$1,433	$700	$1,367	$1,033	$1,033	$1,033	$2,533	$1,533
Interest Expense Long-term	$1,997	$1,976	$2,663	$2,642	$2,620	$2,599	$2,577	$2,555	$2,533	$2,511	$2,489	$2,466
Taxes Incurred	$149	($1,097)	$4,196	$662	$6,792	$1,758	($1,485)	($5,416)	($287)	$10,105	$16,195	$12,576
Net Profit	$595	($4,390)	$16,784	$2,647	$27,168	$7,033	($5,938)	($21,665)	($1,148)	$40,419	$64,779	$50,306
Net Profit/Sales	0.22%	-1.28%	4.04%	0.53%	4.22%	1.45%	-1.04%	-7.08%	-0.22%	5.36%	6.93%	6.80%

Appendix: AMT, Inc.

Table 5.5.1: Sales Forecast

Unit Sales	Jan	Feb	Mar	Apr	May	Jun	Jul	Aug	Sep	Oct	Nov	Dec
Systems	85	115	145	190	245	175	120	100	180	275	350	275
Service	200	200	200	200	244	256	269	282	296	311	327	343
Software	150	200	250	330	430	310	210	180	320	490	620	490
Training	145	155	165	170	225	200	150	150	200	220	250	200
Other	160	176	192	240	200	175	125	100	104	200	250	200
Total Unit Sales	740	846	952	1,130	1,344	1,116	874	812	1,100	1,496	1,797	1,508

Unit Prices	Jan	Feb	Mar	Apr	May	Jun	Jul	Aug	Sep	Oct	Nov	Dec
Systems	$2,000	$2,000	$2,000	$1,829	$1,891	$1,966	$2,132	$2,115	$2,083	$1,966	$1,980	$1,984
Service	$75	$69	$58	$46	$50	$47	$50	$50	$91	$124	$75	$67
Software	$200	$200	$200	$200	$223	$217	$242	$253	$220	$211	$204	$207
Training	$37	$35	$39	$41	$56	$50	$33	$33	$50	$55	$60	$50
Other	$300	$300	$300	$300	$300	$300	$300	$300	$300	$300	$300	$300

Sales	Jan	Feb	Mar	Apr	May	Jun	Jul	Aug	Sep	Oct	Nov	Dec
Systems	$170,000	$230,000	$290,000	$347,500	$463,203	$344,079	$255,789	$211,538	$375,000	$540,761	$693,100	$545,736
Service	$15,000	$13,846	$11,667	$9,231	$12,200	$11,947	$13,450	$14,100	$26,909	$38,418	$24,525	$22,867
Software	$30,000	$40,000	$50,000	$66,000	$95,923	$67,264	$50,923	$45,556	$70,280	$103,326	$126,715	$101,196
Training	$5,365	$5,500	$6,500	$7,000	$12,500	$10,000	$5,000	$5,000	$10,000	$12,000	$15,000	$10,000
Other	$48,000	$52,800	$57,600	$72,000	$60,000	$52,500	$37,500	$30,000	$31,200	$60,000	$75,000	$60,000
Total Sales	$268,365	$342,146	$415,767	$501,731	$643,826	$485,790	$362,662	$306,194	$513,389	$754,505	$934,341	$739,799

Direct Unit Costs		Jan	Feb	Mar	Apr	May	Jun	Jul	Aug	Sep	Oct	Nov	Dec
Systems	85.00%	$1,700.00	$1,700.00	$1,700.00	$1,700.00	$1,700.00	$1,700.00	$1,700.00	$1,700.00	$1,700.00	$1,700.00	$1,700.00	$1,700.00
Service	40.00%	$30.00	$60.00	$60.00	$60.00	$60.00	$60.00	$60.00	$60.00	$60.00	$60.00	$60.00	$60.00
Software	60.00%	$120.00	$120.00	$120.00	$120.00	$120.00	$120.00	$120.00	$120.00	$120.00	$120.00	$120.00	$120.00
Training	30.00%	$11.10	$11.10	$11.10	$11.10	$11.10	$11.10	$11.10	$11.10	$11.10	$11.10	$11.10	$11.10
Other	30.00%	$90.00	$90.00	$90.00	$90.00	$90.00	$90.00	$90.00	$90.00	$90.00	$90.00	$90.00	$90.00

Appendix: AMT, Inc.

Direct Cost of Sales	Jan	Feb	Mar	Apr	May	Jun	Jul	Aug	Sep	Oct	Nov	Dec
Systems	$144,500	$195,500	$246,500	$323,000	$416,500	$297,500	$204,000	$170,000	$306,000	$467,500	$595,000	$467,500
Service	$6,000	$12,000	$12,000	$12,000	$14,640	$15,360	$16,140	$16,920	$17,760	$18,660	$19,620	$20,580
Software	$18,000	$24,000	$30,000	$39,600	$51,600	$37,200	$25,200	$21,600	$38,400	$58,800	$74,400	$58,800
Training	$1,610	$1,721	$1,832	$1,887	$2,498	$2,220	$1,665	$1,665	$2,220	$2,442	$2,775	$2,220
Other	$14,400	$15,840	$17,280	$21,600	$18,000	$15,750	$11,250	$9,000	$9,360	$18,000	$22,500	$18,000
Subtotal Direct Cost of Sales	$184,510	$249,061	$307,612	$398,087	$503,238	$368,030	$258,255	$219,185	$373,740	$565,402	$714,295	$567,100

This page intentionally blank.

APPENDIX A: *Glossary*

Accounts payable
: Bills to be paid as part of the normal course of business.

Accounts receivable
: Debts owed to your company, usually from sales on credit.

Accumulated depreciation
: Total accumulated depreciation reduces the formal accounting value (called book value) of assets. Each month's accumulated balance is the same as last month's balance plus this month's depreciation.

Acid test
: Short-term assets minus accounts receivable and inventory, divided by short-term liabilities. This is a test of a company's ability to meet its immediate cash requirements.

Asset turnover
: Sales divided by total assets. Important for comparison over time and to other companies of the same industry.

Break-even point
: The unit sales volumes or actual sales amounts that a company needs to equal its running expense rate and not lose or make money in a given month. The formula for break-even point in units is:

=Regular running costs/(Unit Price-Unit Variable Cost)

The formula for break-even point in sales amount is:

=Regular running costs /(1-(Unit Variable Cost/Unit Price))

Burden rate	Refers to personnel burden, the sum of employer costs over and above salaries, including employer taxes, benefits, etc.
Capital assets	Long-term assets, also known as Plant and Equipment.
Capital expenditure	Spending on capital assets (also called plant and equipment, or fixed assets).
Capital input	New money being invested in the business. New capital will increase your cash, and will also increase the total amount of paid-in capital.
Cash	The bank balance, or checking account balance, or real cash in bills and coins.
Collection days	See Collection period, below.
Collection period (days)	The average number of days that pass between delivering an invoice and receiving the money. The formula is:

=(Accounts_receivable_balance*360)/ (Sales_on_credit*12) |
Commissions	Gross margin multiplied by the commissions percentage.
Commissions percent	An assumed percentage used to calculate commissions expense as the product of this percentage multiplied by gross margin.
Cost of sales	The costs associated with producing the sales. In a standard manufacturing or distribution company, this is about the same as the cost of the goods sold. In a services company, this is more likely to be personnel costs for people delivering the service, or subcontracting costs.

Current assets	The same as short-term assets.
Current debt	Short-term debt, short-term liabilities.
Current liabilities	Short-term debt, short-term liabilities.
Debt and equity	The sum of liabilities and capital. This should always be equal to total assets.
Depreciation	An accounting and tax concept used to estimate the loss of value of assets over time. For example, cars depreciate with use.
Directory	A computer term related to the DOS operating system on IBM and compatible computers. Disk storage space is divided into directories.
Dividends	Money distributed to the owners of a business as profits.
Earnings	Also called income or profits, earnings are the famous "bottom line": sales less costs of sales and expenses.
EBIT	Earnings before interest and taxes.
Equity	Business ownership; capital. Equity can be calculated as the difference between assets and liabilities.
Fiscal year	Standard accounting practice allows the accounting year to begin in any month. Fiscal years are numbered according to the year in which they end. For example, a fiscal year ending in February of 1992 is Fiscal 1992, even though most of the year takes place in 1991.

Fixed costs	Running costs that take time to wind down: usually rent, overhead, some salaries. Technically, fixed costs are those that the business would continue to pay even if it went bankrupt. In practice, fixed costs are usually considered the running costs.
Gross margin	Sales minus cost of sales.
Gross margin percent	Gross margin divided by sales, displayed as a percentage. Acceptable levels depend on the nature of the business.
Interest expense	Interest is paid on debts, and interest expense is deducted from profits as expenses. Interest expense is either long-term or short-term interest; we make the distinction because interest rates paid are usually higher on long-term debts.
Inventory	Goods in stock, either finished goods or materials to be used to manufacture goods.
Inventory turnover	Total cost of sales divided by inventory. Usually calculated using the average inventory over an accounting period, not an ending-inventory value.
Inventory turns	Inventory turnover (above).
Label	The row titles along column A of the tables are called labels, or row labels.
Labor	The labor costs associated with making goods to be sold. This labor is part of the cost of sales, part of the manufacturing and assembly.

Liabilities	Debts; money that must be paid. Usually debt on terms of less than five years is called short-term liabilities, and debt for longer than five years in long-term liabilities.
Long term assets	Assets like plant and equipment that are depreciated over terms of more than five years, and are likely to last that long, too.
Long term interest rate	The interest rate charged on long-term debt. This is usually higher than the rate on short-term debt.
Long term liabilities	This is the same as long-term loans. Most companies call a debt long-term when it is on terms of five years or more.
Materials	Included in the cost of sales. These are materials involved in the assembly or manufacture of goods for sale.
Net cash flow	This is the projected change in cash position, an increase or decrease in cash balance.
Net profit	The operating income less taxes and interest. The same as earnings, or net income.
Net worth	This is the same as assets minus liabilities, and the same as total equity.
Other short-term assets	These might be securities, business equipment, etc.
Other ST liabilities	These are short-term debts that don't cause interest expenses. For example, they might be loans from founders or accrued taxes (taxes owed, already incurred, but not yet paid).

Paid-in capital	Real money paid into the company as investments. This is not to be confused with par value of stock, or market value of stock. This is actual money paid into the company as equity investments by owners.
Payment days	The average number of days that pass between receiving an invoice and paying it. It is not a simple estimate; it is calculated with a financial formula: =(Accounts_payable_balance*360)/(Total entries to accounts payable*12)
Payroll burden	Payroll burden includes payroll taxes and benefits. It is calculated using a percentage assumption that is applied to payroll. For example, if payroll is $1,000 and the burden rate 10 percent, the burden is an extra $100. Acceptable payroll burden rates vary by market, by industry, and by company.
Personnel burden	Payroll burden. See above description.
Plant and equipment	This is the same as long-term, fixed or capital assets.
Product development	Expenses incurred in development of new products; salaries, laboratory equipment, test equipment, prototypes, research and development, etc.
Profit before int and taxes	This is also called EBIT, for Earnings Before Interest and Taxes. It is gross margin minus operating expenses.
Receivables turnover	Sales on credit for an accounting period divided by the average accounts receivables balance.
Retained earnings	Earnings (or losses) that have been reinvested into the company, not paid out as dividends to the owners. When retained earnings are negative, the company has accumulated losses.

Return on assets	Net profit divided by total assets. A measure of profitability.
Return on investment	Net profits divided by net worth or total equity; yet another measure of profitability. Also called ROI.
Return on sales	Net profits divided by sales; another measure of profitability.
ROI	Return on investment; net profits divided by net worth or total equity, another measure of profitability.
Sales break-even	The sales volume at which costs are exactly equal to sales. The exact formula is =Fixed_costs/(1-(Unit_Variable_Cost/Unit_Price)).
Sales on credit	Sales made on account, shipments against invoices to be paid later.
Short term	Normally used to distinguish between short-term and long-term, when referring to assets or liabilities. Definitions vary because different companies and accountants handle this in different ways. Accounts payable is always a short-term liability, and cash, accounts receivable and inventory are always short-term assets. Most companies call any debt of less than five-year terms short-term debt. Assets that depreciate over more than five years (e.g., plant and equipment) are usually long-term assets.
Short term assets	Cash, securities, bank accounts, accounts receivable, inventory, business equipment, assets that last less than five years or are depreciated over terms of less than five years.
Short term notes	These are the same as short-term loans. These are debts with terms of five years or less.

Starting date	The starting date for the entire business plan system. You set the starting date by setting starting year and starting month, and other datelines will be reset automatically whenever the spreadsheet calculates changes.
Tax rate percent	An assumed percentage applied against pre-tax income to determine taxes. In *Business Plan Pro* we use a single percentage calculation, not a graduated rate or complex formula.
Taxes incurred	Taxes owed but not yet paid.
Unit variable cost	The specific labor and materials associated with a single unit of goods sold. Does not include general overhead.
Units break-even	The unit sales volume at which the fixed and variable costs are exactly equal to sales. The formula is $UBE = Fixed\_costs/(Unit\_Price - Unit\_Variable\_Cost)$.

Appendix B: Index

Hurdle Workbook

Use it with Business Plan Software

This workbook is best used along with either *Business Plan Pro* ™ or *Business Plan Toolkit* ™ (the Macintosh version of Business Plan Pro), published by Palo Alto Software, Inc. It also references Chapters 2-15 of this book.

Use it to Develop A Plan

Take notes for your plan and write draft topics, gather information, and organize your thoughts. Then later you can incorporate this initial work into your plan on the computer. You can also share the main ideas with others, to stir the thinking process.

Use it with Clients, Colleagues, or Students

Give a copy of this book to clients, colleagues, or students. They can use the workbook to prepare drafts of topics, take notes, and gather information. You can use the workbook to absorb their inputs, then create a plan.

Use it with Tables

The workbook anticipates the information you'll want to add to your business plan tables. Use it to start the process, then input your assumptions into the software.

For product information, contact Palo Alto Software, Inc. at:

U.S. Sales:	1 (800) 229-7526
Switchboard:	1 (541) 683-6162
Fax:	1 (541) 683-6250
E-mail:	sales@palo-alto.com
Websites:	www.paloaltosoftware.com
	www.bplans.com

Chapter 2. Initial Assessment

Mission Statement

Start with the basics: your business name, what it sells, where it is located, and the nature and purpose of the plan you are writing.

Write a mission statement to establish your business' fundamental goals. Include a "value proposition," summarizing what benefits you offer, to whom, and at what relative price.

....

....

....

....

....

....

....

....

....

....

....

Keys to Success

The idea of keys to success is based on the need for focus. You can't focus efforts on a few priorities unless you limit the number of priorities. In practice, lists of more than three or four priorities are usually less effective. The more the priorities (beyond three or four), the less chance of implementation.

Virtually every business has different keys to success. These are a few key factors that make the difference between success and failure. This depends on who you are and what services you offer.

....

....

....

....

....

....

....

....

....

....

....

Permission to copy granted only for use with *Business Plan Pro™* or *Business Plan Toolkit™* software. For more information call 1 (800) 229-7526.

PAGE 227

Break-even Analysis

Collect the data to do a break-even analysis. Determine (or guess) your average monthly fixed costs and revenues. For a product business, record your average unit price and average unit cost. What do you have to sell each month in order for your income to exceed your fixed and product costs?

Use the text area to explain your assumptions, and the significance of the analysis.

Assumptions:	
Average Unit Sale	
Average Per-Unit Cost	
Monthly Fixed Cost	
Calculating Fixed Cost	
Rent	
Utilities	
Insurance	
Salaries, benefits, etc.	
Other	
Other	
Other	
Total	

Market Analysis

Do a basic market analysis: list your potential customers by market segment and determine a reasonable growth rate for each segment. Are there enough potential customers for your product or service for you to meet your break-even sales point?

Market Analysis		
Potential Customers	# of Customers	Growth rate (%)

....

....

....

....

....

....

....

Chapter 3. Pick your plan

You will need to choose which topics to include in your plan, and where to insert tables and charts into the text.

Use the generic outline below as a starting point to determine which topics fit into your plan.

Make a note where you'll add tables or charts to illustrate your text.

Add any missing topics that are needed in your plan. Briefly jot ideas for your text under the outline headings.

✓	Outline	Topic	✓	Table	✓	Chart
	1.0	Executive Summary				Highlights
	1.1	Objectives				
	1.2	Mission				
	1.3	Keys to Success				
	2.0	Company Summary				
	2.1	Company Ownership				
	2.2	Company History		Past Performance		Past Performance
	2.2	Start-up Summary		Start-up		Start-up
	2.3	Company Locations and Facilities				
	3.0	Products				
	3.1	Product Description				
	3.2	Competitive Comparison				
	3.3	Sales Literature				
	3.4	Sourcing				
	3.5	Technology				
	3.6	Future Products				
	4.0	Market Analysis Summary				
	4.1	Market Segmentation		Market Analysis		Market Forecast
	4.2	Target Market Segment Strategy				
	4.2.1	Market Needs				
	4.2.2	Market Trends				
	4.2.3	Market Growth				
	4.3	Industry Analysis				
	4.3.1	Industry Participants				
	4.3.2	Distribution Patterns				
	4.3.3	Competitions and Buying Patterns				
	4.3.4	Main Competitors				
	5.0	Strategy and Implementation Summary				
	5.1	Strategy Pyramids				
	5.2	Value Proposition				
	5.3	Competitive Edge				
	5.4	Marketing Strategy				
	5.4.1	Positioning Statement				
	5.4.2	Pricing Strategy				
	5.4.3	Promotion Strategy				
	5.4.4	Distribution Strategy				
	5.4.5	Marketing Programs				
	5.5	Sales Strategy				Annual Sales
	5.5.1	Sales Forecast		Sales Forecast		Monthly Sales
	5.5.2	Sales Programs				
	5.6	Strategic Alliances				
	5.7	Milestones		Milestones		
	6.0	Management Summary				
	6.1	Organizational Structure				
	6.2	Management Team				
	6.3	Management Team Gaps				
	6.4	Personnel Plan		Personnel		
	7.0	Financial Plan				
	7.1	Important Assumptions		General Assumptions		
	7.2	Key Financial Indicators				Benchmarks
	7.3	Break-even Analysis		Break-even		Break-even
	7.4	Projected Profit and Loss		Profit and Loss		
	7.5	Projected Cash Flow		Cash Flow		Cash Flow
	7.6	Projected Balance Sheet		Balance Sheet		
	7.7	Business Ratios		Ratios Table		
	7.8	Long-term Plan		Long term		

Chapter 4. Know Your Market

Market Analysis Summary

This first paragraph is a simple summary. Assume that this paragraph might be included in a loan application or investment summary, so you need it to summarize the rest of the chapter. What information would be most important, if you had only one brief topic to include about your market?

Without going into great detail, you should generally describe the different groups of target customers included in your market analysis, and refer briefly to why you are selecting these as targets. You may also want to summarize market growth, citing highlights of some growth projections.

....

....

....

....

....

....

....

....

....

....

Market Segmentation

Use this topic to explain the potential customers analysis table, which is normally linked to it, plus the market pie chart. Your analysis is based on a list of potential customer groups, each of which is a market segment. Explain how your segments are defined. The market segmentation concept is crucial to market assessment and market strategy. Divide the market into workable market segments--divided by age, income, product type, geography, buying patterns, customer needs, or other classification.

....

....

....

....

....

....

....

....

....

....

....

Target Market Strategy

In this topic you should introduce the strategy behind your market segmentation and your choice of target markets. Explain why your business is focusing on these specific target market groups. What makes these groups more interesting than the other groups that you've ruled out? Why are the characteristics you specify important?

....

....

....

....

....

....

....

....

....

....

....

....

Permission to copy granted only for use with *Business Plan Pro*™ or *Business Plan Toolkit*™ software. For more information call 1 (800) 229-7526.

PAGE 233

Market Needs

This topic is a good reminder that all marketing should be based on underlying needs. For each market segment included in your strategy, explain the market needs that lead to this group's wanting to buy your service.

....

....

....

....

....

....

....

....

....

....

....

....

Market Trends

To describe market trends, think strategically. What factors seem to be changing the market, or changing the business? What developing trends can make a difference? Market trends could be changes in demographics, changes in customer needs, new sense of style or fashion, or something else. It depends on what business you are in.

....

....

....

....

....

....

....

....

....

....

....

....

Market Growth

Use this topic to explain and discuss market growth. Ideally you cite experts, a market expert, market research firm, trade association, or credible journalist, projecting market growth. This is particularly important when your plan is related to finding investors or supporting a loan application because market growth enhances the implied value of your business.

....

....

....

....

....

....

....

....

....

....

....

....

Chapter 5: The Business You're In

This topic summarizes the sub-topics that follow, explaining your type of business. The sub-topics look at the size and concentration of businesses in this group, the way services are bought and sold, and specific competitors.

....

....

....

....

....

....

....

....

....

....

....

....

Permission to copy granted only for use with *Business Plan Pro*™ or *Business Plan Toolkit*™ software. For more information call 1 (800) 229-7526.

PAGE 237

Business Participants

The idea behind this topic is to explain the nature of the industry. There is a huge difference, for example, between an industry like long-distance trunk services, in which there are only a few huge companies in any one country, and one like dry cleaning, in which there are tens of thousands of smaller participants. This topic is supposed to present a summary of this factor.

....

....

....

....

....

....

....

....

....

....

....

....

Distribution Patterns

Explain how distribution works in this industry. Does it have regional distributors, as is the case for computer products, or magazines, or auto parts? Does it depend on direct sales to large industrial customers? Do manufacturers support their own direct sales forces?

....

....

....

....

....

....

....

....

....

....

....

....

Permission to copy granted only for use with *Business Plan Pro*™ or *Business Plan Toolkit*™ software. For more information call 1 (800) 229-7526.

PAGE 239

Competition

Explain the general nature of competition in this business, and how the customers seem to choose one provider over another. In the computer business, for example, competition might, in one part of the market, depend on reputation and trends and on channels of distribution and advertising in another. In many business-to-business industries, the nature of competition depends on direct selling because channels are impractical. Price is vital in products competing with each other on retail shelves, but delivery and reliability might be much more important for materials used by manufacturers in volume, for which a shortage can affect an entire production line.

....

....

....

....

....

....

....

....

....

....

....

Main Competitors

You've referred to competition already, in previous topics, in terms of general factors and the nature of competition. Use this topic to list your specific competitors, and the strengths and weaknesses of each.

Chapter 6. What You Sell

This is another summary topic, that starts a chapter, and introduces the topics to follow. The whole chapter is about the services you sell, so in the sub-topics you will list and describe your products, present detail abcut how they are manufactured, where, at what cost, and by whom, and plans for future product development. This first topic can be a summary in three or four sentences.

....

....

....

....

....

....

....

....

....

....

....

....

Product Description

The previous topic was the summary, so this one provides more detail. List and describe the products your company manufactures. For each product, cover the main points including what the product is, technology, manufacturing cost, distribution, packaging, pricing, what sorts of customers make purchases, and why. What customer need does each product fill? What are the important features and benefits?

....

....

....

....

....

....

....

....

....

....

....

....

Competitive Comparison

Use this topic for a general comparison of your product offering as one of several choices a potential buyer can make. There is a separate topic in the market analysis chapter for detailed comparison of strengths and weaknesses of your specific competitors.

....

....

....

....

....

....

....

....

....

Other Product Topics

Additional details depend on the nature of your business, and the purpose of your plan. If you are a manufacturer or a retailer, you should describe your sources of materials.

Describe the current, and new, technologies which impact your ability to produce these goods or services.

What future products or services are on your drawing board? Is there a relationship between market segments, market demand, market needs, and product development?

List any existing sales literature you will include with your finished plan.

....

....

....

....

....

....

....

....

....

Permission to copy granted only for use with *Business Plan Pro*™ or *Business Plan Toolkit*™ software. For more information call 1 (800) 229-7526.

PAGE 245

Chapter 7. Forecast your Sales

Break down your sales – by product or by service. The best forecasts will list one full year by month, plus three additional years, by year.

You also need to project costs of sales, just as you project sales. Usually you'll use the same sales breakdown for costs as for sales.

Sales

	Jan	Feb	Mar	Apr	May	Jun	Jul	Aug	Sep	Oct	Nov	Dec 1998
Other												

Direct Cost of sales

	Jan	Feb	Mar	Apr	May	Jun	Jul	Aug	Sep	Oct	Nov	Dec 1998
Other												

Explain the Sales Forecast

Use the text to summarize and highlight the Sales Forecast in the detailed sales forecast table, which will print automatically following this text. Your annual sales forecast prints with the text, and the monthlies are in the appendix.

Explain your sales forecast. Emphasize important points and explain assumptions. What growth rates are you expecting for the more important lines, what growth rates in units and in dollars? Why are you projecting your sales at this level; why not less or more? What are the main driving forces behind the sales forecast? How does it relate to your market analysis, your main target segments, your sales strategy and marketing strategy? Is your sales forecast believable? Why?

....

....

....

....

....

....

....

....

....

....

....

Chapter 8. Your Management Team

Use this first paragraph as a summary. As with the other first topics in chapters, it may be used to stand for the rest of the chapter, as part of a summary document. If you only have one or two paragraphs to include about your personnel and management team, this is it.

....

....

....

....

....

....

....

....

....

....

....

Organization

The organizational structure of a company is what you frequently see as an organizational chart, also known as an "org chart." If you have access to a graphic of an organizational chart (from a drawing program, or even one of the specialized organizational charting software packages available), then you can import the drawing into your business plan at this point. If not, you may want to include a chart as an illustration in the appendix. You can also just use the text to describe the organizational structure in words, without a chart.

Permission to copy granted only for use with *Business Plan Pro™* or *Business Plan Toolkit™* software. For more information call 1 (800) 229-7526.

PAGE 249

Management Team

List the most important members of the management team. Include summaries of their backgrounds and experience, using them like brief resumes. Describe their functions with the company.

....

....

....

....

....

....

....

....

....

....

....

....

Management Team Gaps

Specify where the team is weak because of gaps in coverage of key management functions. How will these weaknesses be corrected? How will the more important gaps be filled?

....

....

....

....

....

....

....

....

....

....

....

....

Personnel Plan

Use the Personnel table to prepare a personnel plan, projecting employees, salaries, and departments. Use the text topic here to explain the plan, assumptions, personnel needs, costs, and benefits.

Personnel	Jan	Feb	Mar	Apr	May	Jun	Jul	Aug	Sep	Oct	Nov	Dec
Other												

Chapter 9. The Profit and Loss Statement

Take a deep breath. You've already collected some of the information you need here, so now you can begin to put it together. Again, the goal is to create a plan showing one full year by month, plus three additional years by year.

You roughed out your fixed costs in Chapter 2 – now you'll list the details. You have already forecasted your sales and product costs in Chapter 7. You have your payroll costs from Chapter 8. Remember, you will most likely revise these numbers as you complete this plan. Like any good puzzle, the clues to one piece may be contained in another piece.

Profit and Loss (Income Statement)	Jan	Feb	Mar	Apr	May	Jun	Jul	Aug	Sep	Oct	Nov	Dec
Operating expenses:												
Advertising/Promotion												
Travel												
Payroll												
Payroll Burden												
Depreciation												
Leased Equipment												
Utilities												
Insurance												
Rent												
Other Expenses												
Total Operating Expenses												
Profit Before Interest and Taxes												
Interest Expense Short-term												
Interest Expense Long-term												
Taxes Incurred												

Permission to copy granted only for use with *Business Plan Pro™* or *Business Plan Toolkit™* software. For more information call 1 (800) 229-7526.

PAGE 253

Chapter 10. Describe your Company

Here is your chance to flesh out your notes from Chapter 2. Think strategically, from an outsider's perspective. What about your company and your plan make them unique and successful?

....

....

....

....

....

....

....

....

....

....

....

....

Brief History and Legal Ownership of Company

In this paragraph, describe the ownership and legal establishment of the company. This is mainly specifying whether your company is a corporation, partnership, sole proprietorship, or some other kind of legal entity, such as a limited liability partnership. You should also explain who owns the company, and, if there is more than one owner, in what proportion.

Company History

This topic appears when your business plan options are set for an existing or ongoing company, instead of a start-up company.

For an existing or ongoing company, use this topic to cover past performance. The topic is normally linked to the past performance table, which presents financial highlights for the last three years and starting balances for the next three. Explain why your sales and profits have changed. If you've had important events, like particularly bad years or good years, or new services, new locations, new partners, etc., then include that background here.

....

....

....

....

....

....

....

....

....

....

....

Start-up Plan

This topic is here
because you're set as a
start-up, for a new
company with no history.

Use this text area to
explain the assumptions
in your start-up table that
will be linked to this
topic.

The start-up costs
and start-up investment
table are usually included
after this text, followed
by a bar chart illustrating
your start-up
assumptions.

Start-up Expenses	
Legal	
Stationery etc.	
Brochures	
Consultants	
Insurance	
Rent	
Research and development	
Expensed equipment	
Other	
Total Start-up Expense	

Start-up Assets Needed	
Cash Requirements	
Start-up inventory	
Other Short-term Assets	
Total Short-term Assets	

Long-term Assets	
Total Assets	

Total Start-up Requirements:	
Start-up Funding Plan	
Investment	
Investor 1	
Investor 2	
Other	
Total investment	

Short-term Liabilities	
Unpaid Expenses	
Short-term Loans	
Interest-free Short-term Loans	
Subtotal Short-term Liabilities	
Long-term Liabilities	
Total Liabilities	

Loss at Start-up	
Total Capital	
Total Capital and Liabilities	

Location(s) and Facilities:

Briefly describe offices and locations of your company, the nature and function of each, square footage, lease arrangements, etc. For example, if you are a service business, you probably don't have major manufacturing plants anywhere, but you might have Internet services, office facilities, and telephone systems that are relevant to providing service. It is conceivable that your Internet connection, as one hypothetical case, might be critical to your business.

....

....

....

....

....

....

....

....

....

....

....

Chapter 11. About Business Numbers

Here is where you'll plan for the impact of buying or selling on credit – the two items that create the difference between profits and cash in the bank.

Take a look at your sales from Chapter 7. Consider your Accounts Receivable Collection Days - the numbers of days you will wait between recording the sale and receiving the money. Will you be selling to businesses, on standard terms of net 30? Most businesses expect terms. Have you considered the capital implications of selling on credit?

Will you be buying on credit, like most businesses? How long will you wait, on average, between receiving the bill and paying it. Most businesses take 30 or more days. Will any of your vendors expect prepayment until you have established a credit history with them? Will you be paying any invoices with a credit card as an additional form of financing?

From your start-up table, or your existing balance sheet, list the money you have borrowed, and the repayment terms. How much principal and interest will you have to repay each month?

....

....

....

....

....

....

....

....

Chapter 12. Cash is King

In this section, you'll use the information from Chapter 11 to calculate how your cash flow will be impacted by sales and purchases on credit. Remember that a negative cash balance means you have bounced checks at the bank. If you end up with a negative cash balance in the real world, you will either have to borrow more money, collect payments sooner, or hold your payments to vendors.

Chapter 13. Finish the Financials

The most important item on your balance sheet is your cash. You just dealt with cash in the previous section, the cash flow, and you also explained the assumptions related to cash. The full balance sheet includes all assets, liabilities, and capital.

....

....

....

....

....

....

....

....

....

....

....

....

Permission to copy granted only for use with *Business Plan Pro* ™ or *Business Plan Toolkit* ™ software.
For more information call 1 (800) 229-7526.

PAGE 261

Business Ratios

The business plan software will calculate all of these ratios automatically.

Profitability Ratios:	1998	1999	2000
Gross Margin			
Net Profit Margin			
Return on Assets			
Return on Equity			

Activity Ratios	1998	1999	2000
AR Turnover			
Collection Days			
Inventory Turnover			
Accts Payable Turnover			
Total Asset Turnover			

Debt Ratios	1998	1999	2000
Debt to Net Worth			
Short-term Liab. to Liab.			

Liquidity Ratios	1998	1999	2000
Current Ratio			
Quick Ratio			
Net Working Capital			
Interest Coverage			

Additional Ratios	1998	1999	2000
Assets to Sales			
Debt/Assets			
Current Debt/Total Assets			
Acid Test			
Asset Turnover			
Sales/Net Worth			
Dividend Payout			

Chapter 14. Strategy and Tactics

In this first paragraph, summarize the sales and marketing strategy. Details will come in the following topics, so keep this first summary short, covering just the main points. Remember, this summary may be used as the only paragraph on this topic to be included in a loan application or an investment summary memo, so you don't want to miss the main points.

....

....

....

....

....

....

....

....

....

....

....

....

....

Strategy Pyramid

First, a word of caution: this topic is intended to help you think about strategy, not to make a business plan more difficult. If this framework for analysis doesn't work for you, don't worry about it. This is your business plan, make it your own and remove what doesn't fit.

....

....

....

....

....

....

....

....

....

....

....

....

Value Proposition

Value-based marketing is another conceptual framework, like the pyramid in the previous topic. Like the pyramid, it doesn't have to be in your business plan at all, but we add it here because some people find that the framework helps them develop strategy. Obviously, this has to be a quick treatment. There are textbooks written about value-based marketing, and the business literature on this topic is rich and varied.

....

....

....

....

....

....

....

....

....

....

....

....

Competitive Edge

So what is your competitive edge? How is your company different from all others? In what way does it stand out? Is there a sustainable value there, something that you can maintain and develop over time? For example, a graphic design firm might have its head start in Internet Web design or its Common Gateway Interface (CGI) programming staff as a competitive edge, that puts it ahead of most competitors. An accounting practice might have its very-well-known senior partner, whose books are used as texts. A restaurant might have its excellent location, or its well-known master chef. The competitive edge might be different for any given company, even between one company and another in the same industry.

Marketing Strategy

This topic introduces marketing strategy. Sales strategy comes later. Your marketing strategy normally involves target market focus, emphasis on certain services or media or ways to position your company and your products or service uniquely.

Your marketing strategy depends a great deal on which market segments you've chosen as target market groups. You covered this in the previous chapter, the market analysis, but it is also critical to market strategy. Also, if you've been through the previous topics, including the pyramid, the value proposition, and competitive edge, then you probably have marketing strategy on the way. Obviously, you want to make sure to preserve the same basic focus and themes.

....

....

....

....

....

....

....

....

....

....

Permission to copy granted only for use with *Business Plan Pro ™* or *Business Plan Toolkit ™* software. For more information call 1 (800) 229-7526.

PAGE 267

Positioning Statements

Use this topic for your marketing positioning statements. The positioning statements should include a strategic focus on the most important target market, that market's most important market need, how your product meets that need, who is the main competition, and how your product is better than the competition.

Consider this simple template:

For [target market description] who [target market need], [this product] [how it meets the need]. Unlike [key competition], it [most important distinguishing feature].

....

....

....

....

....

....

....

....

....

....

....

Pricing Strategy

Use this topic to provide detail on product pricing and to relate pricing to strategy. Your value proposition, for example, will normally include implications about relative pricing. Therefore, you should check whether your detailed product-by-product pricing matches the implied pricing in the value proposition. Pricing is also supposed to be intimately related to the positioning statement in the previous topic, since pricing is probably the most important factor in product positioning.

....

....

....

....

....

....

....

....

....

....

....

Permission to copy granted only for use with *Business Plan Pro*™ or *Business Plan Toolkit*™ software.
For more information call 1 (800) 229-7526.

PAGE 269

Promotion Strategy

Think of promotion in a broader sense than simply sales promotion. Think of how you spread the word about your business to your future customers. Think of it in the broader context, including the whole range of advertising, public relations, events, direct mail, seminars, and sales literature.

Think strategically. What, in general, is your strategy about communicating with people? Do you go for expensive ads in mass media, or targeted marketing in specialized publications, or even more targeted with direct mail? Do you have a way to leverage the news media or reviewers? Do you advertise more effectively through public relations events, trade shows, newspaper, or radio? What about telemarketing, the World Wide Web, or even multilevel marketing?

....

....

....

....

....

....

....

....

....

....

Distribution Strategy

What is your strategy for distributing your products? Remember, strategy is focus, so think about emphasizing your strengths and protecting your weaknesses. You should also refer to your discussion of distribution patterns in the previous chapter to consider how your strategy fits in with the rest of your industry.

Are you focusing on a specific channel, area of distribution, or means of distribution? Is there some special advantage you have that you want to emphasize, to differentiate from your competition? Is there anything unique in your distribution plans that your competitors can't imitate? In what way does your plan for distribution emphasize your strengths and move away from your weaknesses?

....

....

....

....

....

....

....

....

....

....

Permission to copy granted only for use with *Business Plan Pro* ™ or *Business Plan Toolkit* ™ software. For more information call 1 (800) 229-7526.

PAGE 271

Marketing Programs

Details and specifics are critical to implementation. Use this topic to list the specific information related to marketing programs in your Milestones table with their specific persons responsible, deadlines, and budgets.

Each marketing program in your Milestones table should appear in this topic, along with relevant details. You may go over them again in the text related to that table, but for this topic you want to cement your sales strategy with programs that make it real. How is this strategy to be implemented? Do you have concrete and specific plans? How will implementation be measured?

Sales Strategy

Describe sales strategy as it differs from marketing strategy. Sales should close the deals that marketing opens. Sales strategies deal with how and when to close sales prospects, how to compensate sales people, how to optimize order processing and database management, how to maneuver price, delivery, and conditions. This topic is the broad summary, to be followed by a detailed sales forecast and a discussion of specific sales programs.

....

....

....

....

....

....

....

....

....

....

....

Sales Programs

Details and specifics are critical to implementation. Use this topic to list the specific information related to sales programs in your Milestones table, with their specific persons responsible, deadlines, and budgets.

....

....

....

....

....

....

....

....

....

....

....

....

Implementation Milestones

The milestones are critical. This is where a business plan becomes a real plan, with specific and measurable activities, instead of just a document. Include as many specific programs as possible. For each program, give it a name, a person responsible, a milestone date, and a budget. The table in the software reserves additional columns for comparing the actual results and the difference between plan and actual results, for each program. It gives you a way to track spending and milestone dates, and you can also sort the table by person responsible, milestone date, budget, and by department.

Milestone	Manager	Planned Date	Department	Budget

Executive Summary

Although this topic appears first in the plan, you normally write it last. Wait until you're almost done so you can include the main highlights. You should cover the most important facts, such as sales growth and profitability and strategic focus, and those facts may change during the planning process.

The contents of the summary depend on the goals of your plan. For example, if you are selling a business idea to investors, then you should include highlights that will invite and encourage potential investors to read on. That might be growth rates, competitive edge, an exciting new technology, etc. On the other hand, if your plan is for internal purposes only, not to be read by outsiders, then your summary would probably not try to sell your plan, but just summarize it. Remember as always to match your plan to your purpose. This is business, not writing class.

....

....

....

....

....

....

....

....

....

....

15: Print and Publish

As you near completion, remember where you started. Form follows function, and your plan started with a business function. It might have been better management and internal communications, raising money, starting a business, supporting a loan document, or some other business purpose. We said "Pick your Plan" in Chapter 2 because a business plan can be many different things to different people. As you go about finishing up and putting it together, keep its original purpose in mind.

Have You Covered Enough? Too Much?

Take another look at the general outline list, on page 230. Do you need to include everything on that list? For example, an internal plan might skip the company chapter altogether, and personnel might also be inappropriate. You might also need to add additional topics that cover your special situation. Some of the more frequently added topics include Exit Strategies, Risks, Special Issues, Next Steps; and of course the business plan should accommodate your business, with your needs, not a standard outline.

Do You Have the Right Tables and Charts?

Take a good look at tables and charts too. If you don't need a market analysis -- which is a rare case, but it happens -- then don't include it. Many plans delete the break-even analysis table and chart. Many delete the personnel plan, because it tends to be particularly confidential, and is therefore inappropriate for internal documents.

Do you Need a Summary Memo?

An important trend in submitting business plans for investors is the summary memo, a streamlined executive summary of 2-10 pages maximum. Investors often prefer just the summary document. If they like what they see there, then they want to see the whole plan. The summary memo should have the key points, such as competitive edge, market needs, defensibility, and of course track records and resumes of main team members. Sell your plan, but keep it short and rich. Focus on real content, not hype.

Permission to copy granted only for use with *Business Plan Pro*™ or *Business Plan Toolkit*™ software.
For more information call 1 (800) 229-7526.

PAGE 277

Know Your Audience

Another important new trend is the steadily increasing demand for research. Investors expect the entrepreneurs to do their homework. You are supposed to know the investors' deal size and industry segment preference. Some venture capital firms want software, early on, and others want biomedical, second or third round. A mass mailing is no longer acceptable.

As for the plan itself, the key is getting to the point, and making the point. Investors won't wade through excess words or unsupported numbers. Nobody has extra time to find diamonds hidden in the verbal or formatting rough.

The Right Presentation

Presentation is always important but only to communicate content. Good charts are dynamite when they make numbers easier to read quickly, and essential when numbers are complex. Good text formatting should make the text easy to read. Use a legible font and a good mix of section headings and subheads and such to make the organization visible. Bullet points are generally easier to read than long paragraphs. Color is good for charts when it makes numbers easier to understand, but gets in the way when used for text.

Fancy paper, expensive bindings, and excessive presentation is not really needed. Make the paper whatever quality it takes to make the plan easy to read, avoiding some of the more fibrous papers that end up interfering with the printed content. Make the binding a good coil or some other binding that will hold up to use, but keep it practical so you impress with content, not expense.

Submitting a plan by email is a matter of recipient's preference. There's nothing wrong with email when your emailee is an email preferrer. Best to make sure, though, because a non-email-user won't like it at all. Don't be afraid to ask, and as long as your target person is used to the net and email (these days most are), they might want to receive the summary memo in email. Don't try to do a whole plan in email text, though.

Notes

Notes

Notes

Notes

Notes

Notes

Notes